Ethnicity and Social Change
(An Anthology of Essays)

Ethnicity and Social Change

(An Anthology of Essays)

Gangmumei Kamei
Professor of History (Retd)
Manipur University

AKANSHA PUBLISHING HOUSE
NEW DELHI-110002 (INDIA)

AKANSHA PUBLISHING HOUSE
4649-B/21, Ansari Road
Darya Ganj, New Delhi - 110 002
Ph.: 23263193 / 9811582579 / 09435116718
Fax: 011-23263193
Email: ektabooks@yahoo.com

Ethnicity and Social Change: (An Anthology of Essays)

Revised & Enlarged Edition, 2008
ISBN 978-81-8370-149-5

PRINTED IN INDIA

Published by Akansha Publishing House, New Delhi and Printed at Aryan Enterprises, Delhi.

Dedicated To

Professor D.P. Barooah

Former Vice Chancellor of Gauhati University
and my teacher who taught me History

CONTENTS

PART-III
HUMAN RIGHTS AND DEVELOPMENT

Preface

"Ethnicity and Social Change" was published in 2002. And it was well received by the reading public. I am delighted that these essays have been prescribed by Manipur University as a reference work for the course of M.A. History. Due to demand from many circles the book has been revised. I have included four new essays and have deleted two essays.

"The Evolution of the Meitei State" was a paper submitted to the workshop on early Manipur jointly organized by the Department of History of Manipur University and the Institute of North East Indian Historical Studies under the initiative of Prof. J.B. Battarcharjee of NEHU, held in Manipur University in September 2007.

"Modernization" is a modified version of a paper submitted to the seminar on Modernization without Westernization held at Kohima on 25th and 26th August, 2007, under the auspices of Jana Jati Vikash Samiti, Nagaland.

"Pluralism, Democracy and Ethnic Relations in Manipur" was the theme of the 2nd Arambam Samarendra Memorial Lecture delivered by me on 10th June 2007. It is published with permission from Dr. Lokendra Arambam, President of Arambam Samarendra Trust.

"Tribal Administration in Manipur" was a lecture delivered by me at the conference organized by All Tribal Students Union, Manipur at Imphal on 27th September, 2007.

I am grateful to Prof. N. Joykumar Singh, Head of Department of History, Manipur University for giving me the opportunity to be associated with the Department of History. I express my gratefulness to Shri M.P. Misra, of the Akansha Publishing House, New Delhi for kind publication of the book.

I thank my daughter Jellu and my son Som Kamei for giving me the assistance in the preparation of this edition of anthology of essays.

Gangmumei Kamei

21st October 2007
Manipur University,
Canchipur

Preface to the First Edition

Ethnicity and Social Change is an anthology of my stray essays written on different occasions. A chance discovery of a compilation of my occasional papers in typescript kept by my former personal assistant, L. Bikram Singh of Manipur University encouraged me to collect my old papers from friends especially, Professor N. Joy Kumar Singh of Manipur University.

Of the papers included in this anthology, the Ethnic Genesis of Manipur is an amalgamation of two papers; the Origin of the Meitei in History of Manipur: Pre-Colonial Period and the Genesis of the Ethnos of Naga and Kuki Chins published by the Naga Students Federation. I added an introductory note on ethnos and ethnicity.

Social Change was written on the basis of the notes of a lecture on social change in Manipur since the 18th century, which I gave at the Centre of south Asia in Jawaharlal Nehru University.

Ethnicity and State Formation (1985) and Education in the N. E. India: Problem of Democratization (1986) were read at the UGC Seminar and UNESCO Workshop organized by the Department of Political Science, Manipur University under the initiative of Professor G.I. Sharma.

Federalism in India is an improved version of my lecture on "Centre-State Relation: Federalism and Autonomy" organized by the Freedom Daily on 12 December 1998. It was a response to an attempt made by a Governor of Manipur to interfere in the functioning of the council of ministers on financial matter; his action violated the spirit of Cabinet system of government. At that time, I was a minister of Law and Legislative Affairs in Manipur government. It was a widely debated and discussed issue.

Regionalism in North East India is a lecture delivered by me in the Commonwealth Parliamentary Association, North Eastern Region Conference at Imphal in 1999.

The Indigenous Peoples and their Rights is a combination of my three lectures delivered during the International Year of the Indigenous Peoples; the first one at Ukhrul, 12, November 1993 organized by the Naga Students Federation,' the second in the International Conference on Tribes and Analogous Peoples at Bhopal, 19, November 1993 organized by the Indira Gandhi Museum of Man, Ministry of Culture, Government of India and the third at the 12th Plenary Session of the UN Working Group on the Indigenous Populations at the UN Human Right Centre on 29, June 1994 at Geneva. I have added the Declaration on the Rights of the Indigenous Peoples.

The Tribal Land System: The case of the Rongmei Naga is an extract of the report of the NABARD sponsored project on the Institutional Finance in Tribal Areas, Council for Social Development, New Delhi and Manipur University (1986). And the Historical Ecology and Technological Development in Manipur is an extract from the report of the DST Project on Endogenous Factors of Development (1985). I am happy that History of Ecology and Environment will be introduced in the Post Graduate course in History of Indian Universities as per guidelines of the U.G.C.

Human Rights in India is a modified version of a paper entitled "National Responsibility on the Protection of Human Rights in India, submitted to the National Seminar on Human

Rights at Manipur University. Colonialism and Colonial Policy is an extract from the lecture on "British Colonial Policy in Burma in the nineteenth century" which I delivered in History Department in 1983. Political Status of Manipur on. the eve of the British Conquest of Manipur, 1891 was submitted to the Jagi Road session of the North East India History Association.

Tribes of the North East India a Historical Perspective, was a paper of a national seminar on Tribal Development held at Nehru Museum and Library in 1987 at New Delhi. It was lost, forgotten and discovered at the collection of Professor Joy Kumar Singh. The Constraints of Development in a Tribal District, was read at the much publicized development seminar at Tamenglong organized by the Ministry of Home Affairs in November 2000.

Emergence of Naga Ethnic Nationality was a lecture at the NSF conference in 1992 and the Village Administration in the Hill Areas of Manipur was an article published in the Imphal Free Press. I am grateful to the editor for giving me a copy of the published article.

This publication of this anthology is more an intellectual exercise for reorienting myself to an academic activism rather than the worthiness of the contents. I would like to acknowledge the help given by my son Dr. Ram Kamei who did the computer setting and for the critical comments on the papers and to my little nephew, Achong, Shri Lankhonlong Kamei and Shri M. Ratankumar Singh, Computer Asst. of Environment & Ecology Wing.

I am also grateful to my wife Lanshailu for creating an academic atmosphere in the 'crowded' life of a public man. I also thank Smt. Pouganglu Gangmei who published the book.

Gangmumei Kamei

PART-I
ETHNICITY AND SOCIAL CHANGE

1

Ethnic Genesis of Manipur

Ethnos

Ethnos is a Greek word meaning "people". Sociologically it has been explained and applied by the Soviet sociologists. According to Academician Yu Bromley, "ethnos in the narrow meaning of the word in the most general form can be defined as a historically formed community of people possessing common, relatively stable, specific features of culture as well as being aware of their unity and the difference from other similar communities". Territorial unity is not compulsory, but the ethnos with their distinctive features are found both in compact as well as dispersed areas.

Ethnic Group and Tribe

Ethnos or ethnic group is an ethnic entity based on race, language, religion and tribal or community organization. An ethnic group shares common features with a tribe but all ethnic groups are not tribes. While a tribal community has the historical prerogative over the sharing of production resources of the tribe, an ethnic group may or may not have such a prerogative. The tribal societies are closed societies while the ethnic groups may or may not be closed societies. Tribes are associated with the primitive technology. According to the anthropologists, a tribal society turns into a peasant society when they come into contact with modern civilization and its production relations. The reality is different. After their contact, they do not necessarily form into a peasant society. But there is change in their cultural and social relation. This interaction produces an acculturation. Some have suggested that such a changing society may be described as the post-primitives who retain their tribal roots and ethos.

Ethnicity

Ethnicity has been loosely used in the sense of ethnic consciousness. Clifford Geertz has defined "ethnicity as an activated primordial consciousness". This is a feeling of belonging of an ethnic group to their ancient roots and their ancestral heritage. This "primordial consciousness" is a psycho-social phenomenon which persists in any society, industrialized plural society of the west or former socialist countries or the newly liberated Third World countries. This consciousness is the prime factor of the formation of an ethnic identity. Despite modernization as a result of spread of education, industrialization, mass struggles and economic development, the primordial consciousness persists. This is a reflection of their distinctiveness and the need to ensure political rights, economic development and cultural protection, free from exploitation. Ethnicity has been the motive force behind the ethnic movements throughout the world leading to the rise of ethnic nationalism. Ethnicity is behind the linguistic and identity movements. Ethnicity is the driving force of the global mobilization of the indigenous peoples. It is because of this "primordial consciousness" that the search for the ethnic genesis, or ethnic roots, is a part of a worldwide phenomenon of ethnic identity assertion.

Ethnic Genesis

The people of Manipur consisting of three major groups, the Meiteis, the Nagas and the Kuki-Chins are strongly influenced by ethnicity or their primordial consciousness.

There is a strong search for their ethnic genesis, their ethnic roots and origin. While the Meiteis are a nationality with a long history of nationhood, the Nagas and the Kuki-Chins are ethnic entities marching towards pre-state or non-territorial nationality. Manipur is a plural society. The population is predominantly Mongoloid with some non-Mongoloid elements, the Arýan and the Tai, who speak the TIbeto-Burman languages.

I. EVOLUTION OF THE MEITEI

The origin of the Meitei is shrouded in mystery. The study on the subject is speculative and controversial. In the middle of the nineteenth century, B.H. Hodgson speculated that the ethnonym, Meitei was 'a combined appellate of Siamese Tai and Kachin Chinese Moy into Moy Tai' (Moitai=Meitei) and that the Meiteis belong to the Moi section of the great Tai race.

T.C. Hodson suggested that it was an outcome of the blending of two terms, "Mei" meaning man and "Tei" meaning separate people, hinting at the blending of seven ethnic groups and tribes. According to an indigenous explanation, Meitei or Meetei was derived from the creation of man by God in his image. *Mee* means image, *Tei [Teiba]* means 'modelled'; modelled after God's image=Meitei. Historically, the term was used during the establishment of the Ningthouja dynasty by Pakhangba in the first century, to mean all the ethnic and social groups who were politically and socially integrated into a cornmon group under the suzerainty of the Ningthouja dynasty.

Aryan Origin ?

Of all the theories of the origin of the Meiteis, the Aryan origin was most enthusiastically propounded and vehemently rejected by the protagonists and their opponents respectively. This Aryan connection was an outcome of the adoption of

Hinduism by the ruling family and the people of valley in the eighteenth century and resultant claim of the descent of the ruling dynasty from Babhruvahana, a scion of the Pandava hero, Arjuna of the Mahabharata. In spite of the best efforts of the great Brahmin scholars backed by the royalty and ruling elite, it cannot be established that the Meiteis as an ethnic group or as a language is Aryan or Indo-Aryan. The fact is that they are neither of Aryan stock nor the Indo-Aryan speakers. However, there is a historical truth that the Meitei community had absorbed the Aryan elements in its fold as many Aryan colonizers, adventurers and immigrants came to Manipur or passed through this land in course of their colonization of or trade with South West China and Southeast Asia as Manipur was on the route of trade and migration in the past and it continues to be so even in the present century. The representatives of Aryan elements are Manipuri Brahmins and the Nongchup Haram (the immigrants from the west, i.e., India) section of the Meiteis. The Brahmins and the Hinduised Meiteis helped the propagation of the claim of the Aryan origin. The identification of the followers of Hinduism with the Aryan speakers, a delibrate attempt for identification of a religion with a language or a race, was the cause of this controversy: The Meiteis as a whole are not Aryan, but there are Aryan elements amongst them.

Mon-Khmer and Tai Connection

Hodgson's suggestion of the Moi-Tai origin of the Meiteis was rejected by T.C. Hodson on the basis of the Meitei being a Tibeto-Burman language and the Tai being the Siamese-Chinese linguistic family though both of them belong to the Sino-Tibetan linguistic family. Hodson writes, "It is difficult specially on linguistic ground to group the Meitheis with the Tai race where the structure and vocabulary of the Meithei language alike agree with those of the TIbeto-Burman". This ethnic blending of the Moi and Tai tribes has been described by an anthropologist as a puzzling ethnological exercise. Though not of the *Tai* origin, it has been conjectured that there was a relationship between the Meitei, MonKhmer and because of historical connection, both conquest and socio-cultural contacts which produced Tai influence on the language and culture of the Meiteis. Recent archaeological findings of the excavations in Tharon cave, Napachik in Manipur point to the existence of Austric speaking Mon-Khmer Austric Mongoloid people in Manipur who migrated to this land before the advent of the Tibeto-Burman speakers. The Mon-Khmer elements were absorbed by later immigrants. "All the archaeological and historical evidences point to the relationship of the ancient Meiteis with the Mon-Khmer and Tai people, but not of Mon-Khmer Tai origin of the people". However, the absorption of many Tai immigrants into Meitei society since the eighth century A.D. and more actively since the fifteenth century has been recorded in the chronicles of Manipur. The clan genealogies also indicate the assignment of clan (salai) and lineage or sub-lineage (sagei), later on Hindu gotras to these eastern (Shan and Burmese) immigrants who are collectively known as the Nongpok Haram (the immigrants from the east).

Tibeto-Burman Family

G.A. Grierson in his monumental *Linguistic Survey of India* has grouped the Meitei in the Kuki-Chin sub-family of the Tibeto-Burman languages. A more appropriate name of this sub-family, in the opinion of many linguists, would have been the Meitei Kuki-Chin. Based on a historical assumption that the Tibeto-Burman and other Mongoloid groups were habitating the upper courses of the Yangtze and the Howang Ho rivers in China in the prehistoric times, Grierson surmises that the ancestors of the Meiteis were among their kinsmen who migrated from China to upper waters of the Irrawaddy and the Chindwin rivers of upper Burma. They lived in the Hukwang valley, the present land of the Kachins before they moved into the Manipur valley. The Kachin connection has been proved by the linguistic affinity between the Meitei and the Kachin. Though the time and manner of migration cannot be easily established, Grierson is generally right in presuming that the ancestors of the Meiteis were among the Tibeto- Burman speakers in South West China, eastern Tibet and upper Burma. Hence, their affinity with the Tibeto-Burman tribes like the Nagas and Kukis who are less advanced than them. In this context, it will be relevant to note that S.K. Chatterjee, identifying the Kiratas of the later Vedas with the Tibeto-Burman Mongoloid, thinks that they might have established themselves in the southern slopes of the eastern Himalayas in eastern India around the beginning of the first millennium before Christ. They were the ancestors of the present Bodo-Kachari tribes of Assam, the Nagas, the Kukis and the Meiteis of the eastern hills.

The Naga Kuki Connection

Greatly influenced by the linguistic and cultural affinities between the Meitei and the hill tribes of Manipur and their folklore, W McCulloch advanced a theory that the major tribes and clans of the Meiteis appeared to have been the descendants of the Naga and Kuki tribes. He observes, "From the most credible traditions, the valley appears to have been occupied by some tribes, the principal of which named Koomal (Khuman), Looang (Luwang), Moirang and Meithei (Ningthouja), all of whom came from different directions. For a time, the Koomal appears to have been the most powerful and after its declension the Moirang tribe. But by degrees, the Meithei subdued the whole, and the name Meithei has become applicable to all... I... think there is...ground to conclude them to be descendants of the surrounding hill tribes. The languages spoken by these tribes are in their prestine state. I conceive then, that in their spoken language, an indication of the descent of the Munnipoorees (Meitei) might be found. Tradition brings the Moirang tribe from the south, the direction of the Kookies, the Koomal from the east, the direction of the Murrings, and the Meithei and Looang from the north west, the direction of the Koupooes (Kabui)." R. Brown also endorsed this view of tribal origin of the Meiteis with a speculation, "Should it be a correct view that the valley of Manipur was at no very distant period almost covered entirely by water, the origin of the Munnipoorees (Meitei) from the surrounding hills is the proper and only conclusion to be arrived". T.C. Hodson, writing in the beginning of twentieth century, made a bolder conclusion. "Two hundred years ago, in the internal organization in village, in habits and manners, the Meitheis were as the hill people now are. The successive courses of foreign invasions, Shan, Burmese, English and Hindu, each left permanent marks on the civilization of the people so that they have passed finally away from the stage of relatively primitive culture with one of comparative civilization but their ultimate homogeneity with the Nagas and Kukis of the hills is undoubted".

The reasons for a conclusion drawn by the British political officer-turned-ethnographers appear to be the tradition of common origin prevalent among the hill tribes that the Meiteis were their descendants as found among the Tangkhuls, Rongmei and Maos, the linguistic affinity between the Meitei, Naga and Kuki-Chin as established by Grierson, the close connection of some Meitei clans with the hill tribes who were in the vicinity of their habitat and alleged similarity of the coronation costumes of the royal couple with that of some Naga tribes, and architecture of the coronation halls of the Kangla with the ritual houses of the chiefs of the Naga tribes. The tribal origin of the Meitei clans was refuted by many writers in the 19th and 20th centuries. True, as Ch. Manihar Singh writes, "there is no legend or tradition among the Meiteis about their common origin with the tribes". But chronicles refer to the migration of individual Meitei heroes or families to the hills and conversion into the society of the

Kabuis, Tangkhul and other unspecified tribes. There was a process of entry of the hill tribes into Meitei social fold. We are not sure of the immediate descent of the Meiteis or Meitei clans from the hill tribes as propounded by Hodson but one cannot deny the Naga and Kuki Chin elements in the evolution of the Meiteis as an ethnic group."

The ethnonym Meitei, whatever the genesis of its derivation, was historically found to have been applied to the Ningthouja clan-dynasty founded by Nongda Lairen Pakhangba and other groups absorbed by this dynasty politically and integrated into the social structure. These tribes, clans or social groups are Mangangs, Angoms, Luwangs, Khabas, Naganbas, Khuman, Moirang, Sarang Leishangthem, Heirem Khunjan, Lera Khongnang, Thanga Kambong, Ulok Ushai, Haokha Lokha, Ningol Laton, Phantek Khuyon, Chakpa, Haorok Konthou etc. All these tribes and groups were socially organized into seven clans which exist even in the present time. Hodson thinks that there might have been ten or more than seven clans: Ningthouja, Angom, Luwang, Khuman, Moirang, Sarang-Leishangthem (Chenglei) and Kha-Nganba which was a combination of the Khabas and Nganbas. Khabas were once a powerful clan before the advent of the Ningthoujas. Heiren Khunjan, a tribe in southwest Manipur, for example, was absorbed into the Ningthouja kingdom and clan and assigned a surname, Heirang Khongjam. For several centuries, the Khumans and Moirangs as principal principalities resisted the Meitei hegemony, though social relationship was already established with them. It is to be understood that all the seven clans or other social groups migrated to all parts of the valley and settled in the clan principalities.

The origin of these pro-Meitei tribes is still obscure and complicated due to the absence of information with regard to their migration before they arrived at Manipur valley. The clan geneologies prepared by the Ningthouja royal court shows common origination from a single divine personality; this may be a later interpolation to create a myth of common origin of the Meiteis which was a necessary ingredient of nation building. The independent clan chronicles and geneologies, like the Moirang Ningthourol Lambuba, Khumanlon, Angornlon, Luwanglon and others show an independent history of their own, though social contacts were established and continued with the Meiteis since or little before Pakhangba's time. The Angom chronicle says that they were, at one point of time in their migration, at Khangkhui (Khanghui) cave in Ukhrul hinting at the migration from the North East. There is a tradition of Meitei (Mangang) settlement at Koubru in North West before they moved into the valley. These tribes in their pre-Meitei social formation moved into the valley from different directions and routes. While it is not possible to agree with McCulloch in his assumption of the Meiteis being the descendants of the hill tribes, his conclusion points to a close social and cultural relationship between the particular Meitei clans or tribes with the adjacent tribes, like the Tangkhul relation with the Angoms and Khaba-Nganbas, the Khuman connection with the Marings and the Anals, the Luwang connection with the Kabuis (Rongmeis), the Moirang connection with the Kabuis and other tribes like Kom, Chiru and Koireng. The adoption or conversion of hill tribes into Meitei society necessitated the assignment of *Salai* and *yumnaks* to the converted tribes who had to perform all the rituals prescribed. This practice is still continuing.

On the archaeological findings before the coming of the Tibeto-Burman speaking Proto-Meitei tribes, there were Mon-Khmer speaking Mongoloid people who were later absorbed by the Tibeto-Burmans. The Indo-Aryans and the Tai (Shans) who came to Manipur in later period were also absorbed. Thus ethnologically and linguistically, the Meiteis are Tibeto-Burman of the southern Mongoloid with Austroloid,

Aryan, and Tai admixtures (including some Negrito and Dravidian elements?). Sociologically, the Meiteis have absorbed these foreign elements and completely integrated them in their social structure. Over and above this strong political and social pressure of absorption, there is the dynamic and all absorbing Meitei language that turned out to be the backbone of the process of the Meiteisation of the various elements in the first millennium of the Christian era. It is most likely that the Meitei as a distinct ethnic, linguistic, cultural and social entity was formed in Manipur valley which was a melting pot of culture. And immediately before they settled down in the valley they must have lived in different places in the surrounding hills and gradually moved down to the *foothills* and then into the heart of the valley as indicated by the clan chronicles. Therefore, the Manipur valley is the homeland of the Meiteis. This valley with its great fertility and favourable topography had always attracted peoples from different parts of the world; likewise, the ancestors of the different clans of the Meiteis came from different directions and built up a settled civilization and evolved into a remarkable nationality.

II. ORIGIN OF THE NAGAS

It is not clear how the name "Naga" was derived. There have been several attempts made by the anthropologists and historians to trace out the origin of this word. Yet, as Verrier Elwin points out, "the derivation of the word is still obscure". Even *four* decades after Elwin made this observation the problem remains unsolved. An attempt has been made to present the explanations made by different scholars and find out the correct position. The issue is complicated due to the continuing process of identity assertion, formation and expansion movement of the Nagas themselves.

In the *Ramayana* and *Mahabharata*, there are references to the Kiratas who have been identified with the Indo-

Mongoloid tribal people of North East India. The Puranas and Epics refer to many Naga dynasties (Naga Vansa). In the *Mahabharata*, Arjuna, the great Pandava hero is said to have married Ulupee, a Naga Princess. Indian scholars have attempted to identify the Naga of the ancient Sanskrit literature with the Naga of North East. This is evidently not correct. The Naga of the Sanskrit literature may be identified with the Nagas, who in their climax of glory came to rule in Northern India after the fall of the great Kushanas before the rise of the imperial Guptas in Northern India, the descendents of whom may be the present Naga Sadhus of central India. Thus it is hard to accept the theory of "Naga" originating from Sanskrit "Nag" meaning serpent. There is no snake worship cult among the Nagas, though the python is revered sometimes and its killing is done ceremonially and elaborately. Some have connected the "Naga"'with Sanskrit "Ng" meaning mountain as the people live mostly in the high hills. Thus implying "hill man."

Long ago in the 2nd century, A.D. Ptolemy, the *famous* Greek geographer of Egypt, in his *Ancient Geography* refers to a group of people known as "Nangalogae" living in Novascium in eastern India. G.R. Gerini, Mcrindle, K.L. Barua, P.C. Choudhury and others have identified the Nangalogae with the Nagas. Nangalogae (Nanga Log) means in Sanskrit naked people (Nanga, naked and Logae (Log)= people).

In the middle ages, the chronicles of the Ahoms of Assam, especially "Ahom Buranji" refer to the Nagas who fought against them. The first reference to "Naga" in the Ahom chronicles dates back to the 9th century A.D. when the Ahom-Tais or Shans were living in upper Burma and had not crossed to the Brahmaputra valley. This reference to "Naga" in G.C. Barua (Ed.) *Ahom Buranji* has been doubted, as the Shan and Burman name for the Nagas was Khyen or Khen. The Muslim "writers including Shahabuddin Talish, the chronicler who accompanied Mir Jumla, the great Mughal general of Aurangazeb in his invasion of Assam in the middle of seventeenth Century A.D. have referred to the Nagas. In the 18th and 19th centuries, the word "Naga" became very popular. The Assamese called the Naga tribes as "Noga". Many European writers had accepted that the word originated from Assamese or Sanskrit or Hindustani "Nanga".

The early 19th century view is well expressed by William Robinson (1841) when he observes, "The origin of the word Naga is unknown; but it has been supposed to have been derived from the Sanskrit word (Nanga) and applied in derision to the people, from the paucity of their clothing; but there seems little foundation for the etymological derivation, as the term has never been known to be applied by the Bengalees to either the Khasias or the Garos with whom they were better acquainted than that with the Naga, and besides, the Garos especially are habitually accustomed to a greater degree of nudity than of the Naga tribes with whom we are acquainted".

Despite the "Nanga" theory of the Nagas which became popular with the Naga's fight against the British and their famous head hunting practice, a new theory of the origin of the 'Naga' was propounded by a British explorer and tea cultivator, S.E. Peal, that it came from the word "Nok" meaning man in some of the Tibeto-Burman languages like that of the Ao, Nocte, Garos, etc. The tribes, it is true, call themselves mostly man or people, indicative of the absence of any class or distinction in social order. EA Gait, the great historian of Assam in 1906, wrote on the subject, "The collective designation by which they are known to the Assamese seems to be derived, as suggested by Holcombe and Peal, from "Nok" which means folk in some of the tribal dialects. When strange parties meet the places, they are said to ask each other term Noke or Nok meaning "what folk are you?" and Nokrang, 'the people of the sky.' In this connection it is worth noting that the Khonds call themselves "Kui Luika" and the Orans 'Ku Nok.' The lengthening of the first vowel sound in the Bengali and English rendering of the word is probably due to the old idea that is connected with snake worship". However, the Nanga theory continued to be more or less accepted when the great anthropologists J.H. Hutton and J.P. Mills, through their magnificent monographs on selected Naga tribes and research papers supported Ptolemy's view. Baron von Hamendorf, 'Naked Nagas', J.P Mills, 'Naked Rengmas' and the colonial authority's practice of presenting the Naga tribal dobashis and dancers in the exotic Naga dresses went a long way to confirm this view in popular mind. The 'Nok' theory was first forgotten till the appearance of Verrier Elwin's *Nagas in the Nineteenth Century* (1959) and *Nagaland* (1960). Elwin writes; "The meaning and derivation of the word Naga has long been disputed. Our chief authority on the Naga tribes, J.H. Hutton, originally thought that it was a corruption of the Assamese Noga (pronounced Naga) probably meaning mountaineer from the Sanskrit Ng, a mountain or inaccessible place. Later he reluctantly recanted this opinion in view of the fact that Ptolémy in the 2nd century and Shihabuddin in the 17th century speak of the Nagas as Nanga or naked. This does not seem a very strong argument. Waddel, on the other-hand explains Noga as meaning hillmen." Verrier Elwin in his *Nagaland* (1960) continues the issue. "The most likely derivation to my mind is that which traces "Naga" from the word 'Nok' or people which is its meaning in a few Tibeto-Burman languages, as in Garo, Nokte and Ao. It is common throughout India for tribesmen to call themselves by words meaning 'man' an attractive habit which suggests that they look on themselves simply as people free from communal or caste association". Thus Elwin's prestigious opinion revives the Nok theory of the Nagas.

Meanwhile, a few Naga scholars who want to discount the colonial writer's views proposed two theories. One is that

Naga was derived from the Kachari word Nokka (Nokhhar) meaning warrior fighters as the Kacharis came into violent conflict with Naga tribes like the Angamis and Zeliangrong. The latest proposal made by R.R. Shimray in his "Origin and Culture of the Nagas" (1985) is that it was derived from the Burmese word Na Ka meaning pierced ears. He also quotes a Thai tradition from Chiang Mai of Thailand that a group of people with pierced ears migrated to Burma and they were known as Nakari'. The British came to know of these people and anglicized their name into Naga. These two theories have created more confusion to the whole problem.

These explanations are not convincing; because, the 'Nok' theory is a generalization of a tribal self image. True, most of the Naga or other tribes use to call themselves by the general term man. But 'Nok' to be applied to the Naga as a general term is not reasonable. The Naga tribes call themselves by their tribal names. In the early period, the name Naga was not known. But it was the outsiders like the Assamese, Bengali and Ahom with whom they had very wide contact, who gave this name to the tribes. For example, the tribes like Angami, Ao, Zeme, Rongmei are known by the outsiders' names, not by their own original names. The Meitei name for all the tribes of Manipur, both the Nagas and the Kuki, is Hau. But after further subdivision, the tribal names like Tangkhul, Maram, Maring, Anal, etc. are also used. Therefore "Nok" theory does not explain much.

Though no final word has been said on the derivation of Naga, it is certain that the name was given by the outsiders-the inhabitants of the Brahmaputra and Barak valleys to mean the Naga. The name was popularized and enforced by the British colonial authorities during the introduction of the their rule in the Naga areas. The problem has been more complicated by the political touch which is adopted to identify a particular tribe as Naga or not, in relation to the Kukis. In Manipur, with R.B. Pemberton's writings, the identification of the tribes as Nagas was started with the colonial contact. Whatever the British officials applied to the Naga Hills was also applied to Manipur tribes. The colonial ethnographers did not bother themselves to give thought on the issue.

The Naga Tribes

The Nagas are concentrated in the states of Nagaland, Manipur, Assam and Arunachal Pradesh of India and Naga Hills of Upper Myanmar. The following Naga tribes have now been identified and located.

Nagaland: Ao, Angami, Sema, Lotha, Rengma, Chakhesang, Yimchunger, Kalya Kangnyu, Konyak, Chang, Sangtam, Phom, Zeme; Liangmai, Rongmei (Zeliangrong), Khiemungan, Puchori

***Manipur*:** Anal, Maring, Moyon, Monsang, Lamkang, Chote, Tangkhul, Mao, Poumai, Maram, Thangal, Zeliangrong, (Zeme, Liangmei, Rongmei, Puimei), Chiru, Kharam, Tarao.

Arunachal Pradesh : Tangsha, Wancho, Nocte.

Myanmar: Konyak, Tangkhul, Phom, Yunchunger, Haimi Pangmi and two dozen tribes and clans.

Assam: Zeme, Rongmei and Rengma.

The Nagas present a picture of unity in diversity. The Nagas themselves feel that they are a homogenous group of race. The Nagas are divided into different tribal and linguistic groups. Every tribe has a unique political organization of their own. All types of political system are found among the Nagas, ranging from the pure democracy of the Angami to the autocratic rule of the Angs of the Konyaks, from the gerontocracy (Tatar) of the Aos to the semi-republic of the Zeliangrongs. In their manners and customs, there are great outward variations. In their racial make up and physical features, there are elements ranging from the Mongoloid to which the majority belongs, to the Aryan and Negrito. Their religions, now grouped into Christianity and traditional religion, have variety with diverse belief and custom. There is difference in rituals and mode of worship.

Despite these diversities, there is a strong fundamental unity, a feeling of ethnic and emotional solidarity and belonging. The hostile topography and ecology provide no bar to the Naga sense .of unity. When the geographical barriers of isolation were broken down by the easy means of communication introduced by the British, it provided a common identity and name. The sense of unity was first imposed exogenously but later on endogenous attempt fostered the Naga sense of unity. The Naga national feeling or Naga nationality is a product of British colonialism, the Second World War, modernization and the Naga movement for political sovereignty. However, the evolution of Naga nationality is not *fait accompli but* an ongoing search for ethnic identity. Thus the concept of a Naga nationality is a new force whose growth has been facilitated by the Naga love for their culture and freedom.

The Nagaising process has produced an interesting psychological phenomenon which leads towards the centrifugal tendency. This is the process of transformation of tribes among some tribes, for example, the Chakhesang, (a combination of Chakru, Kheza and Sangtam= Cha+Khe+ Sang), the Zeliangrong (Zeme, Liangmai, Rongmei = Ze+ Liang + Rong). There is another process of identity expansion among the tribes in Manipur to be grouped under the Naga constellation or under the Kuki-Chin constellation.

Origin and Migration

The proto-history of the Nagas is not fully studied. The available information are scanty and unreliable. The legends and oral tradition which the Nagas relate even today give some gleanings to the past of this fine and remarkable people.

The problem of periodizing the human habitation of their country still remains unresolved. How old is man and his culture in the Naga area? The myth and legends preserved by the different Naga tribes claim that they originated from the land and have been living here from times immemorial. The solution can be- found by the study of the relics of the neolithic and megalithic culture of the Nagas in comparison with some peoples of Southeast Asia and Pacific region which were initiated by J.H. Hutton and continued by others.

Almost all the tribes trace their origin to the cave or holes in the earth. This is a myth reminiscent of the distant echo .of the cave man's style of life of the Nagas. All the southern Naga tribes claim their origin from Makhel in Manipur's Senapati district. Starting from the southwestern tribes, the Zeliangrong of western Manipur have a tradition that they came out of a mythical cave known as Taobhei. They migrated to Makhel, then to Ramting Kabin, a village in a deep gorge, then to Makui longdi, then they dispersed towards three regions, the south, west and north.

The Mao legend points to Makhel from where their ancestors emerged from the earth and refer to Khezakhenoma as the centre of migration. The stone relics still exist both at Makhel and Khazekhenoma which was separated from Makhel. The Tangkhuls of North East Manipur have two traditions according to one of which they originated from Makhel and migrated toward Ithe east and settled at Hungdung. T.C. Hodson records the Tangkhul tradition of habitation in Manipur valley and later migration from that place to the present habitat. Another tradition of the Tangkhuls preserved in their folk songs points to their migration from Samsok (Thuangdut) of Kabaw valley of upper Burma and moved into Imphal valley which they left due to heat and mosquito. There are relics of Tangkhul settlement in the valley.

The Angamis of Kohima also came from Mao area, especially the village of Khezakhenoma. It can be easily seen that the Mao, the Poumei, the Chakhesang and the Angamis are kindred tribes and some writers describe them as quasi-Angami tribes. The Marams have affinities with the Zeliangrong and Tangkhul tribes linguistically and ethnically while they have strong political alliance with the Maos. Other Naga tribes of Manipur like the Marings, Anals, Moyon, Moyon Monshang, Lamkang have the tradition of coming out from the caves, mostly located in south eastern hills of Manipur.

It will be relevant to know the tradition of origin of some tribes of Nagaland. Regarding the origin of the Semas, J.H. Hutton writes, "Like other western Naga tribes, the Semas point to the south as the direction from which they came. They relate the story of Khezakhenoma stone as well as many other folk tales common to the Angamis and Lotha particularly the later. They do not, however, trace their origin south of Mao, but point to Tukabo *(Japvo)* as the place from which they sprang". The Lotha legend points their origin to Khezakhenoma. J.P. Mills writes, "It is narrated that three brothers Limhachan, Izumontse and Rankhanla who were ancestors of the three Phratries of the Lotha tribe came out of a hole near the miraculous stone at Khezakhenoma". Yet another tradition says that the common ancestors of the Lotha, the southern Sangtam, Semas, Rengmas came somewhere near Mao. The Rengma name for Khezakhenoma is Khein Zenyui and both the Lotha and Rengmas agree that they were once a single tribe.

The Aos and the northern tribes have the belief. that men came from the hole in the earth. The Ao cosmogony is relevant to the story of creation prevalent among the Shans and the Japanese. According to the Ao legend, Lunkizungbe was the supreme deity. He was like the wind, he made the sky, he created the sun and the moon and he was the creator of man. However, the earth was created by Lichabe. According to another legend "man is said to have come from the Lungterok (six stones) near the vlllage of Chongliyimti. Six men, the progenitors of the human race came from this place". The Phoms also claim to have emerged from the cave at Lungterok but do not reckon themselves as Ao. The Yimchungers relate that they emerged from Mom village in the extreme east.

It is simply absurd to give credence to the legends indicating an autochthonous origin of the Naga tribes; it can be regarded, from the proto-historical point of view, as a stage of human society and culture through which they passed. Therefore, it is inferred that the traditions of Makhel, Khezakhenoma, Ramting kabin in Manipur and Lungterok in central Nagaland point to such state of life and their routes of migration.

Looking into the affinities between the various Naga tribes with the tribes of island Southeast Asia, like the Dayaks and Ingorots of Indonesia, and the Naga use of artefacts found in the sea, it has been conjectured that the Naga had traversed from south west China to Burma and western Thailand, and to island Southeast Asia and moved north again and entered into the present habitat in North East India and some area of upper Burma.

Ethnic and Linguistic Features

In the racial mosaic of India, the Mongoloid is a segment which dominates the North East India. And ethnologically, the Nagas are the Tibeto-Burmans of the Sino Tibetan groups of Mongoloid who have been described by Indian philologists led by S.K. Chatterjee as the Indo–Mongoloid because of their historical connection with India, especially in North East and the Himalayan region. Dr. S.K. Chatterjee and, following him, many Indian scholars have interpreted the Kiratas of the Sanskrit literature with the Indo–Mongoloid. It has been established that the Mongoloid had contributed to the enrichment of Indian culture as a whole (S.K. Chatterjee 1950). According to him, the Kiratas include all these Sino-Tibetan speaking tribes, Mongoloid of various types race, who entered into or touched the triangle of the cultural entity that is India, the Himalayan tribes (the Nepal tribes and north Assam tribes), the Indian Tibetans, the Khasis, and earlier tribes (of unknown affiliation within the Tibeto-Burman Branch of the Sino TIbetan family) who have now become absorbed in the population of the northern and northeastern India.

The Linguistic Survey of India, conducted by G.A. Grierson in the early twentieth century, established the linguistic family of the Naga as Tibeto Burman. Grierson divides the group into the Naga family and Naga-Bodo sub-family. Now with the entry of a few more tribes of Manipur into Naga constellation, a few Kuki-Chin speakers now are among the Naga tribes.

The Nagas of Manipur

The tribes of Manipur who are now grouped under the Naga fold are among the earliest inhabitants of the hills of Manipur. The name Naga was given to them by the British on the basis of their policy of identifying and classifying the tribes of Nagaland and Manipur. The Naga tribes of Manipur are known by their tribal names. We have already indicated the tribes under Naga fold. But a word of caution is necessary. The tribes like Zeme, Liangmai, Rongmei. Mao, Maram, Thangal and Tangkhul and Maring who have strong tradition of common origin *on* ethnological and linguistic grounds have been called Naga. There are some tribes, like Anal, Moyon, Monshang, Lamkang, Tarao, Chothe, Chiru, and Kharam who have linguistic affinity with the Kuki-Chin, and cultural and political identification with the Naga.

They are, in the words of B.K. Roy Burman, bridge buffer communities between the Naga and the Kuki Chins, who are more attracted towards the Naga ideologically and have accepted the Naga identity.

These tribes occupy different areas of Manipur hills; the Naga ethnic territory was well maintained till the migration of the Kuki-chin tribes during the historical period. The Zeliangrong tribes occupy the western hills of Manipur. The Rongmeis are a widely dispersed community. They had settled down in Imphal valley and the Cachar district of Assam. There are relics to show that the Zeliangrong habitat in the past, reached the edge of the Mizo hills. The Zeme and Liangmci are found in Nagaland; some Rongmeis had recently migrated to that state. The Zeme are also found in the North Cachar hills. The Mao, Poumai, Maram and Thangal inhabit the north Manipur. The Tangkhuls are the most numerous tribe and occupy the hills of Ukhrul. The Tangkhul habitat spreads beyond the Indian border into upper Burma in Somra tract and Naga hills of Burma. Many Tangkhuls have settled down in the foothills and in Irnphal valley. The Marings occupy the Tengnoupal area of Chandel district, whereas the Moyon, Monshang, Lamkang, Anal, Tarao, Chothe are found in Chandel and Chakpikarong area of the same district.

The problem of the origin and migration of the Nagas have not been properly studied by the scholars. They pose as a challenging and intense problem of the Naga history. The oral tradition of Nagas of Manipur claiming to record the account of their origin, tell us more about the migration within Manipur and the trans-Chindwin region. It may be accepted that the Naga tribes were in occupation of the present habitat in the centuries before the Christian era. Like some tribes of Nagaland, Manipur's Naga tribes point to Makhel in Mao area as their place of origin from where they migrated to the present habitat. There are also traditions among the Naga tribes of Chandel speaking dialects akin to Kuki Chin, showing their migration from the Chin hills and Kabaw valley. There is a Tangkhul tradition of migrating from Thaungdut in the Kabaw Valley. The other Naga tribes like Chiru and Kharam who have strong affinity with the Kom and Koireng, point to migration from the southern hills probably south Manipur and Chin hills. The Makhel tradition is quite prominent in the history of Naga migration.

Tangkhul

As indicated, the Tangkhuls point to Makhel as their ancestral place from where they migrated to the present habitat. Another legend also indicates their migration from Samsok (Thaungdut) in Kabaw valley of upper Burma. The latter legend appears to be indicative of transmigration within the Tangkhul country itself. It shows the settlement of the Tangkhul upto the western bank of the Chindwin. Tangkhul was perhaps a name given by the outsiders but there is a view that it was derived from 'Tangkhu', one of the three progenitors. According to T. Luikham, the original name of the Tangkhul is 'Wung'. Regarding the racial composition, the Tangkhul features consist of sharp semiAryan features and Mongoloid elements. There are two groups, the northern Tangkhuls who use spear as tbeir major weapon and the southern Tangkhuls who use bow and arrow as their weapon. Seeing the semi-Aryan features, Sir James Johnstone muses whether they are the remnants of the migrating Aryan hordes of the past, as one of the routes of Indian colonization to Southeast Asia lay through Manipur hills.

Zeliangrong

The Zeliangrong is the combined name of the Zeme, Liangmai, Rongmei and Puimei. The Zeme and Liangmai were known to the British as Kacha Naga whereas the Rongmei and Puimei are popularly known as the Kabui, a name given by the Meiteis of Manipur. The Zeliangrong people, according to their legend preserved in the religious hymns and folk songs, originated from a mythical cave called Taobhei; they moved to Makhel and to Ramting Kabin and then to Makuilongdi. From this settlement they migrated to the south, west and the north. Makhel is thus an important point of dispersal in their migration to the western Manipur and Barail range. How the name 'Kacha Naga' carne to be applied to the Zeme and Liangmai by the British is not known, whether it was the Angami word Ketsu or Ketsa meaning deep forest or from a name of peak named Kacha in Zeme country. Nothing is known clearly about the derivation of 'Kabui'. The ancient chronicles of Manipur refer to Kabui, Tangkhul, Anal and others as very ancient tribes. Poireiton Khunthokpa, an ancient text dealing with the adventures and colonization of Poireiton, records that when he came to Manipur hills, the Kabui, Tangkhul and Anal were already living there.

Mao

Mao appears to be appended to the present tribe of the same name by the neighbouring tribe of Maram and the people call themselves as Ememei (descendents of Emeo). The assertion of T.C. Hodson that Mao is a Meitei name given to the village of Mao does not have corroboration since the Meitei gave the name of Ngamei to Maos and Angami. Sometimes, they are locally known as Shupfomei, descendents *oj* a great culture hero of the same name. The Mao Nagas are concentrated in the confederacy of 16 villages with the village of Pudunamei as the titular head. Poumai is a kindred group of the Maos who call them Kape Mata. Paomata or Poumai'means the descendents of Pao whereas Kape Mata means descendents of Kapeo. It seems Pao or Kapeo are one and same person who was also a descendent of Memeo, the ancestor who was living at Makhel to which the Maos point as the place of origin and a point of migration. The Maram and Thangals are linguistically and culturally allied people. They have affinity with the Liangmei of the Zeliangrong.

Maring

The Marings are among the oldest tribes of Manipur. They are concentrated in Tengnoupal sub-division of Chandel district, bordering Burma. Their main villages are Machi, Khudei Khullen, Lamlong and Khunbi which are very important centres of dispersal in their migration. The name Maring was derived from two words Mi (Ma) and Ring (Mi means men and ring means to live=Living men). There are other interpretations according to which it came from the two words Mi (corrupted to Ma) and Ring (Mi means fire and *Ring* means to kindle; the user or kindler of fire). But there is no authentic historical account about their origin. There is a tradition that the Marings came from Haobam Marak of Imphal valley pointing to a common origin with the Meiteis. However, other traditions point to the migration from upper Burma according to which two original villages are mentioned: Kulisong-song and Vasafa. Some ethnographers divide the Marings into three sections (which are not accepted by the Maring themselves): (i) Those who wear red bordered cloth, (ii) those who wear the black bordered cloth and (iii) those who wear red and black bordered cloths.

Anal

The Anal is a very interesting case of a bridge buffer tribe. Their habitat is sandwiched in the north by the Naga areas of the Maring and Tangkhul tribes, and by the Kuki-Chin-Mizo of Burma and Mizoram in the south, by the Shan dominated Kabaw valley in the east and by the Meitei inhabited Manipur valley. According to Ningthourol Lambuba, an ancient chronicle of Manipur, the name Anal was derived from the Meitei word "Nanba" meaning slippery, as Poireiton, a first century colonizer slipped on the mossy place in their country. G.A. Grierson was also told that it was a Meitei name. The name was in fact derived from the name of the village, Anal Namfou (Lamfou) and Anal Khullen. Anal Khullen was named *after* Angnal or Anal Pa, founder of the village: And later on Anal-Pa was corrupted to Anal Khu (Anal village). The original homeland of the Anal cannot be loca ted precisellу. A comparative study of the language and culture of the Anals and tribes of the Chin Hills of Burma will give a clue to the understanding of the problem.

The Anal oral tradition tells the story of their migration from a cave, under the leadership of Hansu and Hantha. The original name of the tribe was Pakan which included Anal, Moyon, Monshang and Lamkang. The neighbours of the Anals are Chote, Moyon, Monshang and Lamkang tribes. The Chiru, Koireng and Kharam are found in Senapati district.

Before Makhel, from where ?

The Naga tradition of Makhel being their original home does not conclusively prove their antiquity and origin, but their common origin has been believed and accepted because of this popular tradition. As a point of dispersal and migration, the existing relics of Makhel have clearly confirmed the traditions. The following relics are important archaeological evidence of Makhel, 3 miles away from Tadubi.

(i) A Menhir called Tamaratu, stone of Dispersal (Tamara: departure, Tu: stone) with engravings of a man dragging a bull, a cock, a tiger's head, a shield and spear.

(ii) A wild pear tree called Chatebu (Kaji) which was planted at upper Sajouba, near Makhel at the time of their dispersal. It was forbidden to cut a branch of the tree; whenever a branch breaks down a genna is obsered. It is believed that if anybody breaks the branch, he will die.

(iii) A peepal tree (Marrabu), a sacred tree believed to have grown out of the tomb of the first woman who died at Makhel, a very old oak tree.

(iv) 3 stone megaliths called Lino Tu are the stone in memory of the dispersal of the Nagas.

(v) Some polished stones, known as war stone, famine and calamity, rain and thunder stones are preserved in the Headman's house. A sacred shield made of an animal skin kept at the headman's residence of Makhel is believed to have magical power.

Now, wherefrom did they come to Makhel ? The Zeliangrong (Liangmei) folk songs refer to their contact with the Dimasa-Kachari before they came to Makhel. The Poumai tradition found in the hymn of Chazil during the Salaoni festival tells thus: "We came from a floating land, we came from Makhel and we came from Siifid." According to another tradition prevalent among Paomata, Leopaona and Chilevai, the migrating people were led by an old man called Pou to Makhel. Manipur valley was full of water and not suitable for settlement; one group went to the east, and another group went to the north, led by Pou and arrived at Makhel. The "floating lands" may be the small islets of Imphal basin or of the sea coast in the Bay of Bengal. Perhaps, the different groups of Nagas arrived at Makhel from different directions. It has been surmised that the Tangkhuls had migrated from the east, Samsok to Imphal valley. Makhel, perhaps was derived from Mao or Maram word Makheo or Makhre-fu, a place of secrecy.

Some more intensive study based on archaeological, ethnographic and linguistic evidence will be necessary to find out the route of migration of the Nagas. As they are Tibeto-Burman, they must have lived with other groups of the same family in south west China before 1000 B.C. and migrated to eastern Tibet, Upper Burma, then moved into the Irrawaddy valley, Malaysia and Indonesia, and they returned northward and entered north east India through Manipur River, and some tracts of Indo-Burma border to present Naga habitat. The traditions described in this chapter deal more with the migration within their country, before they established their ethnic territory. It is clear that they preceded the Kuki-Chins in the migration to Manipur.

III. THE KUKI-CHIN : ORIGIN AND MIGRATION

The Kuki Chin is both a linguistic group and an ethno-cultural entity. Linguistically, the Kuki-c:hin is a sub-family of the Tibeto-Burman comprising the Kuki, Chin, Mizo (Zo, Zomi) and the Meitei (Manipuri) languages, on the basis of the linguistic classification adopted by G.A. Grierson, in his "The Linguistic Survey of India". As an ethno cultural entity; the term excludes the Meitei, but covers the Kuki, Chin, Mizo (Zo, Zomi) and other cognate tribes and clans. The evolution of this composite name is an outcome of the colonial imposition of a common identity and a search for common ethnic identity on part of the Kuki-Chin-Mizo people themselves. John Shakespeare, a great authority on the Kukis and Lushais wrote in 1912, "The term Kuki is not recognized by the people to whom it is applied." Historically speaking, the first reference was made to the 'Kuki' in 1777, when these tribesmen attacked the British subjects in Chittagong when Warren Hastings was the Governor General of Bengal. According to J.H. Hutton, the name Kuki first appeared in the writing of Rawlins on "the Cuceis or Mountaineers of Tripura" in 1792 in Asiatic Researches (II. xii). E.T. Dalton mentions that the Kukis were first known from an article written by Surgeon Mecrea in Asiatic Researches Vol. VII, on 24th January, 1799 who described the Kukis as "nation of hunters and warriors". T.H. Lewin, another frontier officer and ethnographer, refers to the account of the Cucis or inhabitants of the Hill Tipperah written by J. Rennel, the Chief Engineer of Bengal in 1800. John Shakespeare thinks that these "Cucis were the Rivungs, the advance guard of the great Lushai invasion. Thus the name "Kuki" is not a very old name. 'Kuki' means to their immediate neighbours of Bengal and Tripura, 'hill people' or "mountaineers". The term was arbitrarily applied to them by the British administrators who had a hazy knowledge after their conquest of Bengal and later on, Assam. The Meitei name for the Kukis is Khongsai or Khongjai, and as such R.B. Pemberton (1835) refers to them as "Khongjuees". Khongsai is one of the ancestral lineages of the Kukis. We have the great authority of T.H. Lewin that "The Loosei commonly called the Kookie are a powerful and independent people who are known to the Bengalees by the name of Kookie and the Burmese as the Lankhe". In Manipur, where the great Kuki exodus of the nineteenth century created a lot of ethnic tension and administrative problems for the state, they were both known as the Khongjai and Kukis. In Manipur, the Kukis were identified as distinct and quite separate from the Lushais against whom the British and Manipur launched the Lushai Expedition in 1871-72.

From the British point of view, both administrative and ethnographic, the Kukis were replaced by the term "Lushai" since the Lushai Expedition of 1871. The name was adopted to mean the tribal groups of the later Lushai Hills District, now Mizoram. While the earlier inhabitants of the Lushai hills were the Kukis, they were pushed out of the area by the more aggressive clans who came to be known as the Lushai. According to Shakespeare, the term 'Lushai' is the incorrect transliteration of the word, 'Lushei' which is the name of the clan under which various chiefs of the Thangur lineage, came into prominence in the eighteenth century and was responsible for the eruption into Cachar of the Kukis. Shakespeare continues, "Lushai is used in the wider sense, Lushei being used only for the clan of the name. Among the people themselves, the Lushais are spoken of as Dulian... and the general population is spoken of as Mizo." Mizo was a term used by the people among themselves even in the nineteenth century.

As regards the derivation of the "Lushai", T.H. Lewin thought that it was derived from 'Lu' meaning a head and 'Shai' meaning to cut, a sort of headhunter. Shakespeare did not accept this opinion when he observed, " This of course, is a mistake, as the name of the clan is not Lushai, but Lusei, and though 'Sha' does mean 'to cut', it does not mean 'to cut off' and not being used of cutting off' a man's head" but that such a mistake should have been possible was one of the peculiarities of the population of these hills".

Chin is an old Burmese word which according to Professor C.H. Luce, means 'an ally or comrade' P.K. Lehman thinks that it means roughly the 'unsophisticated'. In modem Burmese, Chin means a basket and B. Lalthangliana interprets it as a "man with a basket". The Chins are concentrated in the Chin Hills of Burma with some distribution in India. After the Lushai Expedition and the ultimate conquest of Lushai hills and formation of Lushai Hills district, the Lushai was widely used.

So also the British conquest of the Chin Hills, and the widely circulated Gazetteer of the Chin Hills written by B.S. Carey and H.N. Tuck (1896) andA.S. Reid's Lushai- Chin land, (1893), and the writings of the British officers who served in Burma and north east India among these tribes, emphasized on the affinity and racial identity of the Chin, Lushai and Kukis.1n Burma and Mizoram (then Lusahi hills), the term "Kuki" was gradually discarded. But in Manipur state, Assam and Tripura, the name is continued. Thus in the beginning of the twentieth century the names, Kuki, Chin and Lushai appeared as settled names in the above mentioned administrative divisions or areas in which they lived.

John Shakespeare with his wide knowledge of the ethnography of these tribes, and before him the linguists and philologists like Stein Konow and G.A. Grierson had strongly and convincingly pointed out the common racial and linguistic affinity of the Kuki, Chin and Lushai. It was Grierson's Linguistic Survey which gave a definite name "the Kuki-Chin", to connote the linguistic sub-family. But, the Kukis of Cachar and Manipur and the Lushais (Mizo) of Mizoram, because of that past political and military conflicts did not maintain any political alliance. Despite this, Shakespeare declared in 1912 that "the feuds between different clans which are always found where permanent villages exist, tend to widen the breach between communities and to sharpen every accidental variation of custom, so that the common origin is soon lost sight of. Nevertheless, there is no doubt that the Kukis, Chins and Lushais are all of the same race". He ascribed clan status to various cognate lineage groups which half a century later were taken as tribes and the terms like Kuki, Mizo, Chin appeared as generic names like the Naga.

It was because of this strong ethnic, linguistic and cultural affinity that the movement for uniting these communities under a common nomenclature, like Mizo, then Kuki-Mizo, and Chin-Kuki-Mizo has been going on. The case of 'Zo' or Zomi is definitely stronger than the rest in recent years. The Zo History written by Vumson is a strong historical basis for such a fraternity.

While the Chins of Burma, Lushais (Mizo) of Mizoram were settled in an administrative area which was more or less coterminus with their ethnic territories, the Kukis of Manipur, Tripura and Cachar had a different story. The Kukis who migrated to Cachar and North Cachar Hills of Assam in 18th century became settled subjects without much trouble. Tarun Goswami has clearly indicated the cordial relationship behveen the Kukis and Tularam Senapati, the ruler of North Cachar Hills and consequently between the Kukis and the Dimasa. Actually it was Stewart and later Soppitt, who were serving officers in these areas and who wrote first on the affinity between the Kukis, Lushai and Chin. The common identity of the Kuki was maintained in Assam (later in Nagaland). The twenty eight clans were recognized as Scheduled Tribes under the category of 'Any Kuki Tribe' in Assam.

Maharaja Nara Singh of Manipur settled the Kukis in Manipur hills with the assistance of Political Agent W. Mc Culloch. They were recruited to Manipur's armed forces. The Kuki Irregulars formed a part of the army of the state before 1891. Maharaja Chandrakriti of Manipur (1850-1886) had a very close relationship with them. Even the rebellion of 1917-1919 was officially called Kuki Rebellion or Kuki Punitive Measures. Official writers like R. Brown (1874) and E.W. Dun (1886), had already indicated the existence of various tribes other than the Nagas, who were settled in Manipur for more than a thousand years but speaking dialects peculiar to the Kuki Chin speech. They have great affinity with the new migrants of the 18th and 19th centuries. These tribes were described by the British writers as Naga and Kuki. As Manipur was an independent country, the British did not have the opportunity of direct administration before 1891; therefore there was confusion over the identification of these tribes. They also invented the term 'old Kuki' to be differentiated from the recent Kuki migrants, and this term was applied to the Manipur tribes with linguistic affinity with the Kukis. And the great authority of John Shakespeare gave a final approval on this term. This distinction of the 'Old' and 'New' Kuki is a misnomer. This classification was based on their linguistic and cultural affinities and difference in the period of their migration to their present habitat, without looking into the differences in their land ownership system, polity system and .their relationship with other tribes of Manipur. The tribes like Anal, Moyon, Monshang, Lamkang who were already in Manipur since the first century A.D. when Poireiton migrated to Manipur. And Tarao, Aimol, Chiru, Chothes were already tribute paying tribes of Manipur in the twelfth century as indicated in Loyamba Shilyen and the Kharam and Koireng who were in Manipur around 14th century.

But the Indian anthropologists also joined in the fray and accepted the Old-New Kuki classification. We may refer to the classification of Kuki Tribes made by J.K. Bose of Calcutta University in 1934, perhaps based on the census of India (1931). But the appearance of William Shaw's book named "Notes on Thadou Kukis" in 1929 claiming the primacy of the Thadous among the Kukis revived the old rivalry and caused the "disintegration" or break up of ,the Kuki fraternity in Manipur. To this was added the tension created by over emphasis given to the " Old and New Kuki" syndrome. Thus, despite, the formation of the Kuki National Assembly which was a Thadou dominated organization to which were admitted all the willing Kuki tribes during the post Second World War period, other Kuki tribes went in for separate tribal organizations. The attempts made by the Aizawl based Mizo Union to unite the Kuki-Chin-Lushai tribes under the banner of a common name "Mizo" were ignored in Manipur except the Hmars who launched a boycott movement in 1949 for integration of their area into the former Lushai Hills. The result of the intra-tribal tension, added to it the jealous consciousness of the tribes to maintain their clan genealogies. The dropping of the term ".Any Kuki Tribe" from the list of the Scheduled Tribes of Manipur in 1956 has led to the recognition of individual tribes belonging to the Kuki fold. Interestingly "Any Kuki Tribe was again recognized in 2003.

During the period of deep internal crisis of identity among the Kuki Chin speaking tribal groups, the Naga national movement gained momentum with a strong emphasis on the ethnic formation of the Naga nationality, which is both a political and sociological phenomenon and a process of "Nagaisation". The "Nagaising" process converted the bridge-buffer communities who were oscillating between the Naga and the Kuki-Chin constellations into the Naga fold and joined the Naga movement. After sometime, the Mizo National Front, tried to organize an insurgency based on Pan Kuki-Mizo fraternity. As the Naga movement was more powerful and deeper, the tribes who are Kuki Chin speakers but having strong cultural affinity and geographical proximity and homogeneity with Naga are completely confirmed within the Naga constellation. The Naga-ising process is still a continuing phenomenon.

The Mizo movement seeking integration with Mizoram, and participation in the *Mizo* insurgency has now, after the end of the Mizo Rebellion, turned into a cultural movement-a Kuki-Chin-Mizo fraternity. This movement is based on the preservation of the linguistic, social and cultural oneness of the people of the group.

The major Kuki-Chin tribes of Manipur are Thadou, Paite, Gangte, Simte, Vaiphei, *Zou,* Hmar, Mizo, Kom, Aimol, Baite, Mate, etc.

Original Homeland and Migration

The antiquity, original homeland and the migration of the KukiChin-Mizo people to the present habitat have been a realm of speculation for the anthropologists and the historians. The historicity of their civilization has been established by their contact with the Shan and Burman civilization in Burma, and with the Meitei state, Tripura, Cachar and the British administration in India. The enquiry into this field assumes two ways. From the Indian side, the enquiry does not go beyond the recounting of their past from the folklore, oral traditions and the British archival records. In Burma, both archaeology and historical linguistics have been utilized to find out the antiquity of their homeland.

There are different waves of migration of the tribes in an extended period. A group of the Tibeto-Burman tribes speaking the Kuki-Chin followed the tribes of the Naga group and the Proto-Meitei tribes into Manipur from the Kabaw valley of Upper Burma, either along the course of the Manipur river and or across the Tengnoupal Hills. So these tribes are the present "bridge buffer tribes" of Manipur sandwiched behveen the Nagas and the Kuki-Chin. Then came the ancestors of the Kuki Chins from their homeland in China to upper Chindwin basin and Kabaw valley in a period covering several centuries in different wayes. An earlier group preceded the main group into the present Chin Hills and lived there for several centuries. These groups, according to Vumson, were Khumi/Khami, Mashi, Khuangsu, Pawaman, Asu, Myhn Reangtu, Yhppy. Then the main group, the present Chins of Burma and Mizo of Mizoram moved into Chin Hills and dislodged the earlier inhabitants from their mountain country. These migrants were Yaw, Asho, Sho, Matu of the southern Chin Hills and clans like Pawi, Lushai and Paite inhabiting the northern Chin Hills. The eaIlier tribes of the northern section were pushed into Manipur, Cachar and Tripura and the remaining section was left behind in the southern part of the Chin Hills. The tribes who migrated *to* Manipur came in *two* waves, the earlier wave was given a misnomer name "Old Kuki" and the later migrants were described by the British as "New Kuki" which was not acceptable *to* the people themselves. The later migrants also quarralled among themselves, the Lusei clans were compelled *by* the Pawis *to* move west into the present Mizoram, the Thadous and Paitemoved into Manipur.

The Tradition of Sinlung

There are two traditions current in both the early and later migrants. One popular tradition is the emergence of the ancestors of the Kuki people from the hole or bowel of the earth or cave. The second tradition is that of Sinlung according to which the ancestors emerged out of a place called Sinlung or Chhinlung. The cave or "bowel" of the earth tradition is a myth current among the Naga tribes also, which is a reminiscence of their cave men's state of life as discussed in the earlier part of this paper. About Sinlung, there has been very serious study. The Hmar folklore refers *to* Sinlung and Shan. The Sinlung tradition has been popularized by the Hmar historians and picked up by other *Mizo* writers. From Sinlung, they moved to a land named Shan. The reason of the exodus is not mentioned. The songs of the Hmar festival of Sikpuiruai reveal that they were living in Shan with great prosperity and cultural festivals were performed. A great famine forced them *to* leave Shan. Both Sinlung and Shan are referred *to* as townships. Therefore, it was presumed that the people must have been in contact with the Chinese civilization and with *some* of the petty principalities in China.

Sinlung has been identified by *some* writers with a small township of the same name on the bank of Chamdo and Szechuan in south China. It is not known whether Shan was a township in the *country* of the Shan people in upper Burma or Kabaw valley where the Shan built up several fortified townships. The gap behveen Sinlung and Shan must have been several centuries in time.

Historicity of their Migration

The historicity of the Kuki-Chin-Mizo migration has been seriously examined. The problem of their migration has to be tackled as a part of the general movement of the people from Inner Asia or mainland China to south east Asia and north east India. E.R Leach, discussing the issue, advances a theory that historical linguistics, archaeology and racial relationship definitely indicate that "the ancestors of these people did indeed came from the north, but they did not come as the social and cultural units we know to-day and cannot be identified with any particular groups of today. Lehman, on the basis of historical linguistics, observes, " History shows, however, that both hills and plain people have moved about within the general region of south west China and south east Asia over considerable distances for many centuries, until the recent past. The apparent close relationship among the several TIbeto-Burrnan languages of Burma (including India) indicates clearly that in the not very distant past, the ancestors of such different people as the Nagas and the Chin belong relatively to unitary speech group".

Due to the paucity of evidence about their past, the historicity of their migration may only be indicated with their relationship with established dvilization or states: Chinese, Tibetan, Shan, Burman, Meitei and the British. The present reconstruction is based on the reliable surmise that the Tibeto-Burman speakers of which the Kuki-Chin-Mizo and the various ethnic groups are important members, lived in China in the 3rd million B.C (around 2500) B. C). The earliest known tribe of Tibeto-Burrnan according to Chinese sources was the Chiang tribes of 2500 B.C who were among the principal historical cultures of ancient China. The Chiang was the ancestors of the Tibeto-Burmans. Their earliest known habitat was in the west or north China in the present day province of Szechuan and mountainous regions of Kansu and Shensi. Their occupation was sheep herding, raising of yaks, ponies and pigs.

Then during,the period of the Shang dynasty of China (1600-1028) B.C the Chiang tribes were the neighbours of the Shang and their relation was full of conflicts and war. The Chiang were still on southwest region of the Shansi and Sensi. During the Chou dynasty which lived in early part of 2nd millennium B.C they were found in northeast China, between the sources of the Yangste and the Jei. The Chinese hostility forced the Chiang tribes to take refuge in northeastern Tibet. D.G.E Hail writes about the Tibeto-Burman: "these people had been mountain dwellers, originally living in the north west of China. The earliest Chinese records coming from the second half of the second millennium B.C called them the Chiang. Chinese hostility forced them to take refuge in northeast Tibet." But he thinks that the Tibeto-Burman migrated towards the south about 1st millennium B.C, S.K. Chatterjee also surmises that the Tibeto-Burmans must have left their homeland in China and moved into eastern India around 1000 B.C. The fighting between the Tanguts who were the descendants of the Chiangs and the Chinese continued during the Han period even. This southward movement of the Tibeto-Burmans took many centuries. According to Than Tun, around 1000 B.C. the Chinese under Ching dynasty made further depredations against them. In order to avoid them, the Tibeto Burmans moved to the south and came to the border of Tibet and Burma. The Kuki-Chin-Mizo in different batches and groups tracked into Burma, through Hukwang valley, to Chindwin basin and the Kabaw valley. Before them, the earlier groups the Proto-Meitei and the Kadu (Sak Kadu). In Kabaw valley, they were confronted by the Kadus who were split into two groups, one further moved to the south in Burma and the other splinter group went into Manipur who according to Lehman, were related to the Sengmai-Andro of Manipur. The Chins lived in the Chindwin basin for a long time. Chindwin means the hole of the Chin. They moved to Khampat in southern Kale-Kabaw valley.

Regarding the possible chronology of their migration to upper Burma, some speculations have been put forward. According to the earliest Burmese inscriptions, the Burmans were in upper Burma in the 9th century A.D. Before them, the Man and the Pyus established kingdoms but did not rule in Kabaw Valley, occupied by the Chin or the related people. Therefore, Professor G.H. Luce of Rangoon University put the entry of the Kuki-Chin people between 4th to the 8th century A.D. The latter period is more acceptable. The people came into contact with the Burmans in the Kabaw valley and a comparatively developed society was built up. From this region an earlier group moved to the west in the present Chin Hills and some to Manipur. Then came the Shan invaders in upper Burma and started conflicts with the Burman rulers during the 12th century onwards. During the earlier period, 8th to 9th century, the Shan of Nanchao had made military raids in upper Burma. However, the Burmese invaders described China as their ally. The Shan penetrated into Kabaw valley and founded several townships at Kale, Khampat, Tamu and Thuangdut. And it was they who gradually pushed the Chins out of Kabaw valley into the hills which were under the occupation of the earlier clans who were the ancestors of the Kukis. These Kuki tribes were greatly disturbed by the Chin migrants around the 15th-16th centuries. This group was split into two: the northern group was pushed into the north by the Lushai clans into Manipur and Cachar around 1700 A.D., and the southern group remained in the southern Chin Hills. The disturbers of the Kukis, the Lushais were driven out into the west in the present Mizoram. They came into contact with the Bengalis who gave them a new name "Kuki" then the Meitei who called them Khongsais and the British who knew them by the Kuki Chin and Lushai. The migration continued throughout the nineteenth and early part of twentieth centuries. Their migration had made them develop migratory nature. But their migration was an aspect of their struggle for survival from the attacks of the more powerful aggressive clans, their search for agricultural land and their need for shelter and peaceful settlement.

2

Social Change in Manipur

What is Social Change?

According to sociologist Wilbert Moore, "social change is the significant alteration of social structure, that is pattern of social action and interaction including consequences and manifestation of such structure embodied in norms, values and cultural symbols" (Moore, Social Change: 1972). Social change is greatly interlinked with social structure; their relationship is complicated. Social changes have been conceived as a phenomenon of progress and decay. The process for the maintenance of the social structure is the social dynamics, and the processes that modify the social structure are social change. Social change is a built-in phenomenon of a society, any change in social relation.

Social structure

Social Structure is the "social relationship" covering regular and repetitive aspects of interaction between the members of a social entity. Social structure covers the features of a society which have certain permanence over time, are inter-related, and determine the functioning of the society or a group within the society as a whole and the activity of its individual members.

Thus social structure is based on the following formulations that

— Human beings form the social relation with regularity and permanence.

— Social life is interdependent and functionally inter-related.

— Human beings are not completely free and autonomous in the choice of their activities but are constrained by the social life and social relationship.

— Idea of continuity, regularity and interrelatedness are features of social life.

In the light of the above explanations, social structure, according to A. R Radcliff Brown, is a "patterned or normative social relation that covers the social activities that conform to the accepted social rules and norms". It is the institutionalized pattern of activities concerning social behaviour that conforms to norms, values, ethical sense etc. And the components of social structure are the institution of property, kinship, marriage, norms, role of groups and individuals. These components are necessary to ensure continuity, regularity and interdependence in a social relation.

Social Evolution

Change, either progress or decline, is a feature of human civilization. Social change is a recurring phenomenon .of human society; customs and norms change, values, ideas and beliefs change, inventions are made and applied, environmental changes lead to new adaptation, revolution or conflicts lead to redistribution or change in the control of power, so on. It has been pointed out that social change has got biological roots. Herbert Spencer linked social evolution (change) ,to biological evolution. L.H. Morgan in his Ancient Society (1876) argued that the cyclical evolution of human society was a process of development from " savage to barbarian, to the civilized", the progress of the nature of form of marriage or kinship was from polygamy to monogamy, from matrilineal to patrilineal. E.B. Tylor applied this theory in the development of religious belief, from animism to polytheism and to monotheism. The Marxian concept of social development shows the movement of the society, through the stages of primitive communism, ancient slavery, feudalism, capitalism and socialism (communism). The social evolution has been now replaced by that of social change. Social evolution is concerned with people and community. The distinction between community and society is to be noted. Community is a group of people who are bound together by common tradition and ties of affection and solidahty. And in society, (social) relations have been contractual, rational and non-emotional.

Social change is a field in which both sociology and history can look into in their own methodological perspectives in the light of the historical sociology or the study of the changes in the society of a particular group in the historical perspective. In such a study, the sociological tools can be applied to understand and analyse the historical data: the outcome could be a social history or a historical sociology. The study on social change has become a study of social history. Some writers have pointed out the methodological difference between the historical and the sociological approaches to the problem of social and cultural change, a difference in the direction of enquiry. "The historian moves from effects to causes, the sociologist from causes to effects. The historian attempts to discover the multiple causes that produced a particular phenomenon, the sociologist, the multiple consequences caused by causes" (Robert Dierstedt, Social Order, 1970).

There is no need to differentiate the two approaches; both are complimentary; and interdisciplinary approach is the best scientific method of enquiry, both history and sociology.

Modernization

Efforts were made to give theoretical explanations to the changes that had come to the new independent countries, fonner colonies and dependencies. The social and economic transformations in these countries after their contact with the colonial rule have been described as westernization or modernization. The noted Indian sociologist, M.N. Srinivas writes, "westernization is used to characterize the changes brought about in Indian society and culture as a result of 150 years of the British Rule and the term subsumes changes occurring at different levels, technology, institution, ideology and values" (Srinivas: Social Change in Modern India: 1972). The term modernization:appears to be more appropriate to describe this transformation in the developing societies. Wilbert Moore observes, "modernization is a total transformation of a traditional or pre-modern society into the types of technology and associated social organizations that characterize the 'advanced' economically prosperous and relatively stable political nature of the western world" (Moore: 1975). Modernization means the process of socio-cultural change by which less developed societies acquire characteristics common to more developed societies. The factors for the socio-cultural transformation in the developing countries are . imperialism including colonization, indirect rule, conquest and military occupation, religious imperialism, migration, trade and commerce and the transfer of knowledge.

Modernization has deeper meaning; and Gunnar Myrdal has enumerated the guiding ideals of modernization in Asia's developing countries, namely, rationality in thinking, planned development, rise in productivity and standard of living, social and economic equalization, improved institutions and attitudes, national consolidation, national independence, democratic form of government, grass roots democratic institutions and social disciplines. (Gunnar Myrdal' *Asian Drama*: 1972). Myrdal has equated modernization with democratic process of nation building based on freedom and equality. So modernization can also be perceived as an over-reaching social change in a country. (See also chapter 5. Modernization)

Factors of Social Change

Social change may be brought about through several processes, namely, the natural environment, demographic situation, technological innovations, economic development, ideas and ideology (religion, political ideology and social philosophy), war, revolutions and social conflicts, social movements and political process. These processes have been described as factors responsible for social change in a society and in an extended period. We may further elaborate on ideas and ideology, technological innovation and economic process causing social change.

Idea and Ideology

W.E Ogburn observes that "all social changes take place through the medium of ideas" giving primacy to the ideological factor of social change. Ideas and ideology are powerful motivating factor in the social change. Ideas and ideology can be taken as one as they are closely interlinked. Religious beliefs, political ideology, social philosophy are subsumed in the ideas and political ideology. Ideology is an idea or system of thought that a people in a society have a moral obligation to believe as supported by the norm of the society. (W.E. Ogburn, Social Change with Respect to Culture and Organization, 1965) It was Max Weber who developed the ideological factor of social change in his classic, "The Protestant Ethic and the Spirit of Capitalism," Weber emphasizes on a religious phenomenon of Protestant Christianity and economic phenomenon of capitalism as the motivating ideology of the western civilization. His theory is not totally accepted, but the role of religion in social change, a political ideology, like socialism or economic system, capitalism influenced the changes in society. They led to radical change in the system of belief, government and economic pursuits.

Technological Innovation

Technology is the most important criteria of measuring the standard of human civilization and advancement of a people. Technology implies tools and implements, machines and equipments and manner of their organization. "Technological change" as Margaret Mead observes, "is as old as civilization and since times immemorial, the ways of the life of whole people have been transformed by the introduction of new tools and new technical procedure such as inventions like the plough, the domestication of animal, writing and use of steams". History of civilization is the history of technological development; invention, application and organization, the wheel, the plough, the boat, the compass, gunpowder, printing press, the steam engine, the telegraph and telephone, the automobile, radio, aeroplane, television and the atom bomb represent the tools of civilization and they have brought tremendous changes in human society. The effects of the Industrial Revolution and Agricultural revolution are the foundation of modern civilization. At the present rate of technological invention, the shape of human civilization may take any form in future.

A society is to be measured by its technological advancement.

The Economic Factor

Karl Marx in his writings strongly stated that the mode of production in material life determines the general character of the social, political and spiritual processes of life. Historical materialism developed by Marx and Engels, is the most influential theory that gives priority *to* the economic process of social change. It has been pointed out that technological changes are dovetailed to the economic process. Technological innovation (inventions) are to be applied, so 'also the formation and extension of markets, change in the property relation with the change in the mode of production, organization of labour etc. There is correlation between economic condition and social situation. Production and consumption, organization of trade and commerce, imposition of taxes and tariffs are important economic processes. Prosperity of a nation is dependent on the economic health. Economic hardship correlates to social unrest, political turmoil, revolution and war. Most of the conflicts in society are economic; and all social conflicts are born out of the economic reason.

Economic development has become most important determinant for the stability or otherwise of a society. Society changes along with the change in economy. That produces change in the polity of the state.

Social Change In Manipur

Social change occurred in Manipur in an extended time frame since the 18th century, more significantly, the 20th century due *to* several factors as explained in the preceding paragraphs. The social change was brought about in Manipur by the processes elaborated below.

(I) Ideas and ideology in the form of religious changes; conversion into Hinduism, Christianity and Meitei-Sanamahi movement have greatly contributed to the social change among the Meitei, the Nagas and the Kuki-Chins. Sanskritization, modernization, desanskritization and ethnic nationalism are issues of the factor.

(II) Wars, conquest and insurgency or rebellion have been the frequent phenomenon in the history of Manipur. The Burma wars, the British conquest, participation in the First and Second World Wars, the Communist revolt, the insurgencies of the Meitei, Naga and Kukis have produced tremendous change in the outlook of the people and in social and economic life of the people.

(III) Colonial rule in Manipur was a landmark in the social political and economic history of Manipur. They destroyed feudalism but substituted it with their colonial system that aimed at the consolidation of the British Empire.

(IV) The technological change is the greatest factor of social change and modernization: The adoption of western technology is a great contribution to the civilizational change in Manipur.

(V) Western education is a vehicle of social change introduced by the British and developed by the succeeding governments in Manipur with the assistance of the Government of India.

(VI) Economic change is another name of social change. Change of the economic system from the traditional economy *to* the colonial economy, and the planned development under the Government of India, and ultimately, the capitalist economy occurred as the phases of economic development.

(VII) Democracy is a political ideology and a way of life. Manipur has adopted this ideology. And it has a deep root in the society.

(VIIl)Emergence of elite is another aspect *of* social development. Elite controls the politics, administration, economy, trade and business and culture of the state.

(IX) The social pressure groups like the youth and student activists and the women activists known as the Meira Paibis have strengthened the role of civil society in the body politic of Manipur.

Sanskritization of Manipur

Manipur had passed through three phases of religious

change; Hinduism in the 18th century which led *to* sanskritization of the Hindu Meitei society based on caste system, conversion of the hill tribes into Christianity since the early 20th century leading to the transformation of the traditional tribal society towards westernization or modernization and Sanamahi religious movement in the mid-twentieth century facilitating a process of desanskritization among the Meiteis.

Historically, Hindu beliefs and practices were already present in Manipur with the migration of the Brahmins to the kingdom and employment of the Brahmin priests for astrological, ritualistic and administrative works, But the first ruler of Manipur who was initiated into Hinduism was King Charairongba (1697-1709) in 1703 and he accepted the Nimandi sect, founded by Nimbarka Charya, a Vaishnav preacher. Then his son, the illustrious Pamheiba or Garibniwaz (1709-48) was converted into Vaisnavism by a Hindu preceptor named Gopal. Das in 1717. And then came Shanti Das, a preceptor of Ramandi cult (worship of Ram as an incarnate of Vishnu) wbo exerted strong influence on the king and the court. People were converted into Hinduism. Hindu cultural practices were systematically adopted by King Garibniwaz under the direction of his preceptor. And the sanskritization was started. However, it was during the reign of Bharata Shai, a son and successor of the great king that Gaudiya Vaishnavism, the Bengal school of Vaisnavism, worship of Krishna as an incarnate of Lord Vishnu was adopted. A new phase of Hiduisation completed the conversion of Manipur into Hinduism.

The process of Hinduisation of the Meitei society may be taken as sanskritization, not exactly in the connotation propounded by M.N. Srinivas (Caste in Modern India, Srinivas 1962). According to Srinivas, "Sanskritization is the process by which a "low" Hindu caste or tribal or other group, changes its custom, ritual, ideology and way of life in the direction of a high and frequently "twice born caste". Essentially Srinivas's sanskritization deals with the upward mobility of a Hindu caste or varna or even the adoption of Hindu practice by non-Hindu tribals. Therefore what happened in Manipur was a result of conversion of the Meiteis into Hinduism that covered aspects including the mobility of caste. Sanskritization is a part of the Hinduisation. But this term has been loosely applied in Manipur. What had evolved out of the jealous Hindu proselytism and resistance by the indigenous Sanamahi cult was that there was a religious syncretism between the two, outward form of Hinduism but Sanamahi' in inner ethos. The impact of Hiuduism was seen in the process of Hinduisation of the Meitei polity of Manipur.

1. Change of the name of the kingdom to "Manipur" and the title of King to "Maharaja".

2. Identification of the royal lineage of Manipur with that of Arjuna's son Babhruvahan of the Mahabharata claiming an Aryan origin.

3. Declaration of all Meitei and royal family as sin.gle Kshetriya clan, though the Brahmins form a separate caste outside the Meitei society. The clan system: known as the Yek-Salai system was a powerful institution which could not be replaced by the Hindu gotra system. But Shanti Das made a syncretism in the caste system as given hereunder.

4. Identification of the gods and goddesses of the Meitei with Hindu deities, for example, Nongpok Ningthou with Siva, Panthoibi with Parvati, Hiyangthang Lairembi, Ireima with Kamakhya Devi Durga etc.

5. Adoption of Bengali language as a medium of ritual and ceremony, adoption of Bengali dress by males but not by women.

Salai	Hindu Gotra	Colour	No. of sub-lineage (Sagei)
1. Angom	Gautama	White	74
2. Ningthouja	Shandilya	Red	131
3. Luwang	Kashyapa	Blue	69
4. Khuman	Madhugalya	Black	111
5. Moirang	Areya Angira	Orange-yellow	80
6. Khaba-Nganba	Bharadhwaj	Green	23
7. Sarang Leishangthem	Vasistha	Grey	50

6. Construction of temples dedicated to gods and goddesses like Rama, Krishna, Vishnu, Hanuman etc.
7. Pilgrimage to holy places of Hinduism in different parts of the country. Ban on indigenous dietary habit, especially, meat eating and drinking of wine.
8. The king as the chief of the theocratic state acted as the head of the religion. And the Hindu religious affairs were administered by the Brahma Sabha. Other non-Hindu indigenous practices and institution like Lai Haraoba continued. Conversion to Hinduism brought orthodoxy and sharp caste distinction between Hindu Meiteis and non-Hindu hill tribes and communities like the Loi. However, Hinduism broadened the Meitei worldview through their connection with the Hindu world of India.

Other social groups who were known by the generic term "Loi" was not a separate caste in the real sense of the Hindu Varna system but it was a social category. The Lois had been gradually provided a low social status. Due to urbanization and need to provide municipal services, a group of people known as Yaithibi also emerged. They were renamed as Hari during the colonial period.

Coming of Christianity

After British conquest of Manipur in 1891, some British mission societies made a plan to convert the Meiteis into Christianity. A young missionary named William Pettigrew was sent to Manipur in 1892. But as a precautionary measure not to provoke the sentiment of orthodox Vaishnavas of Irnphal valley, the colonial authorities did not give him permission to do evangelical work. Of course, he was permitted to go to the Tangkhul Nagas of Ukhrul in 1896 under the sponsorship of American Baptist Mission based at Boston. WIlliam Pettigrew among the Nagas, and Watkins Roberts through the Indo-Burma Thadou-Kuki Pioneer Mission did the evangelical works. Both of them succeeded in their own spheres. The missionaries started mission schools which provided free education and the students of these schools became the first converts. The missionaries were given support by the colonial authorities. The missionaries collaborated with the government in educational administration, production of school textbooks for primary school thildren and census works. They cooperated with the British government in the suppression of the anti-British rebellions, like the Kuki Rebellion or the rebellion of Jadonang and Gaidinliu. They published Biblical literature in Manipuri and in tribal dialects. Christian missions came into conflict with the believers of the indigenous faith which they condemned as animist and heathen. And they also tried to destroy the indigenous cultural and social practices. They wanted to change the tribal life, lock, stock and barrel. With the 'strong support from the colonial authorities, financial support from the sponsoring mission societies and the new converts to Christian faith, they brought about the conversion of a large number of people into Christianity. The most condemned "head hunting" was stopped; inter-tribal congregation and social interactions led to the harmonious relation between the tribes, the Naga and Kuki-Chin. They also posed as savior of the hill tribes from the plainsmen, the Hindus of Manipur valley. Hinduism was supported by the king and the state, Christianity was given support by the colonial authorities. Christianity brought western education, exposure of the tribes to the outside world. After the Second World War, over and above the Baptists, the Catholics and Seventh Day Adventists also carne and started their missions. While the Baptists became indigenised in leadership and organization, Catholics started intensive proselytizing works in all communities. Education is a field of specialization of the Catholic mission: Parishes are established throughout the state. Tribal Catholics are among the most educated group. Catholics are more liberal in their outlook and in their relationship with larger community of Manipur.

Christianity brought change in the social outlook of the converts; education brought job opportunities and they entered the state services, both civil and police. Literary works and inter-community relation are sponsored. The tribal worldview is now broadened. This has been a great factor in the modernization of the tribal society.

Meitei Sanamahi Movement

The Bengal school of Vaishnavism, Gaudiya Vaishnavism, was one of the vehicles of Bengali cultural diffusion: Bengali language, Bengali script, Bengali literature have overshadowed the Meitei identity. As a reaction to this, a young Meitei from Assam, Naoria Phullo started an organization,.Apokpa Marup, for religious, cultural, linguistic revivalism of the Meiteis. They were anti-Brahmin and anti-Hindu, antiBengali script. They tried to establish the separate worship of the Meitei deities Taibang Panba Mapu, Sanamahi, Leimaren and Pakhangba of the indigenous faith.

They came initially to clash with the Brahmin scholars of the court and Hindu Meitei scholars. But in the second half ofthe twentieth century, they had succeeded in the process of desanskritization; abolition of caste system among them, adoption of Meitei festivals and establishment of Sanamahi Temple Board as a counterpart to Govindaji Temple Board to monitor the Sanamahi cult.

If Shanti Das was responsible for Meitei conversion into Hinduism with the support from the royalty, Rev. William Pettigrew, Watkins Roberts and their colleagues with support from the colonial authority, brought Christianity among the hill tribes. And Naoria Phullo and his followers revived the Sanamahi cult. Sanamahi movement looking from a sociological term is an identity assertion based on religion and culture. It has strengthened the forces leading to the regeneration of the Meitei nationalism.

Wars, Conquest and Insurgencies

Manipur had experienced the ravages of wars and rebellions. The kingdom was a theocratic state. Repeated raids by the king of Manipur in the first part of the 18th century into Upper Burma led to retaliatory conquest of Manipur by Burma, culminating in the devastation of the kingdom known as the Seven Years Devastation, (Chahi Taret Khuntakpa) 1819-1826. Burmese imperialism almost obliterated Manipur. Manipur was liberated by Maharaja Gambhir Singh with the British help. Manipur was reconstructed and restored to her prime position in the 19th century. However, British imperial design led to the conquest of Manipur in 1891. Manipur had faced many raids and rebellions, but these two wars, the Burmese invasions and British conquest produced devastating effects on the polity, economy, military organiiation and social relation. But the Hindu caste system was firmly built into Meitei society; there was no structural change in Meitei society. But the relation between the Meitei royalty and nobility with the Burmese and hill tribes underwent a sea change Meiteis became more orthodox; the relation between them and hill tribes became more widened. Burmese conquest did not produce much social change, except destruction and anarchy. On the other hand, the British conquest and subsequent imposition of the colonial rule brought drastic changes in all spheres, social, political, economic and cultural.

The Kuki Rebellion (1917-1919) and the First World War brought the people to the cruel realities of war in the foreign lands and the depredation in the hills. 2000 tribal labourers were exposed to the European world crossing the ocean, working in the war fields of Europe, and visit to Buckingham Palace made an impact on the tribal psyche. Manipur contributed assistance, an airplane and a double company of Manipur state force to the British. The Kuki Rebellion brought about a Kuki solidarity but it was broken by the colonial policy of splitting the Kuki solidarity through a book written by an Anglo Indian official named William Shaw, (Notes on Thadou Kukis, 1929).

The Second World War was more serious. The decisive battles of the War were fought in Manipur hills and Imphal valley. Manipur was exposed to the outside world. Allied forces, their technology, the battles between the invading Japanese and INA and the Allied forces produced a radical change on the people of Manipur. The War had political, economic and social consequences. It was a new chapter in the history of Manipur. After the independence, the Communist revolt of 1948-51 was a peasantry-based armed struggle for establishment of an independent country. Insurgency in Manipur, rise of peasantry and suppression by the state government are of lasting importance. The Naga insurgency in late 1950's and Meitei insurgency in mid 1960's and Mizo-Kuki rebellion in 60's and Kuki insurgency in mid 1980's have got internal and external impact on tribal society.

Rise of ethnic nationalism, though in an incipient form, is a great social phenomenon.

Colonial Rule

Manipur had passed through three forms of political process, Feudalism, Colonialism and Democracy. The British colonial rule was a great leveller and all-embracing. The British introduced the indirect rule in Manipur valley where the Maharaja administered through the Manipur State Darbar, and the rule of the tribal chiefs and village headmen under British ocupension was introduced in the hills. Both valley and hill administration through the State Darbar and President of the Darbar was supervised by the Political Agent.

Feudalism was an economic and political system presided over by the king and administered through the nobility which supervised the ownership and possession of the land. This system was associated with a unique social relationship between the king and the nobles, the king and the subjects, the nobility with the rent paying peasants. The feudal system subsumes ownership of the land and resources of the kingdom being vested with the king and the royalty. In Manipur, feudalism operated through several institutions and practices. While the feudal paraphernalia connected with royalty and nobility was not touched, the British abolished in 1892, the Lallup system which was a feudal service rendered by the subjects to the king, by persons belonging to age group 16 to 60 years. They rendered service to the state, 10 days out of 40 days, both in peacetime and wartime. During peacetime, they were development workers and artisans and during wartime they were peasant soldiers who maintained their own arms. The British also abolished slavery in the state. Abolition of slavery affected the royalty which employed more than a thousand slaves at the time of British occupation of Manipur.

After the abolition of Lallup and slavery, the British introduced house taxes in the valley and the hills. After sometime, hill house tax was retained in the hill, and the land revenue was introduced in the valley. A revenue department was created; land was surveyed and settlement were made and revenues were imposed. Money taxes both in the hills and valley caused a great hardship on the people. Monetization of the economy and administration produced drastic effect on Manipur's society. In the hills, forced labour was introduced again. The British introduced several Indian laws dealing with police, criminal law, revenue, settlement and forests. Forest tolls, ferry tolls, water and electricity. tariff caused great hardship.

Meanwhile, the social oppression by the Maharaja through Brahma Sabha continued unabated. The British did not interfere.

After the Second World War, with the departure of the British, in 1947, democratization of the govermental system was introduced. Manipur State Constitution Act, 1947, provided a monarchy with representative form of government; a legislative assembly elected on adult franchise, Manipur on the first state to have adopted a representati Assembly on adult franchise. However, after merger with India democracy was forgotten; a central government's rule was introduced. Part 'C' state under a Chief Commissioner assisted by an Advisory Council, Union Territory, 1957 with a Territorial Council upgraded to Assembly in 1963 and to full statehood in 1972. Struggle for democracy and representative form of government took a long time for fulfilment. Democracy has given the people, the fundamental right: and freedoms guaranteed by the Constitution of India.

Democracy has taken deep root in Manipur's society. People's participation in law making and decision making, the self-governin bodies have unleashed the people's power and expressed thei aspiration.

So these systems had brought about institutional changes, which produced reactions within both Meitei and tribal society. One reaction was a peaceful revolution in religion, education, economic development, inctllcation of democratic ethos. There was a resistance against the colonial political domination before 1947 in the form of social and political movements like Kuki rebellion, Zeliangrong uprising led by Jadonang and Gaidinliu which was anti-British and anti-imperialistic. The insurgencies raised by the Nagas, Kukis-Mizo and the Meiteis were for the assertion of their ethnic nationalism.

Technological Change

Technological change is the greatest factor of change in a society or even a civilization. Technology means not only tools and implements, machinery, energy either steam or electric power but the manner of organization. It is directly linked up with economic organization or production relation, the division of labour among men, women and children. Technological change is a fundamental vehicle of change in human society and economy. The tribal technology was primitive, dao, hoe and axe. But the Meiteis knew the art of writing quite earlier. The weaponry consisted of the sword, spear, bow and arrow, the arambai, a sling used in the cavalry, other technology consisted of the thangjou, spade, plough, spade, handloom etc.

Manipur's search for improved military technology to match the Burmese guns in the 18th century led her to an alliance with the British East India Company and also to trade agreement on exports and imports between Manipur and the East India Company. British equipped Gambhir Singh's Manipur Levy in the First Anglo-Burmese war (1823-26) with arms and Manipur was liberated. However, Manipur's adoption of European technology was slow and gradual. She accepted the technology in communication, postal system, later on telegraphy (1886). After the British conquest, the flow of European technology was greatly increased; modern means of communication, telegraphy, wireless, printing press, improved roads and bridges, mechanized means of transport (cycle and automobile), use of electricity, modem medicine and health services, water supply and civil engineering constituted the new technology. Further, use of radio, gramophone, type writer, telephone was introduced. During the wars, First World War and Second World War, military technology, guns, machine, airplane were introduced. In the Anglo-Manipur war of 1891, Manipur used muzzle loading guns, the Martini, Enfield and Snider rifles which were no match of the British artillery and improved rifles. A significant improvement of the military technology in Manipur was the introduction of the 303 rifles in 1922 though it was already used during and before the First World War. Mechanized transport, the truck, car, jeeps really revolutionized Manipur's economy, administration and social relation. The people of Manipur responded to the use of the new technology. The standard of living was improved, scientific tools and implements are used for domestic purposes, improved utensils, radio, transistors, improved housing technology, use of corrugated iron sheets and reinforced concrete structure. Then came the television and computers. The agriculture technology, use of tractor and power tiller improved seeds and fertilizer led to a higher productivity. The use of electronic goods, like camera of latest brand television mobile have come to stay. Than came the information technology.

However, among the tribes, the scientific technology has not affected the production system in agriculture or cottage industries. The people excel in heavy type of works, the tribals lack precision and finesse in production. However, the Naga pottery has greatly improved. The agricultural technology is still primitive in jhum cultivation or in terrace cultivation. The hoe is the tool, and in terrace and wet rice cultivation in plain land, the plough, power tiller and tractor are now used. These are the symbols of tribal response to the modem technology. Their nonagricultural skills are confined to house building, handicrafts, weaving and basketry; the dao, hoe the saw, the chisel and plane and the axe are still indispensable tools. The modem technology introduced by the British and now produced and marketed by the mainland Indian manufacturers has greatly influenced the production and consumption pattern of the people and have produced a tremendous change in the society.

Education has always been a vehicle of progress and change. Education in the pre-colonial period was a feudal monopoly. With the coming of the colonial rule and Christian missions, western education was introduced. Western education was a strong motive force of social change in Manipur. After independence there was a rapid growth of education. In 1885, an English school was established by Political Agent Sir James Johnstone and in 1980, a university was founded by the state government. This is the indicator of a rapid educational growth. Education brings a high level of social awareness among the people. It is an instrument of employment, a status symbol and key to success. Manipur has produced a large number of educated men and women, doctors, engineers, teachers, scholars, scientists and lawyers, and civil servants. The change was tremendous. It brought tremendous changes, opportunity for progress. But unemployrpent among the youths creates social unrest and frustrations. Yet eddcation is the key to solve these social and economic problems.

Economic Development is both an inditator and cause of social change. The traditional economy of Manipur in the pre-colonial period was based on simple agriculture, home industries and barter trade. The colonial rule destroyed the traditional economy and brought about a money-based economy; regulation of land tenure system through a scientific land survey, preparation of record of rights, imposition of revenue and house tax and other forms of taxes. The colonial objectives were, as stated above, to keep law and order, to collect revenues and taxes, to exploit the natural resources as raw materials for the home based capitalist enterprises and to provide market for their products. Trade was promoted; the export of rice and timber were touchy subjects affecting the people both in the hills and valley. The Women Agitation of 1939 was a protest against this colonial monopoly of rice export. After merger with India, Manipur had undergone the process of economic changes, development in agriculture, industries, transport and communication, education and health services, expansion of trade and commerce, roads and bridges and housing. The planned development was introduced by the government and it is still continuing; the nation building continues .At the same time, Manipur came under the grip of the consumer oriented capitalist economy of mainland India. A new rich class, both among the urban traders and businessmen, and rural farmers have grown up. The per-capita income rose; gross domestic products increased. The economic forces have shaped the change in society. Economic disparity, regional imbalance, economic deprivation, economic exploitation have led to social and political problems. The economic growth has led to the multiplication of people's problems; demand for basic minimum needs, drinking water, health services, electric power, social welfare and social security services and employment goes on.

Democracy, the rule of the people, has brought changes in Manipur's social life, both among the people of the valley and hills. Democracy has taken deep root in Manipur's social life. With the introduction of the adult franchise in 1948 in the election to the erstwhile Manipur Assembly and participation in India' general elections to the Parliament since 1952 and in the local legislatures like the Territorial

Council and Territorial Assembly, and in self governing institutions and ultimately in the full-fledged state Assembly, have given the power to the people to choose their rulers. They have also enjoyed their rights to elect representatives to participate in the law making and decision making bodies and administer the state. The constitution guarantees the fundamental rights and freedoms to the people. Democracy has activated all sections of the people. There is a strong awareness of their rights among the people. Thus democracy have brought changes in the society. The democratic legislature of the state the self governing institutions like the District Council, Zilla Parishad and municipal bodies have strengthened the people's empowerment. Moreover, the democratic means of discussion, debate and criticism of public issues in press and public forum have come to stay. Democratic ethos have become quite strong and deep rooted.

Elite Formation is an aspect of social change. The expanded government activities led to the rise of bureaucracy, which has become the most powerful section of the people of Manipur. Bureaucray controls the decision making in the administration. Since the Second World War, trade, commerce and other production activities led to the emergence of businessmen. Professional experts in the field of legal matters, engineering, medical and health services, higher and professional education led to the rise of lawyers, engineers, doctors, teachers, writers, scientists and scholars, both among the people of the hills and valley. An elite representing the middle class had emerged in Manipur. They control the politics, government, business, trade and commerce, education and culture of the state. The emergence of a powerful media, both print and electronic, led to a strong and alert public opinion more or less controlled by the elite. Media controls the thought of men. The peasantry both in valley and hills has emerged quite powerful. Because of the bigger number, they dominate *the* democratic process and one notices that the political leaders from *the* rural areas dominate over the urban group in the control of *the* democratic political process.

Social pressure groups, youth and student activists, the most profound and influential women activists known as the Meira paibis, the women torch-bearers, either as prohibition workers or proted of human rights, are important features of Manipur's civil society. The role of Manipuri women in conflict situation is a subject matter of intensive study by the intellectuals, especially by the sociologists. All these changes in society are leading towards modernization. However, change is a continuous process like the course of the river. There is neither end of change, nor end of history.

3

Ethnicity and State Formation in North East India

The purpose of this paper is to indicate the connection between ethnicity and formation of the states in India's Northeastern region. Ethnic factor in the whole body politic of the region has assumed great importance due to the peculiarities of the region. The term, ethnicity is used to indicate ethnic consciousness or sense of ethnic identity of a people or community relating to their political, social and cultural personality. And "State-formation" means the process of evolution, growth or constitution of a people or social group of groups occupying a geographical region into a political society. A state should have the condition of "a human community or people, territoriality, legitimacy and sovereignty." Formation of states is, in other words, the emergence of the state system as a consequence of different phenomena like military conquest, mutual agreement to create and accept a leader of a society.

A state should have an economic foundation, social solidarity and cohesion, capacity to manage religious affairs, an able political leadership (Weber's charismatic leader) with a government backed by a military establishment. The concept of one folk, one state or one nation, is based on principle of nationality which is linked with the ethnic principle. However, these conditions cannot be logically or rigidly applied to India which is a multi-nationality nation. Again the use of the term "State" in this paper has different connotations. (Independent State, Princely States under British paramountcy and autonomous states within the Indian Union) according to the changilig status of the political units of Northeast India which had passed through different stages, ancient and medieval, colonial and post-colonial periods of India's history. For further examination, reference can be made to historical evidences of the region.

The region is a mosaic of cultures and races. This phenomenon is a consequence of her continuous interaction with the 'orthogenetic' ciyilization of India and China, and the "synthetic" civilization of Tibet and Southeast Asia according to L.K. Mahapatra. Despite her publicised geographic isolation, movement of people or migration into the region is a continuing process. These various groups established their habitat in the mountains and river valleys of the region, the Brahmaputra valley and the Manipur valley being the two great cradles of civilization.

Ethnic profile of the region consists of the Indo-Aryans and Mongoloids. (The Tibeto-Burmans, Siamese-Chinese and Austro-Asiatic). While the Indo-Aryans occupied the plains of the Northeast, the Mongoloids occupied both plains and hills with greater concentration in the hill regions.

In ancient period, the kingdom of Pragjyotisha-Kamrupa was developed by the Hinduised Bodo ruling dynasties in the Bramaputra valley; then, principalities of the Bodo Kacharis, Chutias etc. grew up in the same valley in the medieval period. The Ahoms from Upper Burma invaded Assam in the beginning of the thirteenth century and established a kingdom absorbing the petty principalities and chieftainships. This Ahom kingdom lasted till.the first part of the 19th century when it was conquered by the British.

The Khasi-Synteng states in Khasi and Jaintia Hills kept their independent identity till the British adyent. They were kept under the British paramountcy.

In Manipur, the Meitei kingdom was built up in the early centuries of the Christian era, and this had a very long career till British conquest in 1891 and she became a princely state under the British paramountcy. Tripura also passed into same status like Manipur. Another aspect of the British expansion was the conquest of the hill tribes and establishment of their areas into various districts. For example, the Naga areas were constituted into Naga Hills District and the Mizo (Lushai) areas into Lushai Hills District. The tribes living in the southern slopes of eastern Himalayas were brought under political control and later on brought under the North-Eastern Frontier Agency (NEFA).

In the pre-colonial states of the region, especially the Khasi states Jaintia, Kachari and Chutiya kingdom, ethnicity was a deciding factor in the formation of the states over and above other factors accompanying such a formation. The kingdom of Assam established by the Ahorns was a plural society. The Ahom rulers were foreigners and there Were various ethnic, linguistic and religious groups in Assam. But the foreign rule was accepted by the local population.

Formation of Meitei state was started with the foundation of the Ningthouja kingdom by Pakhangba in the first century of the Christian era. The Meiteis were occupying fertile territory which was inhabited by kindred ethnic groups with the knowledge of agricultural technology They were brought under a single political authority and integrated into a single social organization by Pakhangba and his successors. The rulers of the Ningthouja dynasty provided both political and social leadership and ultimately controlled the religious affairs. They also followed a liberal social policy of integrating other kindred tribes and clans under a single Meitei social melieu which emerged as a greater nationality. Ethnic identity of the Meitei was extended and developed into nationhood in the later period

Colonial Impact

Colonial rule had demoted the status of all the principalities of Muttak, Cachar and Jaintia, to that of districts; even Upper Assam which was the heartland of Ahom state was divided into a few districts.

The Khasi states, Tripura and Manipur were put under the British paramountcy while other areas were incorporated into the province of Assam. In all tribal areas, loosely administered tribal states and Hinduised kingdoms, the introduction of British Indian revenue system over land and collection of taxes greatly affected their economy. Monetization of their economy and emergence of private property produced greater destabilizing effect on tribal society and economy Triibals and other natives were administered under the British India law. Modernizing influences were also brought due to the introduction of European technology, new laws, western education and new values through teachings of Christianity. But the British policy of isolation of the hill tribes from the other Indians, had prevented the free and ruthless exploitation of the tribes, their land and natural resources, though it had sharpened' the hill-plain dichotomy which was already in existence between them due to religious and cultural differentiation. Another important effect of the colonial rule was territorial and administrative identification of the two great ethnic groups, the Nagas and the Mizos by the formation of two districts, Naga Hills and Lushai (Mizo) Hills. These administrative units gave geographical expression to the Naga or Mizo concept of identity. Mikir Hills district was another example, but the Bodo Kacharis who were scattered throughout the Brahmaputra valley and North Cachar Hills were not given such an administrative opportunity. The Khasis, Jaintias and Garos were also constituted into districts. The tribes of Manipur, the Nagas and the Kukis, were not constituted into such administrative units. The territorial integrity of Manipur and Tripura was kept intact. Ethnicity was widely applied in the administration of customary laws, regulation of social relation, land tenure system and nature of political institutions of the tribes. For example, the identification of a tribe with the Naga group or Kuki group is a complex issue. Very interestingly, the colonial identification was responsible for the shifting of identity among some bridge buffer tribes in Manipur hills.

Thus ethnicity was employed both by the colonial administrators and the tribal elite for different purposes, one for administrative convenience and the other to build up an expanded identity formation, a process described by B.K. Roy Burman as proto-nationalism. Another significant consequence of the colonial rule was the emergence of the private property which was reinforced during the post-independence period. The tribes tried vehemently to prevent the alienation of tribal land and forests. So the tribal attachment to land and forests could not be destroyed by the colonial rulers despite their profit motivated raw material-market oriented policy towards their natural resources. But capitalist economy had totally absorbed the plain districts. The spread of Christianity among the tribes changed their world view and value judgement. Of course, Sanskritization process continued in the princely states of Manipur and Tripura and among some Assam hill tribes. Revivalism of tribal religion and culture was started among the Khasis and some Naga tribes. The Indian liberation struggle had its impact on Assam and to some extent in Manipur where the Congress became the source of inspiration for the people. It is true that national freedom struggle could not penetrate much into the tribal regions though we may mention the uprisings of Jadonang and Gaidinliu against the British which was identified by Pandit Jawaharlal Nehru as a part of the Indian freedom movement.

Second World War and Indian Independence

The eastern frontier of India, especially Nagaland, Manipur and Mizoram, became main battlefields of the Japanese invasion during the Second World War. The whole Northeast was affected both physically and mentally. This war produced a ferment in the minds of the people. This was further accentuated by the impending departure of the British from India. These various ethnic groups and the princely states were naturally very much concerned about their political future. They had earlier resisted British penetration into their territories which were never properly brought under the Ahom rule or any other rule except the British. So the idea of "getting back the lost freedom and one's homeland" became primary concern of the people. The concern for the future was reflected in the formation of tribal organizations, the prominent among them being the Naga Hills Tribal Council (1945) which was renamed Naga National Council (1946) whose prestige was so high that it concluded an agreement with the Governor of Assam and even Prime Minister Jawaharlal Nehru agreed to accept the NNC as a sort of national law making body of the Nagas, the Mizo Union (1947) and the United Mizo Freedom Organization, the Eastern India Tribal Union etc. Several tribal organisations were formed in almost all parts of North East hill regions. The British administrators and influential observers openly pleaded for the separation of the tribal areas from India. One head of a district presided over a meeting of the Mizo Chiefs demanding the option to join Burma. The tribal leaders were however opposed to any idea of continuation of the British colonial rule. By 1947, their demands were formulated into the establishment of an independent Nagaland for the Nagas and creation of an independent Mizoram or the creation of a hill state.

So, when Independence was granted in 1947, the British province of Assam including the hill districts became a part of Dominion of India by the right of transfer of power. The State of Manipur under the Maharaja introduced a responsible form of Government (1947-1949). Instead of the British Political Agent, a Dominion Agent or Dewan of the Government of India was posted at Imphal. Tripura also continued to have similar relationship with the Government of India.

There were three schools of political thinking in north east India in 1947. The most vocal section was the Indian nationalists represented by the Indian National Congress in Assam and the state Congress parties in the princely states. They wanted to strengthen the national government's hold over the region. The second one was the protagonists of the creation of independent states for the Nagas and the Mizos. The Naga independence was spearheaded by Naga National Council under the leadership of A.Z. Phizo and the Mizo independence was mooted by the United Mizo Freedom Organization. A.Z. Phizo and T. Sakhrei, General Secretary of NNC, tried to make common front.of the Nagas and Mizos but failed. However by the time of independence, NNC had signed the famous Nine-Point Agreement with the Governor of Assam, which would be reviewed after ten years in 19.56. The Mizo leadership dominated by the Mizo Union was engaged in the movement for the abolition of the Mizo chiefship, rather than taking up the independence issue. A section of the Assam hill leaders represented by Shillong-based leaders who wanted participation in national Government proposed the idea of a hill state with district level autonomy to protect the tribal rights over land, custom and traditions. The third group was the Communists who organized revolutionary movements in Manipur and Tripura.

Indian Response

The Indian response to the demand of ethnic autonomy and complete independence and the insurgency in the princely states came into two ways. Nehru's liberal paternalistic policy was found expression in the granting of autonomy at the district level, for full protection to the tribal rights to land and customary usages. At the same time, Sardar Patel's iron hand was rcllected in the merger of Manipur, Tripura and Khasi states. While the Khasi states were incorporated in the autonomous Khasi and Jaintia Hill District, Manipur and Tripura were merged with India and converted to Part 'C' states under a Chief Commissioner since 1949.

It may be of interest that Manipur, Tripura and Khasi states were represented by A.C. Guha, a non-resident representative, in the Constituent Assembly. The Naga National Council under A.Z. Phizo refused to be associated with the Constituent Assembly. Nothing short of independence was acceptable to NNC. Mizo reaction to autonomy was indiffere'nt, in the sense that they did not welcome the Bordoloi Sub-Committee which visited Aizawl over the autonomy issue, but they did not oppose it either and accepted the autonomous district council. However very soon, the province of Assam with democratic legislature and autonomy for the tribal districts, and Part 'C' state status for Manipur and Tripura under the Central Government which was a continuation of the colonial arrangements, could not meet the aspirations of the separatist Nagas, autonomy oriented Khasi, Garo, Mikir and Mizo leadership, nor the democratic nationalists of Manipur and Tripura.

But one thing is clear that the constitutional and administrative changes were evolved to meet the ethnic aspiration. This was a problem of integration of these ethnic elements to Indian national life. The national leadership could not clearly explain the concept of Indian nationalism. This created an atmosphere of mutual fear, distrust in the minds of both sides.

Naga Independence Movement

Naga independence movement is a multi-faceted phenomenon. It is a search and assertion of the ethnic identity of the Nagas, articulated by the Naga elite and represented by the charismatic personality of Phizo. It is a process of absorption of various tribes into a common generic name "Naga" for the different tribes brought under a single administrative roof and law, accompanied by introduction of English education and Christianity spread by the supporters of the colonial rule. Despite the absence of a common language, the Nagaization process is still continuing and the movement has undergone transformation in its character, from purely nationalist to Marxist ideological colouring.

Reorganization of States

By 1950, Northeast India had three categories of administrative units: Province of Assam, Part 'C' States of Manipur and Tripura and the North Eastern Frontier Agency (NEFA). There were also demands for creation of various provinces or states in North East after 1947. Mention may be made of the Poorvanchal Pradesh to be carved out of Tripura, Cachar, Manipur and Lushai Hills which was reportedly proposed with the blessing of some central leaders; it was rejected by the people concerned. The Hill,State to be carved out of Assam hills was being talked about and later on persued by the All Party Hill Leaders Conference (APHLC). There was also a demand for granting of restoration of democratic rule in Manipur. These demands coincided with demands raised in other parts of the country for reorganization on linguistic principle. And the States Reorganization Commission was constituted in 1954 to look into the matter. The SRC recommended the creation of states on linguistic principle. As regards the north east India, the SRC recommended the constitution of the State of Assam with Assamese language as its basis. The SRC did not accept the demands of the hill state, upgrading of Manipur and Tripura to full State; on the contrary, the SRC recommended the merger of the two states into Assam as districts. At the intervention of Prime Minister Jawaharlal Nehru, Manipur and Tripura were converted into Union Territories in 1957.

What the SRC recommended was the continuation and expansion of modern Assam created by the British.

Creation of Nagaland State

The intense armed conflict in Nagaland went unabated for several years. The government of India made very cautious response to solve the Naga problem which had military, human and political aspects. The Naga Hill Tuensang Area (NHTA) was created in 1957, accepting partially the bringing of the contiguous Naga areas under one unit. Later on in 1960, the Naga Peoples Convention negotiated with Prime Minister Nehru for the creation of State of Nagaland to solve the Naga problem. The creation of a State for a group of people claiming common ethnic identity was a fresh principle in the formation of States within the Indian Union. For the first time, the ethnic principle was introduced in the Indian federal system. Granting of full statehood to Nagaland in 1963 evoked similar demands for statehood for Manipur, Tripura and hill areas of Assam with multiplicity of both language and ethnicity.

Demand for Hill State

The demand for the hill state comprising the autonomous hill districts of Assam was going on for some years. Prime Minister Nehru promised Scottish pattern of autonomy for these areas. Then Pataskar Commission was appointed to look into the problem. Later on, the idea of autonomous hill state was mooted. The demand for the hill state was based on the need for tribal solidarity of the various ethnic groups inhabiting Garo Hills, Khasi, Jaintia hills, North Cachar and Mikir Hills (now Karbi Anglong) and Mizo Hills; it was not purely on ethnic principle but it had elements of ethnicity. The Nagas did not join this movement from the very beginning. There was internal stress and strains and ultimately, the Mizos backed out of the movement. This demand was pressed hard during the period after the creation of Nagaland.

Mizo Uprising

Mizo Independence movement which was started as early as August, 1947, got revived during the serious famine in Mizo Hills in 1960. And famine relief measures in the district was taken up and later on the Mizo National Front was founded. The Mizo uprising broke out in February 1966. Their aim was the creation of an independent Mizo state through an armed revolution. Like the Naga movement, Mizo movement is a nationalist movement. All Kuki-Lushai tribes were brought under the Mizo identity. Their ethnic identity is further reinforced by linguistic affinity which is not present among the Nagas who use a foreign language as their lingua franca.

Reorganization of States, 1972

It is clear that the Naga and Mizo movements are based on ethnicity and to some extent on language. Demands for statehood for Tripura and Manipur were based neither on linguistic affinity nor ethnic identity but on the historic reason of being former kingdoms. The demand for the Hill State was perhaps similar to that of Manipur and Tripura in the sense that they had common administrative framework both under the British and Indian governments.

There was also another on-going demand for the creation of Udayachal for the Bodo-Kachari plain tribals of Assam in the Brahmaputra valley. It is both linguistic and ethnic demand launched by the Plain Tribal Council of Assam (PCTA). It was changed to Bodoland demand. So the political aspirations of the people in the region range from sovereign states, autonomous regions, statehood in the Indian Union, to merger with a greater unit or creation of a district even. The policy of the Government of India on meeting the aspirations of the various ethnic groups and political units was spelled out in the States Reorganization Act of 1971 by which statehood was granted to Manipur, Tripura, and the Khasi-Jaintia hills and Garo hills were constituted into the state of Meghalaya, thus fulfilling the demand for the Hill State (District of North Cachar and Karbi Anglong opted for the State of Assam). Mizo hills were upgraded to Union Territory of Mizoram and NEFA was constituted to Union Territory of Arunachal Pradesh and then to full fledged statehood. It is clear that only in Mizoram the ethnic principle was applied. The central government is following a pragmatic approach towards the formation of States in Northeast India.

The ethnic principle had greatly suited the demand of the integration of Mizo areas into Mizoram and Naga areas into Nagaland. This had also suited the demand of the Udayachal state or Bodoland and Ahom-Mongoloid state in the Brahmaputra valley and similar demands, If the linguistic principle is applied, Tripura may be partitioned into Bengali-speaking and Tripuri-speaking units which are not practicable at all. Then by the linguistic principle Cachar may be separated from Assam. Karbis are demanding separation from Assam, though in a mild from. Balkanization of Assam is now a historical fact. If the socio-economic problems of the various groups of the region are not properly looked into and solved by the rulers both in the centre and states, there is a possibility of further conflicts which would disturb the boundaries of existing States and Union Territories.

In conclusion, the formation of States and Union Territories, whether on ethnic principle or historical or administrative consideration, was the creation of the institutional frame as a part of the Indian federal system to fulfil the aspiration of the people and at the same time to channelise the gradual participation in greater Indian national life. By no means the reorganization of States in India is complete; and it is most likely that Northeast India may also be reorganized at one time or another. But Indian democracy has proved its capacity to meet the expectations and aspirations of the different segments of the people.

4

Evolution of the Meitei State: The Process of State Formation in Early Manipur

STATE AND STATE FORMATION

State, according to the classical political thinkers, is "a people occupying a definite territory, having a government which has an external sovereign relations". To the sociologists, the state is a social organization which has given expression to the existing relation in a society and to the ideas pertaining to power; authority, force, justice, property and the laws. The ancient Greek and Roman thinkers thought that the state was coterminous with the society. So, the state is essentially a social institution with the basic features, such as, population, territoriality, legitimacy (power and authority) and sovereignty.

To the Marxists, the state was a structure created by the propertied class to manage the complex social relationship and to protect the interests of the rich and powerful class. According to Frederick Engels, the distinguishing features of the state are the territory, establishment of the public power, imposition of taxes, introduction of public debts and the authority of the bureaucracy of the state.

Therefore, the state is the highest form of human institution ever created by man. A German philosopher, Hegel describes the state as the march of God on Earth.

The State Formation is the process of evolution of a people or a social group occupying a territory into a political society through the different stages and phases of social and economic function. The political society is the state. However, there is not a single accepted paradigm to explain the process of state formation.

According to Ronald Cohen, "there is no clear cut or simple set of causal statement that explains the phenomenon of the state". However, he explains the process of the state formation thus, "The formation of state is a funnel like progression of interactions in which a variety of pre-state structures responding to the different determinants of change are found by other unresolvable conflicts to choose additional and more complex laws of political hierarchy. Once a particular solution is hit upon, the structural features of the adaptation and benefits cause these politics to converge culturally and socially to the early states"(Anthropology of Political Evolution, 1975).

Romila Thapar in her *Lineage to State* (1984) more or less concurring with Cohen's view observes, "State formation is a complex process in which a range of factors may be crucial and may apply to varying situation. There will be no single factor of state formation. The form of the state would vary according to the nature of the origin". It is not proposed to go into the origin of the state speculated by political philosophers and sociologists. However, it is necessary to understand the typology of states for a clear perception of the process of state formation.

Typology of the States

The states have been classified into four categories; the early states and modern statcs; pristine (primary) and secondary states. Henry Claessen and Peter Skalnik in the *Early State* (1978) classify the states into the early and modern. The early states are simple, non-industrialized and pre capitalistic, and the modern states are complex, industrialized and developing.

Morton H. Fried in his *Evolution of the Political Society* (1967) classifies the states into pristine state and secondary state. The pristine state is also known as the primary state. This classification is on the basis of the natural evolution or the external sponsorship. Pristine states like the primitive societies are simple, early, original, primary and lacking in development. Secondary states are found due to the pressure from the existing states. In most case, secondary states are sponsored by the developing existing states which impose their model on the new state formation.

Evolutionary Process

The formation of the pristine states has been explained by two theoretical formulations; the evolutionary process as proposed by Fried and the conflict process as propounded by Frederick Engels.

According to Fried, the pristine states passed through the three stages with corresponding social and political formations as given hereunder.

	Form of Social Formation	Polity Formation
1.	Egalitarianism [in a primitive society]	Band and Tribal polity
2.	Ranked Society [Diversified Society]	Chiefdom
3.	Stratified Society	State

Conflict Process

The Marxian theory of state formation was propounded by Engels in his *Origin of Family, Private Property and the State* (1884). He explained the formation of the states on the basis of intra-societal conflicts and forms of class struggle through four stages of social and political development as follows.

1. Primitive Communism
2. Emergence of Private Property
3. Formation of Social and Econoril ic Classes
4. Emergence of the State

According to Engels, the primitive communism was the first stage of social formation in which there was no property, no trade and commerce, no class of rich or poor, and no despotic ruler. In course of time, the individuals started acquiring things from the common or community's pool of resources (wealth) and it was legitimized and the private property as acquired by the individuals emerged. The creation of the private property led to the concentration of the property or wealth into the hands of the few and it led to the formation of the social and economic class which possessed the wealth. A dominant class among them tried to perpetuate their control over their private property. In order to protect the interests of the dominant class, a military power was created. And out of this, a structure of productivity due to technological development and surplus products were created. Trade in surplus commodities resulted in the change of the economy from consumption or subsistence to production of commodities for exchange. This type of economy necessitated the growth of middlemen, entrepreneurs and capital. The class structure so evolved is perpetuated through the state. This theory explains the evolution of the states in European context.

However, Marx's model of state formation for the oriental states including India, known as the Asiatic Mode of Production has not been able to explain the evolution of the state in India. Thus it has not been accepted.

Romila Thapar explains the evolution of the pristine state in Vedic period as the transformation of the lineage society to the state. Lineage was "a corporate group of unilinial kin with a formalized system of authority as the binding force". There was "transformation of the lineage system to a combined lineage and territorial group and to a sharper stratification of the chieftainship (chiefdom) which was germinal to state formation".

In the context of state formation in Manipur, there was the evolution of the primary or the pristine state in ancient and medieval period. The process of state formation was on the basis of evolutionary process. But the exact evolution of the state was, as pointed out by Romila Thapar, the transformation of the lineage-based society to state: lineage based clan chiefdom to the state.

State Formation is also regarded as a process of cultural evolution. It has been rightly said that the creation of culture is a great human achievement by the use of which the society tames and governs their members, create and maintain their complex social organization.

Culture has technological, economic, religious, artistic and recreational functions. All of these depend on the ability of the political aspects of culture to integrate and protect the society. A society grows or declines depending on the ability to preserve the authority. The growth and decline of a culture also depends on the ability of the state to preserve its culture and civilization.

Coming back to the pristine states, we focus on the factors contributing to the emergence of the pristine society and state.

Claessen and Skalnik mention the major factors: growth of population and pressure of population war, war machine, threat of war, conquest, progress in production and creation of surplus, imposition of tribute, affluence, ideology and legitimization and the influence of the existing states. These factors are applicable to the case of Manipur.

FORMATION OF THE MEITEI CLAN CHIEFDOMS

The Meiteis in ancient Manipur had developed a lineage based social system and resultant polity formation which ultimately emerged as clan chiefdoms and principalities. Historical texts and literary works refer to a large number of ethnic and social groups in ancient Manipur valley. They were the Proto-Meitei social groups like the Mangang, Angom, Luwang, Khaba, N ganba, Khuman, Moirang, Sarang, Leishangthem, Heiram Khunjam, Chenglei, Haorok Konthou, Manting Mara, Lera Khongnang, Thanga, Kambong, Ulok Ushai, Haokha-Lokkha, Ningol Latam, Phantek Khuyon, Chakpa. There were hill tribal communities like the Anal, Tangkhul and Kabui (Rongmei).

These tribes and social groups except the hill tribes were socially organized into the seven clans of the Meiteis during the reign of King Nongda Lairen Pakhangba who founded the Ningthouja dynasty. The clan genealogies give the account of the origin and geological trees of the clans concerned showing their historicity. Myths were created to provide the background of the origin of the clans which were constituted into the Meitei social fold.

Pre-Pakhangba Polity Formation

There are historical references to a large number of pre-Pakhangba chiefs and rulers who ruled in different periods of the traditional Meitei Age known as the Chak; Hayi Chak, Haya Chak, Langba Chak and Konna Chak. Of these accounts, Kangbalon, a chronicle which is supposed to have been compiled during the reign of Khuyoi Tompok, the successor of Pakhangba gives a brief account of several rulers and chiefs. Kangba was the first chief of the Meiteis. His successors were Maliya Phambalcha, the founder of the Era of Maliya Phambacha, Nongdamhan,and Taohuireng who faced a slave rebellion, Kaksuba, Tonkonba, discoverer of the wild paddy, Pitingkoi, Lambicha, Sopaiba, Puthiba, the inventor of the plough, Kuptreng and Sentreng. The accounts of these rulers present a picture of the emerging chieftainship. But we cannot establish the historicity of their rule in a chronological frame.

The Clan Chiefdoms

The clan among the ancient Meitei was both a social and political institution. This duality in the nature and function of the clan is a unique feature of the Meitei lineage system. The clan is known as the Salai, which literally means the ancestor god of the lineage (Sa means Sagei, Lai means god). There was no salai system in the legendary period though there are references to the sagei (lineage or families). It was during the reign of King Pakhangba that seven clans were regrouped and recognized as the part of the Meitei social system. The seven clans were the Ningthouja, the royal clan (the Magang), the Angom, Luwang, Kha-Nganba (combination of the Khabas and Nganbas), Sarang Leishangthem (combination of Sarang, Leishangthem and Chenglei), the Khuman and the Moirang. Each of the clans had a territorial region. Smaller groups were absorbed into the seven clans along with their territory. Credit should be given to Pakhangba for the creation of the Meitei Salai system which was the connerstone of the Meitei society and state.

The clan was both a social category and a polity formation when the seven clans were created. Each clan or salai had a delineated territory which became the political space of the clan chiefdom. The name of the clan was identical to the name of the clan territory. A clan spoke a similar language or dialect. Later on all the clans spoke the Meitei language which was an outcome of political hegemony of the Ningthoujas who called themselves as the Meitei. However, in a clan territory, people of other clans also migrated and there was the salai system within a clan territory or principality.

The chief of the clan was called Piba, the social head of the clan. He was originally the head of the lineage (sagei) and head of the village inhabited by his kinsmen. The Piba was expected by his clansmen to be the protector of the clan lands including the agricultural lands, forests, rivers and lakes. The chief of the clan by his moral and social authority, and physical prowess organized a group of armed kinsmen for defence of the land and protection of life and property of the community. The Piba became ultimately the protector of the land and people within the clan territory. So the Piba, the social head of the clan became the political authority with his command over the armed militia who were voluntary soldiers. With this authority the Piba became a Ningthou (chief or king) of the clan within the clan territory which ultimately had become a principality or a chiefdom.

The concept of clan land as a communal land and clan territory had emerged. Thus the land within clan chiefdom was owned by the clan in common while the individual families established individual land holdings. They enjoyed the rights to the common land like the .forests, rivers and lakes. The Ningthou's foremost duty was the protection of the people and territory. He exercised the power of the military force for the performance of this duty. The members of the clan, later on the inhabitants: of the principality were to render military service under the command of the Ningthou. It was the beginning of the military service known as the Lallup. The chiefs also established individual ownership of lands out of the common lands of the clan. He compelled his kinsmen and other subjects to render service to him for agricultural products. He acquired enough food grains for the maintenance of royal households and the administrative establishment. He asked the subjects to cut timber from the forest for making houses in the royal palace and for manufacturing of boats.

In return the chief was given the responsibility of performing the royal religious rituals for the clan and the chiefdom with the help of the priest. He combined.,in himself the role of the Piba (social head), Ningthou (king) and the high priest. The king was the Piba of his clan only and not of other clans.

The clan genealogies give the list of chiefs of the clans who became rulers. The clan chronicles give brief accounts of the history of the clan. However, of the clan chronicles, the Moirang chronicles and the Khuman chronicles give their political history and the account of their polity. The Angom, Khaba, Nganba, Sarang, Leishangthem did not have separate polity. They accepted feudatory status in the court of the Ningthouja kingdom. Angom Ningthou or the chief of the Angom, Luwang Ningthou or chief of the Luwang occupied the feudatory position in the Ningthouja courts.

Support to the chiefdom, or the chief came in form of tribute, either in kind or services from the population, lesser clans and ethnic groups at the village levels who came under their hegemony or control. As the Piba of the clan, the chief got support from the heads of the sub-lineages (sagei) and the kinsmen of the clan as a whole.

Romila Thapar, writing on the state formation in the Vedic period observes," A state is generally associated with the political authority which "functions within a territorial unit, delegates its power to the functionaries, is financed by revenue collected from those who contribute on an impersonal basis to its maintenance and acts as an instrument of integrating social segments identified not merely by ritual roles but also by economic function".

This was exactly the task carried out by the Ningthouja dynasty on the evolution of the Meitei state.

BEGINNING OF THE MEITCI STATE: FOUNDATION OF THE NINGTHOUJA DYNASTY

The establishment of the Ningthouja Kingdom at the Kangla, the heartland of the Meitei State, by Nongda Lairen Pakhangba marked the beginning of the evolution of the Meitei State. The emergence of the Ningthouja dynasty was an outcome of the struggle between the various ethnic groups and clan chiefdoms. There were also various ethnic groups who assumed the clanhood within the Meitei society. There was always a bone of contention among them at one time or the other for the occupation of the Kangla which was a seat of political power, religion and culture of the Meiteis. In the Meitei psyche, the Kangla was regarded as the navel of the earth and the centre of the Meitei worldview and universe.

Pakhangba occupied the Kangla after defeating his rivals, the Khabas and Poireiton, a leader of the colonizers to Manipur valley in the first century A.D. Pakhangba was supported by several clans, the Angom, the Luwang, the Mangang, the Khuman, the Moirang and the Chakpa. The royal chronicles describe him as the founding monarch of the Ningthouja ruling family. Pakhangba Phambal (the coronation of Pakhangba) records that Pakhangba was given the title of Meidingu, a corruption of Meitei-Ngu, the Lord of the Meitei. He was the first monarch to have performed the coronation ceremony. He was the founder of the Meitei monarchy. His reign saw the reorganization and improvement of the Meitei social and political structure.

He organized the proto-Meitei ethnic groups into the seven clans of the Meiteis. He became the head of the Meitei social confederacy. And he was the head of the Meitei state. The fact that Pakhangba was crowned the king of the Meiteis led to a query whether the ancient Meiteis had developed the concept of monarchy and Pakhangba just succeeded to assume the monarchy of the Meitei state. If we were to believe the proto historical accounts of political formations before the emergence of Ningthouja dynasty, the Meiteis had already developed the concept of monarchy. There are also references made by Yaibirok, the mother of Pakhangba, who made serious attempts to make her son assume the kingship of the Meiteis at Kangla. We are short of historical evidences to trace the paraphernalia of a polity before the accession of Pakhangba on the throne of Kangla. He created the administrative machinery of a state which was followed by his successors. Every king of Ningthouja dynasty who ruled in Manipur from 33 AD 1955 traced direct descent from Pakhangba.

The Growth of the Meitei State:

The Meitei kings ruled the country from Kangla. They gradually established their control over the forest rich plain areas of the basin of the Imphal and Iril rivers in northern Manipur valley, which was a part of the Ningthouja kingdom. The forests were cleared and agriculture was developed in the upper reaches of the two rivers. In the early stage, the broadcasting and shifting cultivation (Pamlou) were adopted. Later on they took to wet rice cultivation. In the central part of the valley, there were swampy areas with a large number of lakes and marshes which were required to be drained continuously. The water from the swampy areas were drained through the three rivers, Imphal, Iril and Nambul. The kings employed the labour of the people through the Lallup system in dredging the rivers, correcting or changing the courses of the rivers. Irrigation was undertaken by the state. These rivers provided the waterways. The swampy areas and the lakes were traversed by waterways in which the dug out canoes were used in large number. The state penetrated into the thickly forested Nongmaijing hills and to Koubru mountain for the supply of timber and collection of forest products, catching of wild elephants for the royal stable and the armed forces.

With access to and control over the fertile plains of northern Imphal valley and the forests of the surrounding mountains the Meitei state had acquired enough resources to strengthen and expand the state. There was enough population for engagement in state sponsored irrigation works. They also organized the militia as the Meitei was a martial race. The control of the menace created by the wild animals like the tiger, leopard and wild boar was effected by the state. Thinly populated areas were inhabited by the immigrants.

The State under Naothingkhong

From the first century to the 8th century, the Meitei state made a gradual expansion. Naothingkhong Phamban Kaba, a historical text dealing with adventures and coronation of Naothingkhong gives a portrait of a well developed state structure. His kingdom came into contact with the Shans of the kingdom of Pong of Upper Burma. Samlung, a prince and a brother of Pong King Sukhampha visited Manipur valley and stayed for ten years at Pong lngkhol (Homestead of the Pong) on the lril river. Contact with the Shan was a significant development in the expanding relation of the Meitei state with a foreign country. The king married a Bengal princess Chingngurembi, a princess from the west.

The Naothingkhong Phamban Kaba gives a reference to the agricultural development. The people of the Ningthouja, Khuman and Luwang clans were devoted to wet rice cultivation. The hill tribes like the Shelloi Langmais among whom Prince Naothingkhong took shelter and married a tribal girl named Petanga took to shifting cultivation or pamlou. There were always plentiful harvests. The historical text says that there was surplus in the production of food grains. Fishing was another means of livelihood. There were conflicts and quarrels over the exercise of fishing rights over the streams and rivers.

The state machinery was developed to some extent. The coronation ceremony, the elaborate coronation costumes and participation of the members of royalty and nobility in it show that there was an elaborate administrative hierarchy and rituals which were the symbols of a developed state. The military system was well organized. It consisted of cavalry, foot soldiers and riverine navy. The weapons were sword, spear and shields. The Lallup was mentiod but it was perhaps in a rudimentary stage.

The Loiyamba Shilyen: The first written constitution of the Meitei State

Loiyamba (1094-1120 A.D) was a remarkable king of Manipur. The formation of the Meitei state was almost completed during his reign. He issued a royal edict entitled,"Loiyamba Shilyen" in 1110 A.D. The edict has been described as the first written constitution in the history of Manipur. It deals with the status and working of the monarchy, privileges of the royalty and nobility. Working of the different administrative departments, functions of the various state officials, and the distribution of economic occupation to different social groups or lineages among the subjects, the maintenance of the abodes of deities:, functions and duties of the priestly class. It gives a picture of the fully developed Meitei state system.

The Royal chronicle refers to the creation of six administrative divisions which were the precursor of the Pana system of district adtpinistration. The divisions were Khongchalup, Khongbilup, Angoubalup, Nongmailup, Khurailup and Khongjenglup. The Loiyamba Shilyen mentions four panas.

Lallup System

For the first time, the royal chronicle mentions the existence of the Lallup system in Manipur during the reign of Loiyamba. Lallup was the feudal service rendered by the male subjects between the ages of 16 to 60 years, to the state. Each able-bodied subject had to render labour of ten days out of forty days. Lallup covered both military and non military development works. Lallup literally means war organization. Perhaps it was originally a military service which extended to non-military activities of the state. The development of the elaborate Lallup system was the manifestation of the emergence of feudalism in the social, administrative and political s,tructure of the kingdom of Manipur.

Loiyamba Shilyen has projected a well-organized state, society and economy of Manipur. The agrarian economy was supplemented by the growing cottage industries of handicrafts and textile. It was so much developed that the state had to regulate the organization of these activities. The edict shows the emergence of the artisan class.

The monarchy was fully entrenched and the king was becoming very powerful. The nobility was strengthened and the hierarchy of the nobility was mentioned. The paraphernalia of the court etiquette had become very elaborate. The edict mentions the duties and functions of the king and royal families.

The priestly class was regulated by the state. The king assumed the social and religious headship over and above his royal functions. The state was projected as the regulator of the economy.

EMERGENCE OF THE NATION STATE: KYAMBA (1467-1506 A.D)

Four centuries after King Loiyamba, the Meitei state

under King Kyamba attained the status of the nation state. The power of the Meitei state was reflected in the military aggrandizement and territorial expansion. The whole valley of Manipur with the regional principalities was brought under the direct rule of the Ningthouja dynasty. The Khuman principalities could not survive long and in the fourteenth century it was merged with the Meitei state. The principalities of Moirang continue to maintain its independence for many centuries. They could maintain their political structure due to their resource available in the surrounding hills and the Loktak lake. However by 1432 King Ningthoukhomba of the Ningthoujas defeated the Moirang principalities which was absorbed into the Meitei state. The hill tribes in the foothills were kept under political control. The hills between Manipur valley and Kabaw valley were kept under political supremacy though in Burma there was no direct rule over the hill tribe. The most significant achievement of King Kyamba'was the conquest of Kabaw valley in Upper Burma.

Conquest of Kabaw Valley: Treaty Relation between Manipur and Kingdom of Pong

King Kyamba made a joint military expedition in the Chindwin basin in Upper Burma, along with King Khekhomba of the Mau Shan Kingdom of Pong. The two kings made conquest in both banks of the Chindwin river. Kyamba conquered Kabaw valley and several principalities in the west bank of the river. Khekhomba conquered the territories to the east of the Chindwin.

"Pong Meitei Lamyen Lairik" (the treaty fixing boundary between Meitei and Pong)

This text is an account of the treaty made between King Kyamba of Manipur and King Khekhomba of Pong. There was an agreement made between the two kings that the Kabaw valley in the west of Chindwin river was given to Manipur. And the territories to the east of Chindwin were given to Pong. This treaty was the confirmation of the conquest of the territories by a formal treaty between the two independent countries. By this treaty, the international entity of Manipur was recognized by a powerful kingdom of Upper Burma in the 15th century. The sovereignty of Manipur was now internationally recognized. The state formation had attained the ultimate stage.

King Kyamba introduced internal reforms. According to Cheitharol Kumbaba, the first was the Pana system. He established two Panas; Ahallup and Naharup. It has been conjectured that the "Pana" was a Shan word. Loiyamba Shilyen mentions several panas.

Chronicle keeping and calendar

Kyamba introduced the practice of keeping the royal chronicle known as the Cheitharol Kumbaba and the Cheithaba system of counting years from 1485 A.D. The peaceful reign of King Kyamba saw the expansion of the territory of Manipur, incorporation of Kabaw valley and the Shan population of the valley to the population of Manipur. The kingdom attracted immigrants from the mainland India particularly the Brahmins.

The evolution of the Meitei state in a long period of 1500 years was an example of the evolution of the pristine (primary) state formation. The Meiteis who were organized by King Pakhangba into a single state and society became a nationality during the reign of King Kyamba. The Meitei language was the backbone of the Meitei nationality. And the kingdom of Manipur had become a nation state. The Meitei was the nation and the state was Kangleipak which was renamed Manipur in the 18th century.

REFERENCES

Ch.Manihar Singh (Ed), *Naothingkhong Phambal Kaba* (In English translation), Imphal, 1986

Frederick Engels, *Origin of Family, Private Property and the State*, Reprint, Moscow, 1977.

Gangmumei Kamei, State Formation in North East India: A Review, Presidential address of North East India History Association, Kohima Session, 1986

Gangmumei Kamei, *A History of Manipur* Vol I: Pre colonial period, Delhi, 1991

Henry, J.M. Claessen and Peter Skalnik (Ed), The Early Sate, The Hague, 1978. Frederick Engels, *Origin of Family, Private Property and the State*, Reprint, Moscow, 1977

International Encyclopedia of Social Sciences, Vol. 15, p. 150

Kh. Chandrasekhar (Ed), *Loiyamba Shilyen*, Imphal, 1984

Kh.Yaima (Ed) Pakhangba Phambal, Imphal, 1967

L.M. Singh and N. Khelchandra Singh (Ed) *Cheitharol Kumbaba* Imphal, 1967

Meitei Pong Lamyen Lairik, MSS supplied by B. Kulachandra Sharma and extracts reproduced in N. Khelchandra Singh, *Ariba Manipuri Sahitya Itihaas*, Imphal, 1969

Ronald Cohen and E.R. Service (Ed), *Origin of the State: the Anthropology of Political Evolution*, Philadelphia, 1978

Romila Thapar, *From Lineage to State*, Oxford University Press, Bombay, 1984

5

Modernization

What is Modernization?

Modernization in sociological terms, is a process of social change, a current form for an old and continuous process. Modernization means the "transformation of a society from a traditional, rural and agrarian society to a secular, urban and industrialized society". Modernization is the latest form of human civilization in its historical march which passed through the three stages.

Emergence of the primitive societies and communities;

Transformation of the primitive societies into civilization;

Evolution of an industrialized modem society as a result of the industrial revolution.

Historically the North West Europe covering England, Belgium, France and Germany, was the original base of modernization from where it had spread to other parts of the modern world since the nineteenth century taking different forms and assuming different scales.

Ethos of Modernization:

"Modern" literally means "of the present and present times". "Being modern" derives meaning and momentum by comparison and contrast with, and rejection and negation of what preceded it in time. The ethos of "being modern" which characterize modernization are, according to the sociologists, individualism, specialization, rationality, secularization and abstraction.

A modern or modernized society is based on the individuals rather than the agrarian or peasant communities, the social group or the community. The institutions in a modern society and state are assigned the performance of limited specialized tasks with a highly developed division of labour. Specialization is a mark of modernization. Rationality is an aspect of modernization. Man's thinking and action are based on rationality. And rationality is the base of secularization. We find that rather attaching rights and prerogatives to the particular groups or communities or being guided by customs and traditions, modern institutions are governed by rational laws, general rules and regulations which derive legitimacy from the method and finding of science. Rational thinking and scientific attitude are essential characteristics of being modern.

Modernization has two aspects: social and political. In social aspect, as noted above, modernization is the process of social change with a large percentage of economic components. Truly speaking, a modern society is an industrial society. A modern society is based on industrialism. In other words, industrialism is the backbone of a modern society. Again industrialism is a way of life; it covers economic, social, political and cultural changes. A society becomes modernized after undergoing a comprehensive transformation of industrialization. An economic change occurs due to industrialization. It is based on the technological change and change in the mode of production: use of machine instead of hand, factory not home as the place of production, mass production instead of home based small production. The industrial sites have become the work place and people move to the towns and cities where industries are located. This is a movement of people from rural or village to urban centre and towns. Thus urbanism has emerged. And it has become a way of life in a modernized society. The city has become the symbol or reality of the industrial society as a whole.

While family was the unit of production in the pre-industrial society, work in the factory had become the identity of the worker. The family has become fragmented with a highly developed division of labour. Nuclear family has emerged. In social structure, the economic status of the worker has assumed a great primacy. Modernization as a result of industrialization led to secularization and rationalization.

Political Modernization

Political modernization is the process of the changes in the structure of the political system of a modernizing society. Historically it means the totality of the changes in the political structure and culture affected by the process of modernization. And this process covers secularization, industrialization, commercialization, social mobility, restratification, higher standard of living, rise in literacy and educational development, national unification and the people's participation in the government.

Thus, the political modernization also means the transfonnation of "pre-modern" traditional polity to a post traditional modern polity. It also means the growing capacity of the people to develop political or economic structure to cope with or resolve problems of a country, to absorb and adopt the continuous change for attainment of the societal goals. The political modernization is based on the principle of equality in the political structure. It is reflected in the democratic fonn of government and functioning of the nation states.

In the second half of the twentieth century, many Western and non-Western countries had undergone the process of modernization with varying degrees: Developed, Developing and Underdeveloped. Modernization with the latest trend of globalization of economy has made the modern society a sort of a world society. History has shown both the Western and non-Western routes to modernity. The Western experience of industrialization is a model of world industrialization. But a new dimension and approach has been adopted in the modernization of the non-Western nations, particularly, Japan, Russia, China and India. Japanese model is unique in the sense that she is industrialized on her own tradition.

There is also a better understanding of the oriental ideas, philosophy and religion among the people of the west, Buddhism and Hinduism have been better understood. It is well known that Asia particularly India had contributed to the development of mathematical science which was adopted by the western scientists. The Chinese technology of printing and gun powder were adopted by the west. Even Christianity was born in Asia.

Westernization

Among the social scientists, economists and sociologists, there are two opinions on the defining term to describe the process of social and economic transformations in the Third World. The well known Indian sociologist, M.N. Srinivas proposed that such a change might be called as westernization. He observes," westernization is used to characterize the changes brought about in Indian society and culture as a result of 150 years of the British rule and the term subsumes the changes occurring at different levels; technology, institution, ideology and values" (Srinivas, *Social Change in Modem India*, 1972). However, other sociologists think that the phenomenon of change out of the contact between a non-western society with a western country may be described as modernization. To them, modernization is a global phenomenon which covers the process of change in India.

It is in this context that Wilbert Moore describes modernization. He says,"Modernization is a total transformation of a traditional or pre-modern society into a type of technology and associated social organization that characterize the "advanced" economically prosperous and relatively stable political nature of the western world" (Moore, *Social Order*, 1975). He thinks that modernization means the process of socio-cultural change whereby less developed societies acquire characteristics common to more developed societies.

At the same time, the theory of Srinivas comes into contrast with the popular Indian view according to which westernization means, "making the oriental people or country to adopt ideas, ideals, institution, systems, structures, living styles and values of life of the west". This concept of westernization implies the loss of cultural identity and national personality. It implies the absorption and assimilation by foreign culture. It is therefore presumed that westernization means the aping of the west which is harmful and should be discarded.

Srinivas's study of westernization, sanskritization and secularization does not lead to a gloomy interpretation as presented above. India maintains her identity, her nationality, her cultural heritage and new interpretation and reform of her religion despite the onslaught of the Anglican ideas during the colonial period. There is no much qualitative difference between modernization and the concept of Srinivas.

If we examine the characteristics of westernization and modernization there is no much of a qualitative difference. However, modernization appears universal and westernization sounds parochial and Eurocentric. Modernization has an aura of value, standing on the side of the good while westernization, as Srinivas himself says is ethically neutral. Regarding the process of change in the third world countries, Gunar Myrdal tends to agree with other sociologists that it is modernization. He analyses the characteristics of modernization in the countries with the following factors.

"Rationality, planning for development, rise of productivity, increasing standard of living, social and economic equalization or egalitarianism, improved institution, national unification, national independence and national consolidation, political democracy and democracy at the grass roots, social discipline and democratic planning" (Myrdal, *Asian Drama*, Abridged Edn, 1972).

This is what is happening at least in modern India. The scheme of modernization is not an imposed one. It is to be rooted in the soil of the newly liberated countries.

Models of Modernization

(i) The western model originated from north-west Europe and was spread to United States, Canada, Southern and Eastern Europe, South Africa and Australia.

(ii) The non-Western model was first developed in Japan, and was later on spread to Russia, Turkey, China, India and Israel.

(iii) Extension of the Western model to the Latin America.

(iv) Africa and Arab world are grappled with the different models of modernization and forces of change.

At the end of the twentieth century, the western industrialized nations had established their control over the global economy. The polarization of the nation states on the basis of ideology led to the East-West divide of the world. But it came to an end with the break up of the Soviet empire. A new mode of polarization on the basis of industrialization and national wealth known as the North-South divide of nations had emerged. North represents the rich nations of the Northern Hemisphere and South represents the poor nations of the Southern Hemisphere (except Australia and South Africa). Now there is no escape from modernization and no end to modernization. Modernization had become global and universal; modernization is an inevitable process of history.

Emergence of the Postmodern Society

Out of the tremendous economic growth as a result of industrialization in many countries, a new aspect of economy has grown up in form of the "Service Economy". A service economy is marked by great expansion in education, health and other welfare service.

The needs of the modernized societies are fulfilled by the "knowledge class" consisting of professionals (teacher, doctor, lawyer, banker), the scientific and technical workers. There also grew up new industries like aeronautics, space and nuclear industries and information technology which are created by developments in pure science and theoretical research. Theoretical knowledge of social science, particularly in economics, finance and commerce is applied to the management of the national economy. Modernization has pushed these developments to a larger dimension of change. An American sociologist, Daniel Bell (*Coming of the Post Industrial Society*) has described these "fantastic" changes in economy and management of the economy, mostly global, as a move towards "postmodern or post industrial society". Many think that the analysis of Bell sounds immature. But a new phenomenon of change in the process of modernization is occurring.

Post modernism is used to refer to the style or movements within the literature, painting, the plastic art and architecture. It is originally meant to concern with the aspects of aesthetic reflection upon the nature of modernization. However, sociologically as pointed out by Anthony Giddens (The Consequences of Modernity), post modernity refers to something different. He says, "If we are moving into a phase of post modernity, this means that trajectory of social development is taking us away from the institutions of modernity towards a new and distinctive type of social order. "Post modernism" might express an awareness of such a transition but does not show that it exists".

No Modernization Without Indigenization

The process of modernization has shown that modernization cannot be brought about by the transfer and implantation of the modern institutions in the transitional societies of the modernizing countries. The lesson learnt from the failure to implant modernization to a country was that modernization must be systematic. It requires the involvement of the indigenous people in the process and their acceptance of the process of change. Institutions cannot be transfered they have to be transformed. So the indigenization of the process of modernization is called for. Lifeways cannot be adopted, they have to be adapted according to genius of the indigenous people.

An alien civilization and culture cannot be implanted on a people of a country with an ancient civilization and culture. India is in the process of modernization. India has become a strong political power and an economic giant. India has adopted Western science and technology and ethos connected with it. She has adopted democracy. She is the greatest democracy in the world. She has adopted secularism based on rationality and her cultural heritage. India is a great country with a strong civilizational roots, the religion, philosophy and culture.

In the early years, India was in search of a model of modernization which had a great economic component. A socialist model and mixed economy were kept in freeze. She is marching towards free economy, and state planning for development with a committed societal goal of welfare state. India's modernization is based on the syncretism of modern technology and scientific rationalism with the cultural and spiritual value of Indian civilization; a synthesis of modernity and tradition; India is a plural society; unity in diversity. The Indian model is to provide all round welfare and development to all sections of the society.

Modernization of Indigenous Tribes of Manipur:

The indigenous tribes of Manipur like their counterparts in North East India have been passing through a process of social, economic and cultural change which we may call modernization. The change was brought about by the Western technology introduced by the British in the colonial period and by the massive economic development introduced by the Government of India in the post-independence period. They have participated in the democratic processes in Manipur. They have accepted western education with great enthusiasm and have made a substantial progress. They have participated in the governance of the state and joined bureaucracy. They are exposed to liberal ideas and Christian religious philosophy and ethos. The evangelical Christianity was spread among all the tribal communities. It has been projected sometimes as a process of modernization and progress. But they are also facing a dilemma, after achieving educational and economic progress. They want to preserve their culture and identity. A nation cannot prosper on the alien ideals of life. It is to be rooted in their heritage and identity. They have strong sense of identity which is to be accommodated into a greater Indian identity and nationhood.

Modernism has been projected as a norm of change in the tribal society. The tribal society is not yet modernized as their mode of production is agricultural and their lifestyle is tribal and rural, though they have adopted the western dress and the lifestyle among the elite by using the electronic gadgets and other consumer goods. But the technology used by the people in mode of production is not yet modernized. Modernism has come to mean an adoption of western mannerism and lifestyles rather than the real change in the means of production.

In the present perspective there is no way of retreat from modernization which is raging the country. The problems connected with modernization have increased tremendously. These are to be resolved. And for this a rational modernization based on Indian genius and wisdom without aping the west is called for.

REFERENCES

Anthony Giddens, *The Consequences of Modernity*, 1990. Stanford.

Daniel Bell, *The Coming of the Post Industrial Society*, 1974. London.

Gunnar Myrdal, *The Asian Drama* (An Abridged Edn), 1972

M.N. Srinivas, *Social Change in Modem India*, 1972. New Delhi.

Wilbert Moore, *The Social Order*, 1975.

6

Emergnece of the Ethnic Naga Nationality

The Nagas are now an ethnic nationality of Asia. The Naga nationality is an outcome of the Naga liberation movement which based on Naga nationalism. Several factors have influenced the emergence of the Nagas as a nationality. A look into the trends in modern Naga history will enable us to understand the unique and complex phenomenon. Colonialism, Second World War, the Naga struggle for sovereignty and the Indian response to accommodate the Naga aspirations within Indian Union, are factors responsible for the present Naga situation.

In other words, Naga nationalism is an outcome of the British colonial rule, the Second World War and the subsequent disintegration of the British Empire and Naga fight for independence. The emergence of the common ethnic identity of the Nagas was a gift of British colonialism as they grouped the tribes under a generic name "Naga" for administrative and ethnographic purposes. A feeling of separateness of the Nagas from the mainland Indians naturally emerged during the rule of the British who conquered and brought them *under* a regular administration. This created a sense of unity among the Nagas, The fundamental unity in diversity expressed in the feeling of pride in being a Naga is one of the strongest factors of Naga nationalism.

The ravages of the Second World War focused the world attention on the Nagas in whose territory the most decisive battles of the second World War in Asia were fought. The Nagas were exposed to outside world. And their contact with the Japanese and the Allied forces broadened their worldview. Taking advantage of the impendingg British withdrawal from India and Burma coupled with the fear of being transferred to the succeeding governments, the Naga people wanted to protect their fundamental rights over land, customary practices and social institutions .and declared independence from the British rule and proposed to carve out an independent Naga Country in the India-Burma border. They also raised the demand of the right to self-determination before the British departure from India. While the succeeding Indian Government and Government of Burma claimed to rule over the Naga areas of Assam, NEFA, Manipur and Somra Tract, the Nagas resisted this as a continuation of the colonial rule and the imperialist policy against which the Indian people and the Burmese fought so admirably. This resistance occurred in the form of military conflict between India and the Nagas. The Naga struggle was spread to all Naga inhabited areas of India and Burma. The struggle became a pan-Naga phenomenon. This struggle was a dual process of integration of the Nagas under one political banner and social absorption into the Naga ethnic identity, which the author has written elsewhere as the process of Nagaisation. The struggle became internationalized when the Nagas took external aid from the foreign countries despite Indian Government's stand that the Nagas are Indians and their problem is an internal affair of India. The Government of India responded in the form of formation of an autonomous state within the Indian Union which has been named

"Nagaland". Many moderate Naga leaders accepted the Nagaland State within Indian Union but the Nationalists continue to fight for independence.

A state should have a people, a definite territory, a government having both internal and external independence or sovereignty. There are tremendous efforts to establish the ethnic identity of the Nagas and identify the ethnic territory of the Nagas. The ethnic and cultural boundaries of the Naga habitat transcend the existing political boundaries within India and international boundary of India and Myanmar. The Naga population is found in the State of Nagaland, in Cachar and North Cachar Hills and Karbi Anglong of Assam, Tamenglong, Senapati, Ukhrul and Chandel districts of Manipur, some areas of Arunachal Pradesh of India and the Naga Hills (Somra Tract) of Myanmar. But the Nagas do not have a common homeland under one political roof. And the present efforts of the Naga nationalists are directed towards this goal. The existing boundaries of the political units in the north east India and upper Burma do not constitute a barrier to the ethnic and nationalist movement of the Nagas.

The Nagas are not under one political unit. They are under the administration of different political units of India and Myanmar. If the United Nation's Charter and relevant resolutions are to be correctly interpreted, the Nagas are a people fighting for national liberation. A reality has to be noted in this context that a large section of the Naga people have accepted the Indian Constitution and participated in free India's democratic political processes. The failure of the political talks between the Nagas and India in the late 1960's and 70's and the failure of the movement for integration of the Naga areas into Nagaland, the unwillingness of the elitist leadership of this state to share the benefits of their state with outside Nagas, and the split in the Naga liberation movements have been responsible for the present Naga imbrioglo. The talks between the Government of India and the Nagas have been a protracted one, One hopes, the talks will lead to a viable political settlement.

The massive decolonization process in Asia and Africa under the aegis of the United Nations with its declared objective of independence for subject nationalities fighting for independence has led to the emergence of many new nations, big and small. There are about 190 members nations of the UN. However, the neo-colonial forces specially the capitalist forces have compelled many ethnic nationalities of the world to fight for the protection of their social, economic and political rights on the basis of the right to self-determination of their national destiny. In this, ethnicity has become a strong factor; it is the core element of the nationalist assertion.

The idea of "one state, one nation" was the European concept of nationalism and nation state. But after the Bolshevik revolution, the multi-nationality nationhood was introduced in the former Union of Soviet Socialist Republics. Stalin's policy towards the nationalities was vigorously followed. India is another example for a quasi-federation of plural linguistic and ethnic groups and a multi-nationality nation. India's ideals of democracy, socialism and secularism have provided the constitutional basis for accommodating ethnic minorities like the Sikhs, Nagas, Mizos for constituting their states on the basis of ethnicity.

But the Sikh movement for Khalistan, the Kashmiri's fight for an independent Kashmir, the Tamil fight for an independent Tamil homeland in Sri Lanka, have impact on the ethnic aspiration in the Indian sub-continent.

The breaking up of the old Soviet Union into fifteen independent republics based on nationalities during the regime of Gorbachev in December 1991 raised the whole issue of ethnic nationalities. Nationalism has been proved to be stronger than communism. The breaking up of Yugoslavia and the consequent civil war and proposal for the formation of ethnic federation with autonomy to each ethnic group, is a great example of the powerful role of ethnicity in the formation of State. The separation of Czechoslovakia into two nations, the Czech and the Slovakia, is another example.

The assertion of the indigenous Amerindians to regain their land and natural resources which were taken by the white colonizers in Canada and Central America and their pressure on the UN to recognise the right of the ipdigenqus people led to the observation of the year 1993 as the Year of the Indigenous Population. The fight of the Kurdish people of Iraq, Turkey and Iran is counterpart of the Nagas in the middle east. In Asia, the indigenous ethnic people are fighting for national independence. In Burma, the Chin, the Karen insurgents are fighting for independence. The Meiteis of Manipur are now fighting for an independent country. The Pakhtoons and Sindhis are revolting against the oppressive rule of Pakistan; Tibetan struggle for regaining of Tibet is quite well known.

No one can predict the future of history. But, if the trends in contemporary Naga history and politics are any indication, the Nagas are going towards a unified polity. Nationalist movements throughout the world have been a long struggle. Whether Nagas would be able to establish an independent country or they would satisfy themselves by living in India would be decided by the Naga themselves. With a strong sense of unity and solidarity, the Nagas are marching towards unity and common ethnic identity which are reflected in social, political and cultural terms. Ethnic nationality of the Nagas is now a reality.

PART-II
FEDERALISM AND COLONIALISM

7

Federalism in India

Federalism

Federalism is a mode of government that unites separate states or polities within an overarching system. Such a system is called a federation which is a compact or union of states. "Federal" is derived from the Latin word:' federe", meaning to unite in a compact. Federalism permits its constituent units to maintain their own political integrity; the government is organized as a union of states, having two centres of power, the federal and the state. Federalism implies that there is constant need for coordination between the centre and the states and among the organs of the state itself. Federation or federalism is not a rigid or static political concept. It has transformed itself to meet certain political exigencies and compulsions. Federalism differs from one country to another. But certain characteristics are common to all federal systems.

Written Constitution

A federal system should have a written constitution. The federal structure and relationship are created and guaranteed by a written constitution framed by the representatives of the constituent states or provinces of the union. The United States of America. a classic model of federation, was established by a convention of the thirteen states (former

British colonies), popularly known as the Philadelphia Convention of 1789. The written constitution of the United States was adopted by this Convention. The provinces of Canada were constituted into a federation by an Act of British Parliament. The Indian Constitution which established the Republic of India was framed by a Constituent Assembly consisting of the representatives of the provinces and the princely states which apted for the Daminion af India after independence in 1947. The supreme authority of the constitution is accepted; and it regulates and enforces the federal structure and the laws af the union which bind the people, the government at the centre and the states. Such a union is born out of the covenant for perpetuity. The written constitution is to be interpreted by the Supreme Court of the Union. Judicial review is normally empowered to the judiciary.

Non-centralization

A federal constitution provides for the devolution or division of powers among a number of self-sustaining institutions, the two sets of government at the centre and the states. Such a devolution of power in the American federal ethos is currently termed as the non-centralisation which empowers the government, peoples with its various interests to participate in the exercise af the political power through the democratic process. This is in contrast to the tendency of centralisation or hegemonic over-centralisation in a new federation like India

Division of Power

A federal constitution spells out the division of power between the federal government and the states with an objective to ensure neutrality and equity in the representation of the various groups and interests in the whole polity. The subjects are divided between the federal gavernment and the states. And the powers are also distributed in the constitution between the two sets of government. The aim is to secure to the diverse interest groups, ethnic, linguistic, religious ar regional, the local (state) autonamy and representation by giving them power bases in the form of states ar regional political formation like the federal or union territories as federally administered areas. In actuality, every state or province has a history of its own; therefore, the regional interests are usually the foundation of the integrity of these political formations. We see the rise of regionalism or sub-nationalism in all countries having federal ar unitary farm of government. Federal structure with guarantee for state autonomy has turned out to be a reliable device which enhances the ability of the federal system to function as a vehicle of political and social integration. Federal territorial democracy in the states and provinces ensures the political integrity of these units and jealously guards their political baundary to maintain their entity and integrity within the federation. Can a federal government destroy the political map of the states? The Indian constitution gives to the Indian Parliament an overriding power in respect of state formatian in the Union. This has raised a number of controversies. History has shown that the federation like the United States, Canada and Switzerland are quite successful whereas that of India, Malaysia, Nigeria and Latin American countries suffer from certain inadequacies. This is mostly concerned with natianalism of these countries. The maintenance of the federal system requires that the nation and the states should have complete self-governing institutions of their own. There is also contractual sharing of the public responsibility by the federal and state governments in respect of policy making, financing and administration. Federal systems are quite stable and long lasting. However a federal system shauld be endowed with a favourable environment of political co-operation and self-restraint. The respect for local and regional autonomy and voluntary political participation are necessary for the success of a federation. Democracy is the key to the success of federalism. The frequent use of force to maintain domestic order is not conducive to the federal pattern of government. The rise of ethnic natianalism or insurgency in the multiethnic federation is one of the threats to federalism. The system is also successful in the countries which have campetent human resource or leadership to run the government and the resources to ensure an equitable economic development.

Is India a Federation?

According to Article 1 of the Constitution, India, that is Bharat, is a Union af States. The Indian polity has all the basic features of a federation.

1. Dual Government: Central or Union Government and State gavernments.
2. Distribution of powers between the Central Government and the State gavernments.
3. Supremacy af the Constitution in all affairs and matters.
4. Authority af the Judiciary to interpret the Constitution.

India is a Union of States with the federal features. But the founding fathers did not visualize a federation in the classic model of the United States. Dr. B.R. Ambedkar declared that Indian Constitution was federal in normal times and unitary in abnormal times, during emergency created by war, rebellion or political instability. It was a sort of federation with a great commitment to maintain Unity, Integrity and Independence of the country.

Is India a Quasi-Federal State?

Though the Indian jurists and political scientists are aware of the peculiar nature of the Indian Constitution in respect of the relation between the Union and the State Governments, several foreign commentators emphasized on the federal features of the Constitution. It was K.C. Wheare (1951), an American scholar who described India as a quasi-federal state. Granvile Austin (1966) termed the Indian, polity as a co-operative federalism.

Federalism as a Basic Feature of the Indian Constitution

Federalism is the concept that a state is to be a union of states with a central government and governments for the constituent states with a sharing of power with a written constitution and the power of judicial review given to the Supreme Court of the country. But not a single word like federation or federal occurs in the Constitution of India which has 443 Articles and 12 Schedules (the original being 395 Articles and 8 Schedules).

But it was the Supreme Court of India which pronounced in Keshavananda vs. Union of India 1973 S.C. 1461 that federalism is one of the basic features of the Indian constitution. It was in Bommai vs. Union of India, A 1994 S.C. 1918, that a 9 judges Supreme Court Constitution Bench reaffirmed that the Constitution is federal and federalism is one of its basic features.

Co-operative Federalism

The term "Co-operative Federalism" is used by the western writers to indicate the changing trend of the relation between the federal authority and the state governments in the United States, Canada and Australia. Instead of competitive stance, there should be co-operation between the federal government and the states; there has emerged a co-operation between the two due to the necessity to meet the problem of defence and security of the country and the protection of the national interest. Justice Sarkaria in his report of the Commission on

Centre–State Relation has widely used the term "Co-operative Federalism" which is quite different from the classical or traditional federalism and the quasi-federalism. The Planning Commission in its 9th Five Year Plan document on Basic Approach during Prime Minister H. Deve Gowda's time, has devoted a chapter on co-operative federalism. It may herald a new era in the Centre-State Relation vis-a.-vis economic and social planning of the country.

Centre-State Relation: The Key Issues

Centre-State relation is a vital area of the federal polity which is being continuously assessed by the political scientists, political parties, judiciary and the leaders of the government through several committees and commissions, specially the Commission on the Centre-State relation under the Chairmanship of Justice S.R. Sarkaria (1983-88).

Over-centralisation of power in the central government reducing or encroaching on the powers and functions of the states has raised the issue of the basic features of the Constitution in respect of its federal structure. A fresh debate whether India is a federal or unitary state is going on.

The central government is alleged to have usurped the subjects given in the Concurrent List of the subjects given in the Seventh Schedule leaving little for the States, thus giving more power to the Union than which was contemplated by the founding fathers of the Constitution.

The office of the Governor has become controversial. The institution of the Governor of the State which is the pivot of the Centre-State relation was utilised by the Union Government to destabilise the state governments by imposing President's Rule by misusing the Article 356 of the Constitution.

There is a pressure on the Centre by the States on the allocation of resources to the States. There is a strong feeling that resources are allocated by the Centre to the States based on reasons other than economic.

Planning Commission which is not a constitutional body has become a super economic cabinet of the country almost becoming a Leviathan in the distribution of resources to the States. There is also discrimination in the allocation of the centrally sponsored schemes.

The issue of more autonomy of the states and nature of the Indian federation has been considered seriously in many circles.

Distribution of Powers between the Centre and the States

The Constitution provides exhaustive provisions regulating the relation between the Centre and the States based on the federal principles of distribution of powers as given in the three Lists of the Seventh Schedule known as I. Union List, II. State List and III. Concurrent List. Several parts of the Constitution deal with the relation between the Centre and the States as enumerated below.

1. Legislative relation
2. Administrative relation
3. Financial relation
4. Role of the Governor
5. All India Services
6. Inter-Government Councils
7. Economic and social planning

Legislative Relationship

The 7th Schedule provides the distribution of subjects in the three lists. The Union List contains 97 subjects on which the Parliament has to legislate; the State List has 66 subjects while the Concurrent List has 47 subjects. All the residuary subjects are reserved for the Parliament. The laws passed by the Parliament have jurisdiction all over the country except those areas specified by the constitution. The State legislature will pass laws on the subjects of the State List which will be operative within the boundaries of the states concerned. When Parliament and the State assemblies have the power to legislate on state law, the former will prevail. The central laws dealing with amendment of the constitution and those relating to the treaties with foreign countries are subject to the ratification by the state legislatures. It has been noticed that the Parliament has increasingly taken over subjects of the Concurrent List for central legislation. Exceptional circumstances have led to the expansion of the Parliament's legislative powers. The Parliament can pass law concerning the national interest, emergency, agreement between the states, the implementation of treaties with foreign countries and failure of constitutional machinery.

Executive Power

Executive power is conterminous with legislative powers. However executive powers of the laws concerning the subjects of the Concurrent list rests with State governments. And the Centre has the power to give directives to the States a) in normal times b) during emergency and c) during the proclamation of the financial emergency.

Financial Relationship

Financial relationship is a very important aspect of State-Centre relationship in view of the sharing of resources like the state share in revenue proceeds of the central government, awards of the Finance Commission and allocation of plan funds. The external aids have been an area of great tussle in the financial relationship between the Centre and the State. The Reserve Bank of India and the finance ministry of the Centre regulate the fund flow to the States including budgetary spending. The bigger states with larger amount of revenue want to have greater autonomy in the financial relationship.

Administrative Relationship

The central government can issue directives to states for the implementation of certain laws and the programme of activities under the national policies. It also delegates power to the states to carry out respective action plans. The All India Services like the IAS, IPS and other services are employed in the state governments. The role of the intelligence and the investigating agencies like the IB, SIB, CBI etc quite well known. Besides these, there is also inter-state councils whid are not effective; there may be inter state commerce commission under the initiative of the central government. The North Eastern Council (NEC) as a regional development agency for the north eastern states working. In this administrative relationship, the central government through various constitutional provisions and relevant laws tries ensure the unity, integrity and the sovereignty of the nation and preservation of the Constitution.

Economic and Social Planning

India is committed to the welfare state (a co-operative common wealth) Therefore planning for economic and social development has been taken up by the central and state governments. Both central and state plans are formulated and implemented in a tenure of five years. Five Year Plans are now an important feature of Indian planning. Resource mobilization and resource allocation by the central government is a key area of the whole process of development planning in the country.

Planning Commission

Planning Commission was created by a decision of the Cabinet. But it has assumed a super cabinet role in the planning and allocation of resources of the states. This power of the Planning Commission ought to be curbed by a constitutional measure. There are complaints that the Planning Commission is influenced by the ruling party in the centre in the allocation of resources to the states on political considerations. The autonomy of the states has been greatly marginalised by this extra constitutional bodr

National Development Council

Another extra-constitutional body in the planning process is the National Development Council consisting of all the chief ministers and with the Prime lvlinister as the chairman. NDC is the final authority which gives approval to the plan proposal.

Role of the Governor

The Governor is the constitutional head of a state. He is a link between the Union government and the State governments and an agent of the Union goyernment on specific areas during normal times [Art. 239(2)] and in abnormal times [Art. 356(1)]. The Governor is empowered with use of discretion in discharge of his function in the following areas.

1. Choice of Chief Minister
2. Testing of majority of the parties in the State assembly
3. Dismissal of the Chief Minister
4. Dissolution of the State assembly
5. Recommendation of the President's Rule in a State due to failure of constitutional machinery
6. Reservation of legislative Bills of the State for the President's consideration.

Article 163(1) says, "There shall be a Council of Ministers with the Chief Minister at the head to aid and advise the Governor in exercise of his functions, except in so far as he is by or under the Constitution required to exercise his functions or any of them in his discretion". This section clearly shows that the cabinet form of goverriinent enjoins on the Council of Ministers and the Chief Minister to run administration of the State but the Governor has got discretionary powers in relation to the above listed functions on specific occasions. It will be of some interest to mention that the Sarkaria Commission records the opinion of various states and the political parties in respect of Governor's office. They range from the abolition of the institution of the Governor to the increase of the powers of the Governor and to the maintenance of the status quo. The Sarkaria Commission makes several recommendations in respect of the mode of appointment, tenure of the office and use of his discretionary powers etc.

The relation of the Chief Minister and the Governor of a State is provided in Article 167 which runs thus:

"It shall be the duty of the Chief Minister of each State

a) to communicate to the Governor of the State all decisions of the Council of Ministers relating to the administration of the affairs of the State and proposals for legislation,

b) to furnish such information relating to the administration of the affairs of the State and the proposals for legislation as the Governor may call for".

According to this provision, the Chief Minister has to keep the Governor informed of all decisions of his cabinet. At the same time, whatever information the Governor calls for is to be provided by the Chief Minister. But this does not provide for the intervention of the Governor in day-to-day functioning of the government which is an exclusive reserve of the Chief Minister and his Council of Ministers.

The Governor and Article 356

The power given by Article 356 to the Governor makes him an agent of the central government in the event of the failure of the constitutional machinery in the State and eventual introduction of the President's Rule in the State concerned. Since the past experiehce has shown that the President' s Rule was imposed by the central govrnent mostly on political consideration based on the recommendation of the Governor, the office of the Governor has become a matter of controversy. There is a strong demand for abrogation of this Article, or limited use of it. The Governor's office is highly responsible for judicious application of this Article.

Autonomy of the States

A State is a constituent unit of the Indian union. But Parliament has the power to alter the boundaries, rename and admit new state or create new states (Art. 1,2,3,4). Because of the common judicial system for the whole' country with central control over economic and social planning, the states have been greatly marginalised. States were reorganized and created from time to time to fulfil sub-national and regional (ethnic) aspirations. With the centralist parties ruling at the Centre in most part of the post-independence period, in the name of national interest, unity, integrity and independence of the country so also in the name of nation building, the states have become too dependent on the Centre. There were instances of discrimination in the installation of new governments, on the dissolution of Assemblies and consequent introduction of President's Rule and distribution of fund by the Planning Commission. As a response to this process of overcentralisation, there have been demands for more autonomy for the States, increase in the financial power of the states and increase in resource distribution. This demand goes along with the growth of regional political parties. Autonomy, regionalism and federalism are the popular issues in the Indian politics. The over-centralisation of the Indian polity will affect the healthy relation with the states. (States of Jammu and Kashmir and Nagaland are provided with different types of autonomy).

Position of the States

We have to examine the position of the States in the Indian Republic. Are they mere administrative units created for administrative convenience or are they constituent units of the Union based on linguistic, ethnic, regional and sub-national consideration? The centralist parties have tried to whittle down the power and autonomy of the States by insisting on the need of a strong Centre to maintain the unity, integrity and independence of the country. At the same time the states which are ruled by regional parties or parties other than the ruling party at the Centre, clamour for the autonomy in the financial power of the States and for redefining the distribution of powers given in the Seventh Schedule. There is a demand for restructuring of the Indian Constitution on federal principle to ensure unity and diversity in a plural society like India.

Status of the States

Autonomy of the State is greatly limited under the Constitution, But the States which are formed on the linguistic and ethnic principle have built up strong regional and sub-national foundation. The states have asserted their own distinctive identity and regional interest. Regionalism within Indian nationalism has softened the divisive and isolationist stance of the regional and ethnic political parties. The Supreme Court has made very significant intervention in respect of the States within the Indian Union. The latest judicial pronouncement on the subject is made by the Supreme Court in its judgement in Bommai vs Union of India

1994. This nine-member Bench has given a landmark judgement on the status of the States of the Indian republic. The judgement says, "The fact that under the scheme of the constitution greater power is conferred on the Centre *vis-a-vis* the States, does not mean that the States are mere appendages of the Centre; within the sphere allotted to them, the States are supreme". It further says that federalism in the Indian Constitution is not a matter of mere administrative convenience but one of principle. The judgement declares that States have their own independent existence; they are not satellite nor agents of the Centre. This judgement has strengthened the federal roots of the Indian Union with great emphasis on the independent existence of the States. The demand for autonomy of the States has been given a big push. At the same time, it has been confirmed that federalism in India is a new kind of federalism to meet India's peculiar situation.

More Autonomy for the States?

Most of the regional parties and some leaders of national parties have raised the issue of restructuring of Indian polity on federal principle. Their demand for more autonomy centres around the following points.

1. Equal representation of the States in the national Parliament irrespective of the size and population, at least in .the upper house.

2. Restructuring of the distribution of the subjects of the three lists of the Seventh Schedule, namely, limitation of the central subjects like defence, external affairs, finance and currency, external trade and commerce, communications, federal legislature and judiciary and federal public service commission, restructuring of the Planning Commission etc.

3. Even if the above two categories are not immediately

possible, the States should be given more financial powers to facilitate development planning etc.

Federalism and State autonomy will continue to dominate the State Centre relation in the coming years. However there should be harmony between the regional interest and the national interest. Regionalism within the nationalism will be accommodated by federalism and autonomy for the States. The strong States will strengthen the nation. Federalism is not non-conducive to the growth of nationalism. A sort of co-operative federalism will be more appropriate answer to some of the problems of Centre and States relation of the Indian republic.

8

Regionalism in North East India

Regionalism

Regionalism is a loose perception for the protection and preservation of a regional identity, may be cultural, linguistic or ethnic, and for promotion of the regional economic and political interest. Emergence of regionalism in Indian polity is a natural expression of the democratic will of the people for extension of autonomy based on federal features under the Constitution. It is also a response to the hegemonic centralism of the Government of India controlled by the national parties representing the capitalistic and chauvinistic vested interests. The earlier odium attached to regionalism as parochial and separatist has vanished with the changing perception of the national parties as a result of their failure to form government at the centre without the help of the regional parties as their allies. Regionalism within the parameter of Indian nationalism is a contemporary political reality. Nationalism has come to terms with regionalism. Regionalism is a healthy and constructive force to protect the regional interests of the body politic of a multi-nationality nation like India. Regionalism does no longer mean parochialism and xenophobia.

Emerging Regional Identity

Northeast India as a region is a geo-political entity developed or enunciated by.the British to serve their co!onial objectives to expand their empire, exploit the resources of the region, and due to the strate necessity, push the frontier to the borders of Tibet, China and Burma

They created the province of Assam based on the ancient kingdom of Ahom and with the amalgamation of the hill areas inhabited by various ethnic and tribal groups. The heterogeneity and multiplicity of the ethnic groups came to the fore after India's independence in the form of different political and social movements of the these groups. The region with its cultural and social pluralism, has emerged as a distinctive entity in the country's national life. This regional identity is the legacy of a long history and a rich cultural heritage: the ancient Hindu kingdom of Kamarupa, the Ahom kingdom of Assam, the kingdoms of Manipur, Tripura and small tribal principalities which were brought under the hegemony and administrative control of British colonialism. The roots of the emerging identity are found in the multiethnic, multi-lingual, multi-religious and multi-cultural characters of the various social groups in this region. The democratic and socialist goals of Indian Republic with its policy of secularism which provides the opportunity of ethnic identity assertion, coupled with comparative geographical isolation and social insularity, have given a new dimension and meaning to this identity. However, this region appears to be different from the rest of this country; at the same time, there are intra-regional differences in the form of ethnicity, social and economic situations, and political aspirations which are being resolved, thanks to the dynamism of Indian democracy, by the formation of the seven States. Nation building on democratic basis is an ongoing process in north east India. Freedom and democracy released their ethnic and linguistic aspirations in the form of political and social movements. These aspirations and their manner of the expression of these ideas have taken the form of regionalism and sub-nationalism or newly formulated ultra-nationalism.

The Northeast is a region; but within the region, there are contradictions and efforts have been made to resolve these differences by the government parties and related forums of the region. This heterogeneity and multiplicity of the social and ethnic groups have been the constraints in the evolution of common regionalism. But it released the regional forces, the strong motive force for the economic development, linguistic and ethnic assertion. This has been aggravated by the evil effect of the partition of the country in 1947. These have made the Northeast distant from the mainland India not onlylin terms of geographical distance alone but a psychological distance. Ignorance of the people of the mainland about the people of the periphery, the Northeast, creates a lack of understanding between the two.

Problems of the Northeast

The psychological state is complicated by the economic backwardness of the different units of the region and the failure to develop the region. Disparity in the level of economic development is a strong factor in the emergence of regionalism. The greatest endogenous factor is the strong urge of the people to preserve their cultural, linguistic and ethnic identity. The ethnic aspirations are expressed through various political movements. The Northeast India is in a turmoil. The region is beset with insurgencies, Naga, Meitei, Tripuri, Assamese and Bodo movements. These militant or revolutionary movements are more or less ethnic nationalist movements expressed in a violent form. These political expressions are to be accommodated by the national government at the political level. The reaction of the Central government is in the form of counter-insurgency measures, granting autonomy to the erstwhile tribal districts and princely states into states under the Indian Republic with varying degrees of autonomy.

Counter-insurgencies have resulted in the human right violation. The policy enunciated by the different leaders at the time of independence is worth recalling. Mahatma Gandhi's humanistic stand was one of non violence and voluntary participation in the free and democratic Indian Republic, as he was reported to have told the Naga leaders in 1947. Pandit Jawaharlal Nehru's policy of paternalism was the dominant Indian response to the problem resulting in the creation of new States and autonomous districts to accommodate the people's desires, creation of Nagaland, statehood to Manipur; Tripura, Meghalaya and creation of Arunachal Pradesh and Mizoram. The Government of India was rudely shaken by China's invasion of India in 1962. India's policy towards the region was concentrated on strategic need of the defence forces. However; after this traumatic experience, we saw the major political initiative being made. It was in line with Sardar Patel's policy of integration of princely states and pushing the frontier to the borders of Tibet and China, a continuation of the British 'Forward Policy'. In the economic front, the North Eastern Council and special category state status given to the states or region cannot meet the rising aspirations of the people. The expectations of the' people are also exploded. Feelings of neglect still persist despite the ongoing nation building process. The problem of insurgency, economic underdevelopment and social egalitarianism call for serious examination. The Government of India has established a Ministry of Development of North Eastern Region (DONER) to give special attention to the region.

Regionalism and Federalism

Meanwhile, several regional political parties have proposed federal restructuring of the Indian polity and granting more autonomy to the states. Hence, the rising support for regionalism in the region. The leaders of the region and political units should evolve a workable solution to these problems. As per Supreme Court's judgement of 1973 and recommendation of the Sarkaria Commission as approved by the Inter-State Council of the Government of India, federalism has been accepted as a basic feature of the Indian Constitution. But necessary constitutional amendments have yet to be made to make Indian Constitution really federal. Regionalism strengthens federalism. It implies respect for the autonomy of the States or the Indian republic which is a union of States. The Supreme Court in the famous judgement in "Bommai vs Union of India 1994" has decreed that "states" in the Indian republic are not appendages of the Centre but they are distinct entity and supreme in their assigned sphere. This means that the autonomy of the States is constitutionally guaranteed. Strong States make a federal government strong. Federalism is the order of the day. But the Central government, particularly the ministry of home affairs, refuses to see the reality and does not recognize the writing on the wall. They still are suffering from the colonial hangover and belief that they inherit the imperial system. The use or misuse of Article 356 of Indian Constitution is an intensely debated issue. Holding out the threat to introduce President Rule in the States is anachronistic to the vibrant Indian democracy. This attitude is the negation of the democratic will of the people who send their representatives to the Assembly to govern their respective states. Democracy has taken deep root in the Northeast and it cannot be destroyed either by the home ministry or chauvinistic national parties nor by the insurgents. Nation building is a process of strengthening Indian democracy. Regionalism, federalism and autonomy are the reality in the politics of the Northeast India.

9

Colonialism and Colonial Policy

Empire, imperialism and colonialism have almost the same connotation, but of varying public popularity and are linked up with colonial relationship between the colonizing powerand colonized people. "A colonial relationship is created when one nation establishes and maintains political domination over a geographically external unit inhabited by people of any race and at stage of cultural development". This relationship is the foundation of the colonial system which is designated to mean "an arrangement by which a mother country attempts to bind her colonies by commercial ties with the primary objects of promoting her own economic advantage".

Most of the studies of administration of European colonies both settlers and exploitation are on this colonial system. This system was based on Mercantilism of Europe which was a policy of e.xploitation of the colonies for the benefit of the mother country. So imrerialism and colonialism were born out of the imperial or colonial relatiohship. Stephen Neill writes, "the term colonialism appears to be a recent arrival in the languages of the western world taking the place of the older and now familiar 'imperialism'. It is used as a term of reproach implying that the only aim of colonial rule has been the exploitation and impoverishment of the weaker, and defenceless people and that its only results have been the destruction of what was good in ancient civilization and the multiplication of measureless evils". Yet colonialism or colonial rule has been for centuries an inevitable phenomenon as any other historical phenomenon: conquest, emigration and subjugation happened in history. "Colonialism", Rupert Emerson writes, "is the establishment and maintenance for an extended term of rule over an alien people that is separate from and subordinate to the ruling power". It is also a specific form of human emigration and therefore details a contact, mostly clash of cultures of the colonizing and colonized peoples, especially the impact of a technologically and spiritually (theologically better organized) more powerful culture on a weaker one. At the root of colonialism lies the impact of capitalism on the precapitalist world, mostly the Asian and Africans. The impact of capitalism involves the introduction of new social needs, of money economy, market production, hired labour, migration of labour, dissociating them from village community, its morals and custom.

In order to cope with such a situation, a political system, either colonial or national has emerged specially to deal with the clash of unequal social forces. In the colonial context, the colonial administra tion was designed under a well formulated policy to safeguard the interests of the mother countries which are capitalist countries. Lenin's famous thesis that imperialism is the highest form of capitalism is relevant to the study of colonial policy and administration in Asian and African countries. In short, a feature of European colonialism is the domination of an alien minority, administrators, businessmen and soldiers, asserting racial and cultural superiority over the subjugated people. It is as pointed out by George Balandier, a contact between machine oriented civilization with Christian origin, a powerful economy based on capitalism and a rapid rhythm of life and a non-Christian civilization with a low level technology and a backward economy and a slow rhythm of life. It also marks the imposition of European technology on the Asian and African countries and extension of European ideas and methods in the colonies and dependencies.

Colonial Policy

A colonial policy is the general principle followed by a colonizing power to regulate the colonial relationship between her and her dependency. The colonial policy is the reflection of the national ethos and ideals of the colonizing powers at a given extended period of time. Therefore, it has been frequently mentioned that the colonial policy is a metropolitan affair and colonial people do not have much say, because the colonial policy is framed with reference to the interests, real or imagined of the colonial power. The colonial policy is only one aspect of the national policy which is based on its own social philosophy. Therefore, this policy is framed in terms of broad general concept which dominates the national outlook and reflects the emergence of new general ideas. The methods of colonial policy vary according to difference in the social, economic and cultural conditions in respective colonies, and for the same reason find their analogies in comparable circumstances elsewhere; but the aim and standard of policy are dictated by the social ideal and by the interests of the colonizing nations. A colonial policy would have political, economic, cultural, social and moral objectives for the attainment or maintenance of which an administrative machinery is created to work in the colonies. Since colonial relationship involves two social systems, two or more cultural patterns, two civilizations, two different levels of technology and economy, a colonial policy is designed with deeper connotations and implications. Ideas, ideology, interests, social norms are built into a colonial policy. So, as Logemann observes, "a colonial policy means the framing of a social order that provides for an acceptable modus vivendi in an oriental society wherein, the westerns have penetrated, have settled and are carrying on business",

As already mentioned, European colonialism has passed through three phases of historical development, each was influenced by the dominant economic and social philosophy prevailing in the mother country. From the 15th century to the end of the Napoleonic war, the colonial powers were following the Mercantilist philosophy that colonies existed for the benefit of the mother country. Mercantilism came under strong criticism of the economists espcially by Adam Smith. Between the Congress of Vienna of 1815 to the 3rd quarter of the 19th century liberal attitude was adopted towards the colonies. The liberal philosophy of *laissez faire*, Darwinism and the Utilitarianism were the foundations of colonialism. When the Laissez Faire declined to some extent in the second half of the nineteenth during the period of great colonial expansion and rivalry among the European powers, the rest of the countries took to Protectionism. Imperialism and empire building were the most popular and the prestigious slogans of the period.

Protectionism and liberal ideas were behind the great imperial expansion under-taken by the European powers.

Colonial Administration

The colonial powers created administrative machineries to administer their colonies. And the art and practice of colonial administration was quite well known to the imperial and colonial powers from very early times, and it had become a highly specialized major part of the goyemment and a major phase of the national policy of the concerned countries. The objectives of the colonial policy are implemented through the administrative machinery. As explained elsewhere, the principles underlying the colonial administration are the reflections of the dominant national social philosophy of the time. When Mercantilism was the motivating philosophy of the political economy, the administration of colonies was carried on by the military leaders assisted by the Christian missionary priests and civil representatives of the mother countries, great trading companies with charters guaranteed by the governments, established trading posts in the Orient, they openly or surreptitiously joined the struggle for grabbing of territories and became masters of a large tract as dependencies. These companies built up administrative cadres to administer the colonies. They had both civil and military establishments and enjoyed freedom of action in colonies with least interference from the home countries. During the Mercantilist era, the administration was geared at the exploitation of colonies for the benefit of the mother countries alone, it was thought that the primary concern of a colony was to act as a source of raw materials and a market for finished products. Thus the development of industries in the colonies was discouraged; trade was monopolized by the government or the Chartered companies or nationals of the colonizing country. Shipping was controlled and other financial restrictions were imposed on them. There was resistance to this excessive restriction; and the American Revolution was such a violent resistance against the colonial system based on Mercantilism.

After the Industrial Revolution, the colonial administration was influenced and guided by the liberal ideas of Europe, namely utilitarianism and laissez Faire which affected not only economic affairs but also religion, literature and politics. Mercantilism was replaced by Laissez Faire leading to complete free trade. The colonial administration was manned by men professing liberal ideas with the more attention given by the home government in the second half of the 19th century, the governments started sponsoring colonial expansion, which was backed by a powerful industrialization and a keen competition for markets. The government took over the administration of the colonies administered earlier by the trading companies. The form of government remained almost the same. The agent generals of the companies were replaced by Governors or Representatives of the Crown with plenipotentiary powers and subsequently the colonies were given a sort of representative form of government. Despite all this tremendous expansion, the governments more or less looked upon them as trading posts or pawns in the strategic games of empire building. But when the industrialization in the colonies was financed by the capital from the mother countries, the national outlook was changed; and the colonial administration was made to keep order and stability to ensure industrial enterprises prosper. The colonial administration became a national concern during the end of the nineteenth century as a result of the large scale capital investment in the colonies. The form of colonial administration reflected the mood of the home government The English colonies were given parliamentary or representative system of government while the France adopted the tradition of assimilation and centralization.

The elaboration of governmental functions led to the extension of colonial administrative machinery in the home governments like the department of colonial affairs; in England, the office of the Secretary of State for colonial affairs was created in 1854 and in France a special ministry for the colonies was created during the Third Republic. Such colonial office coordinated the entire colonial policy of a country, supervised administrative officials watched colonial finance and exercised the authority of the crown or parliament or assembly.

The administrative structure of the colonies differed from colony to colony but, in the main was dependent on a colonial civil service which comprised officials selected on the merit system. The officials and members of the colonial services were trained as specialized professionals in the administrative schools and colleges. The East India ompany's school at Fort William at Calcutta was established in 1800; the East India College was established by the British at Haileysbury near London. The French and the Dutch established similar schools.

With these highly qualified administrative personnels at the top civil service the colonial governments also employed the natives in the administrative structure mostly in the army and police force, then native teachers in the educational service and judges in the judiciary. The colonial administration was highly controlled by the home government either in war or peace, external or internal affairs. However in British colonies and dependencies, local self-government or representative form of government was introduced in a limited. scale. The autonomy granted to the British colonies devolved financial responsibility on them.

The scope of the colonial administration was related to the objectives of the colonial policy: Since a colony was to be a source of raw materials, market and in some as a place of industrial enterprise especially plantation industry, the administration was geared to obtain three main objectives; to maintain law and order, to collect revenues through a well formulated taxation system to meet the cost of administration and adjudicate judicial matter. Therefore, the administration's scope covered the army and police for defence, conquest and to keep internal order to ensure stability in the colony; then an elaborate system of taxation, including land revenue, customs and different types of taxes, then a fiscal administration was well developed. The next was the civil service to administer both the law of the colonizing power and law of the indigenous people. A well conceived judicial system was primary step in the establishment of a settled civil government. In order to administer the private law of the indigenous people, like Hindu and Muslim law in India, and Budhist law in Burma, the national laws were applied to the nationals of the colonizing country. Naturally, judiciary had faced difficulty in the choice of its members as it had to deal with multiple laws.

The colonial administration being influenced by this liberal ideas ltilitarianism adopted welfare programmes for the population like establishment of schools, colleges, university under an educational policy, the public health programrne, the public works which undertook the construction of road and transport, roadways, railways and shipping, development of postal system. Thus, the taxes collected from the people were ploughed back in term of such social activities. The administration undertook social reform programme like the abolition of Sati in India.

The colonial administration utilized the services of the Christian mission to legitimize their rule over the conquered people and to facilitate the westernization of the indigenous society. However, the established world religions in these colonies could not be easily changed while among the less developed societies where such world religions did not enter, Christianity made indent and produced far reaching impact. These were in short the objective, structure and scope of the colonial administration.

Colonial Policy in Operation

Such a policy was introduced in India and Burma. As stated above Mercantilism was the guiding principle of the British policy. The East India Company with the charter given by the British Crown spearheaded the conquest of India and exploited the riches of the newly conquered kingdoms. The East India Company established the government in India with the civil and military organisation recruited and paid by them. In the beginning of the 19th century, when Mercantilist policy was abandoned, a new policy of Laissez Faire or free trade was adopted. The Utilitarianism of Jeremy Bentham was the main political philosophy guiding the colonial policy in India.

When Burma came into contact with Europe or Britain she presented a portrait of a medieval Asiatic society. Her ruler refused to have intercourse with the outside world and with modernity. But economic imperialism provided the necessary stimulus to the European domination of Southeast Asia including Burma: This European expansion was strengthened by the Industrial Revolution with the invention of the steam engine, railways, steamship; electricity and telegraphy. And Burma came under the British rule after the Industrial Revolution which had transformed the economic, social and political relationship between Europe and the East. The early phase of the British conquest of Burma, 1826 was a period when Mercantilism was being replaced by Laissez Faire and Liberal ideas. And the British colonial policy reflected, as Furnivall writes, ' the Liberal Doctrine of economic freedom, freedom of trade, enterprise and proper and equality before law. But Liberalism was not merely a sordid philosophy of self-interest. That everyone should be allowed to pursue private interests in any way was not forbidden by law and that economic progress was a sufficient guarantee of general welfare, both material and moral. Liberalism was not merely a policy but a faith. Naturally it was a period when the British policy in India was in a stage of transition. The process of transformation from a body of merchants to a full-fledged government was not yet complete. Misra writes, "The end of the Company's trading rights accelerated the pace of two of the forces which the Imperial policy of Lord Wellesly (1798-1819) had released. The first was economic while the second was political, together they shaped the character of the Indian administration. The economic force was that of Laissez Faire, a free trade, economic interests comprising both colonial and imperial blend. It was an antithesis of monopoly interests in trade and of regulatory trends in government. Based on the principle of free competition, the government tendency of the Laissez Faire was to restrict the scope of the state activity and to make the executive government subject to the control of free representative institutions... The political force was that of imperialism. It was represented by the crown and the British Parliament". The East India Company had been reduced to a status of the trustee of the British Government in political affairs.

This new policy was discussed between eminent colonial administrators like Raffles in Malaya, Munro in Madras, Elphinstone in Bombay and other scholar statesmen who manned the services of the company. James Mills, a protagonist of the new policy was the leading figure in India House and Sir James Mackenzie taught the officer probationers at the East India College at Haileysbury. Further Lord William Bentinck the new Governor General (1828-1835) was a staunch supporter of the liberal policy.

Colonial relations were essentially economic and colonial administration was conditioned by economic laws. Therefore, the British colonial policy made a turning point in 1870 in the transition from a policy of Laissez-Faire to active participation in the economic development of the colonies. The British capital was invested in the construction of railways and increased ocean going shipping since 1860. The opening of Suez Canal in 1869 marked a new era in the economic, social and political relation of Europe with the East. The new era had a new philosophy. If Liberalism was a combination of the practical common sense of Adam Smith and utilitarianism of Jeremy Bentham, with the humanitarian ideals of Rousseau and French Revolution, the new philosophy had a dual origin from Darwin's principle of survival of the fittest, it had derived justification of efficiency, and from St. Simon, Robert Owen and other socialists of various schools, the doctrine of social justice. These ideas applied to colonial policy in the new environment gave birth to modern imperialism. The liberals earlier demanded free trade with the colonies, but the capitalists who were products of the free trade demanded a more active and intensive colonial policr At the end of the 19th century, there was tremendous colonial expansion and simultaneously a growing sense of social justice demanding welfare for the colonial people which was reinforced by the European pretensions to justify their imperialism on moral ground of civilizing the non European.

REFERENCES

B.B. Misra, *Administrative History of India 1834–1947*, Oxford University Press, New Delhi, 1970.

Hans Kohn, *Reflection on Colonialism in Ideas of Colonialism*, Stranse-hupe and Harry W. Hozard, New Youk, 1958.

J.H.A. Logemann, *One World and Diversity of Culture in Methods and Principles of Colonial Administration*, Edited by, E.W. Evans, London, 1950.

J.F. Cady, *History of Modern Burma*, New York, 1968.

J.S. Furnivall, *Colonial Policy and Practice London*, 1948.

Rene Raunier, *Sociology of Coloneis, vol. 1*, Routledge and Kegan Paul, London, 1948.

Stephen Neill, *Colonialism and Christian Mision*, Luther–Worth Press, London, 1966.

10

Pluralism, Democracy and Ethnic Relations in Manipur – A Critique

Pluralism

What is pluralism? Paul R. Brass in his *"Ethnicity and Nationalism"* (1991) put forth a simple description of pluralism as a "system that embraces a multiplicity of social, cultural, economic and political groups and that does not permit the imposition of the ideas, values, culture or language of a single (dominant) group on others". In social and political thoughts, pluralism would mean "the autonomy" enjoyed by different groups within a society of multi-racial, multi-religious, multi -linguistic and multi -cultural state. Pluralism implies that the existence of such groups within a state is beneficial to the state or nation. Pluralism has become a unique feature of both democratic and communist states and societies in modern times.

This idea is philosophically linked with the theories of Pluralism and Monism, many and one. As opposed to the monistic theory of unity, there are philosophers who believe in the multiplicity and diversity of things as more stable and important factor. It was William James (1842-1910), an American philosopher who developed the philosophy of pluralism. In his "Pluralistic Universe" (1910), William James held that "the problem of the one and the many is the most central of all philosophical probes".

This philosophical perception has been adapted to the political, sociological and cultural issues of the modern civilization, state and society, because diversity has become institutionalized in modern states and societies.

In the early decades of the twentieth century when the "melting pot" theory of the American nationhood as reflected in the vigorous programme of "Americanization" of various ethnic immigrants of the United States was discarded, the idea of cultural pluralism grew up. They discarded assimilation and opted for integration or harmonization, co-existence of cultures. Many American policy makers and sociologists argued that assimilation was not a desirable goal but Americanization would benefit by preserving many separate cultures, blending of the admissible features of various foreign nationalities. This policy gave a great push to pluralism. In India, in the early years of the Republic, there was a widespread talk of Indianization of the people living in the periphery. There was no popular taker for such a theory.

Ethnic pluralism

Ethnic diversity is generally regarded as the main cause of pluralism. Ethnic diversity was the legacy of conquest, trade and immigration, sometimes colonial immigration or voluntary immigration to the countries which provided opportunities for employment and settlement. Historically, an ethnic diversity was created when a group or groups of diverse ethnic peoples were brought together by conquest and put under the rule of the dominant group to which belonged the rulers. Ethnic diversity posed no problems for the big European colonial empires until the beginning of the twentieth century. The central empires under the control of the nation states of Europe required political unity and social solidarity. But nation states and ethnic diversity were diametrically opposed to each other. Naturally problems grew up sooner or later.

The colonial powers of Europe had attempted to find solution to the problems caused by the social, linguistic and religious diversity in the policy of assimilation and acculturation of the diverse groups - whether forced, induced or voluntary. But in actuality, the ethnicity of the social groups or communities becomes more profound and sharpened when they are undergoing an ethnic competition with each other. This competition may be for the assertion of their identity and for a share in the governance and the enjoyment of the state resources. Assimilation does not easily happen as each group asserts its identity; each one of them is concerned not only with material interest but also the symbolic emblems like its identity. Therefore, there are opposition to this policy or concept of assimilation which is being replaced by the policy of integration. We may further note that integration may be understood as the harmonization of the social and cultural relationship based on emotional integration. The sense of mutual belongingness is the basis of emotional integration.

Thus ethnic diversity in most of the newly liberated Third World countries led to the emergence of ethnic pluralism. And a plural society is a social order consisting of institutionally segmented cultural groups living side by side, yet without mingling in one political unit or a nation. In most cases, one dominant cultural or ethnic group monopolizes the political power, controls the state and the government, dominates-over other groups. However, in modern states these groups, either collectively or individually as citizens are entitled to the fundamental rights guaranteed by the constitution and the laws of the land. They are entitled to participate in the governance of the country. A plural society was thus born *out* of the "cultural incompatibility of its plural parts". This incompatibility sometimes enabled the dominant group to use "the state" as the instrument of domination leading to the despotism of the majority ethnic or cultural group.

Pluralism, however, theoretically subsumes both as conflict and co-existence, competition and harmony among the citizens are to be regulated and protected by the state. This also implies that pluralism is to be guided by toleration and mutual respect among the plural parts. More often that not, conflict becomes inevitable due to the divergence of interests and competition for the control of the political power and the economic resources of the state. As most of the modern states operate under an accepted constitution and the appropriate laws, despite the conflict and clash of interest there is also co-existence among the groups. In order to avoid conflict and ensure mutual co-existence, the elites of the ethnic and cultural groups make appropriate alliance, enter into compromise and decide to collaborate in a democratic state so that they share the power and resources of the state. The constituent ethnic groups, despite competition and rivalry, collude to make the state a centre of power and the distributor of resources. The state has been made a source and promoter of new national values. The state assumes a pre-dominant role in a plural society. In a democratic state, pluralism is based on the combination of toleration, interdependence, identity, self-respect, protection of the minorities, a unity in diversity. Further, in India, the national ideal of secularism strengthens pluralism.

Pluralism in Manipur

Plurality is a unique feature of Manipur, her polity society and culture. Manipur is a classic example of a plural society. Ethnic and social pluralism is the basis of the state and society. Ethnic diversity in Manipur, as history shows, is the legacy of her long history. The social composition of her people consists of the indigenous Meiteis who are the dominant group, the indigenous Naga tribes who live in the northern and northeastern and eastern hills of the state, the immigrant Meitei pangan (Manipuri Muslim) who are an indigenized community, and the immigrant Kuki-Chins who migrated to Manipur in different periods of history, and other communities who migrated from mainland India. The ethnic diversity was the result of the conquest of the hill tribes by the Meitei state, settlement of the immigrants in the state by the Kings of Manipur assisted by the British Political Agency.

Manipur is a historically evolved state. The long march of Manipur, in time and space, started from the prehistoric times. The first historical kingdom was founded in the first century of the Christian era by King Pakhangba who founded the Ningthouja dynasty. The kingdom was further developed during the reign of Loiyamba (1078-1122) who promulgated a decree known as the Loiyamba Shilyen which is regarded as the first written constitution of the kingdom. It had become a full- fledged sovereign state during the reign of King Kyamba who conquered the Kabaw Valley in 1471 and annexed it by a treaty with King Khikkhomba of Pong, the Mau Shan state of Mogaung in upper Myanmar. It reached the status of a little empire in the 17th Century as the boundary of the kingdom was pushed beyond the Chindwin river in upper Myanmar. Garibniwaz extended his empire into the heartland of Myanmar up to Sagaing on the Irrawaddy near Mandalay, the capital of Ava during the first half of the 18th Century. In the process of the expansion of the state into the surrounding mountains, the various Naga tribes who inhabited the hill ranges overlooking the valley and along the trade routes to Assam and Myanmar were brought under the political control, though no direct rule was established over them. With the conquest of the Kabaw Valley, the Shans and other ethnic groups living in the western part of the Chindwin basin became the subjects of the empire. In addition to the immigration of early batch of the Kuki-Chin groups, the influx of the Kukis into Manipur in the 19th Century, which was a process of immigration of the Kukis, Paite and kindred tribes, brought in new elements to the growing diversity of the population of Manipur. The earlier Kuki-Chin groups like the Hmar, Kom and kindred tribes came to Manipur in and around the 14th century. However, with the transfer of the Kabaw Valley to Burma in 1834, the Shans and inhabitants of that Valley ceased to be the subjects of Manipur. However, there was a social absorption of the Kabaw (Shan-Tai) into the Meitei social fold when they were in Manipur. Other immigrants like the Aryan Brahmins, the Muslims and the trading communities came to Manipur in different periods of history. By the end of the 19th century, after the British conquest of 1891, Manipur had become a multi-ethnic state, and pluralism had taken deep roots.

Problems of a Plural Society

Manipur had become a sovereign nation state by the 15th century. The kings of Manipur followed a liberal social policy towards the peoples who accepted the suzerainty of the Meitei kings. They were the tribes who were later brought under the Naga identity by the British. The Shans of the Kabaw Valley and some of the earlier Kuki -Chin tribes, were popularly known by the misnomer nomenclature of "Old Kuki", an invention of the British ethnography. There was no bar to the integration of these people into the Meitei social fold. However, the lack of communication, absence or near absence of trade, the King's or state's relation was not beyond the collection or offering of the nominal annual tribute. No Lallup was imposed on them before 1735. They were not disturbed and left to themselves. The king did not interfere in their polity so long as they expressed their loyalty to the king. The writ of the state was confined to the villages along the trade routes only. After conversion into Hinduism in the 18th century and introduction of a mild form of caste system, the social policy of the Hindu monarchy and nobility had undergone a great change. The process of integration of the tribal population into the Meitei social fold was discontinued. A hiatus between the Hindu Meiteis and tribal communities, who were the followers of the indigenous faith, was created. The process of integration was not perhaps completely stopped. There are historical evidences of conversion of not only individual tribesmen but even whole tribal localities into Hinduism and their complete absorption into the Meitei social fold. The process still continues sporadically, confined mostly to the inter-marriage families.

In the nineteenth century, the Kuki influx added a new complexity to the social diversity of Manipur. The Muslims or the Meitei pangan who were settled in Manipur since the 17th century were partially integrated into Manipur while they adopted the Manipuri language (Meitei) as their mother tongue as a result of their marriage with Meitei women and acceptance of the lineage (*Sagei*) system imposed by the state. In the twentieth century, both ethnic and religious diversity had emerged. The adoption of Hinduism by the Meiteis, conversion of tribes onto Christianity created a religious divide and the opportunity of integration was lost.

Colonialism also created further problems for the plural society. During the period of the colonial rule or even earlier to that, ethnicity was adopted as criteria for the identification of the hill tribes into the two identity constellations, the Naga and the Kuki. Affinity with the Nagas of the neighbouring Naga Hills was adopted to identify a group of indigenous tribes as Naga. And the affinity with the Kuki tribes of Assam, (North Cachar and Cachar), Chin and Lushai Hills was adopted to identify a group of tribes as Kuki. These generic names were not used by the tribes themselves who were ignorant of the name but they were imposed on them by the colonial administrator. It was R. B. Pemberton (1835) who refers to the Kookies or Khongjai and Nagas among the tribes. William McCulloch in "The Account of the Valley of Munnipore and surrounding Hill Tribes" (1859) mentions the two identity formations, Naga and Kuki. He listed some tribes as belonging to Kuki group and some tribes as belonging to the Naga group. The classification of William McCulloch, though arbitrary, was more or less adopted by the subsequent writers like R. Brown, T. C. Hodson and John Shakespeare There were additions and modifications in the list of the tribes by these writers.

Ethnic pluralism was contained by the Meitei State (mostly due to the ignorance, disunity and weakness of the tribes). The colonial rulers exploited the ethnic diversity in order to strengthen their rule in Manipur. Conflict and clash among the tribes were to be solved by them by excluding the Maharaja and his government from the administration of the hill tribes of the state. The British tried to project themselves as the saviour of the tribes.

With the coming of democracy, a progressive social outlook had emerged due to rapid educational achievement, economic progress and exposure to the outside world brought about by the Second World War. The social barriers which plague the relationship among the plural segments are breaking down gradually. The ethnic pluralism has been to some extent harmonized by the power sharing by the various cultural groups in the democratic government of the state. The democratically elected leadership has controlled the politics of the state. At the same time, the elites representing the political, bureaucratic, economic interests - including professionals like doctor, engineer, teacher, writer, intellectual and journalist - have greatly influenced (or controlled) the political leadership and the government machinery. The differentiation between the rural peasants and urban white collar employees and commercial class had emerged. The social differentiation has emerged in the ethnic groups, the bureaucracy, the political leadership, business interests, the church bureaucracy and tribal peasantry. There is tension and rivalry among the various ethnic groups in the state bureaucracy which greatly influence the ethnic relationship and their attitude towards the state. This may not be necessarily the outcome of pluralism but mostly of cut-throat economic competition in a capitalist economy.

The problem of inter-ethnic conflict and tension, and intersocietal hiatus exists in the state. This calls for serious introspection. Indian nationalism has come into conflict with ethnic nationalism. At the same time, there is the inter-ethnic identity assertion which is quite a formidable phenomenon. The process of nation building and national integration have to accommodate the ethnic aspirations and identity assertion. Manipur is facing all the negative problems of a plural society. However, it is undeniable fact that pluralism is the basis of the state of Manipur. True it has great constraints; but it has also intrinsic advantage and opportunity to solve these problems. Pluralism is the basic structure of the state of Manipur. It has preserved the identity of the various ethnic groups of Manipur. Pluralism has not so far succeeded in evolving a common identity of the people of Manipur. Amartya Sen's theory of multiple identities in a state exactly fits into the pluralistic state and society of Manipur. But a common aspiration of the people can be evolved if pluralism is properly managed by a conscious state. Manipur state is a partnership of her varied people.

Democracy

Manipur passed through three types of polity - monarchy (feudalism), colonialism and democracy. Democracy coincided with the attainment of freedom from the British in 1947. Manipur experience with democracy had three phases:

(i) The first phase was the experiment with the constitutional monarchy (1947-49) under the Manipur State Constitution Act, 1947.

(ii) The second phase was the post-merger period when th Indian Constitution was introduced followed by a long spell of central rule. Thereafter, a limited democratic institution in the form of Union Territorial Council (1957) and Territorial Assembly (1963) was introduced.

(iii) The third phase was the introduction of full statehood in 1972 and its concomitant paraphernalia like the full-fledged Legislative Assembly, the cabinet form of government and a judiciary.

The participation of the people in the democratic process started during the interim period prior to the attainment of the Independence. The passage of the Manipur State Constitution Act of 194 7 heralded a new era of democracy. This constitution envisaged a constitutional monarchy for Manipur. This constitution in the articles 44-55 laid down the fundamental rights and duties of the citizens. The subjects of the kingdom were guaranteed the status of free citizen.

I quote Article 52, which says "there shall be guaranteed to all people, justice - social, economic and political- equality of status and opportunity before the law, freedom of thought, expression, belief, faith and worship, vocation, association and action, subject to law and public morality".

The Constitution provided for a 53-member Legislative Assembly elected on adult franchise, a council of ministers headed by a chief minister appointed by the Maharaja and a Chief Court. Election was held in 1948 for the Assembly. A council of ministers was appointed. And democracy, for the first time in the history of Manipur, started functioning.

By a coerced Agreement imposed on Maharaja Bodh Chandra Singh, Manipur state was merged into the Dominion of India on 15 October, 1949. The merger put the constitutional experiment to an abrupt end. Manipur was placed under the category of Part 'C' state and was administered by a Chief Commissioner on behalf of the Government of India. The state was transformed into a Union Territory in 1957 and granted full statehood in 1972.

A limited form of democracy which was resented by the people, both pro-merger and anti-merger, was introduced. It was an arbitrary action on the part of the Government of India. India adopted her constitution and was declared a Republic. A full democratic system was introduced in India. However, Manipur was given a step-motherly treatment. Elections were held in 1952 to send representatives to the Parliament. An Electoral College of 30 members was also elected. The status of Manipur was downgraded to that of a Union Territory with a powerless Territorial Council (1957) which was transformed to the Territorial Assembly in 1963.

The long central rule of 23 years (1949-1972) was condemned by the people as the extension of the colonial rule - instead of the Political Agent or Dewan, there was the Chief Commissioner (later on Lt. Governor). Manipur's Legislative Assembly was abolished. There was a prolonged agitation for the grant of statehood to Manipur. There was resentment and bitterness coupled with a sense of betrayal in the minds of the people.

Denial of the democratic rights produced a feeling of deprivation among the people. They resorted to different kinds of rebellions and insurgency; this led to the emergence of ethnic nationalism, which was a challenge and threat to Indian nationalism.

We have to note that the Legislative Assembly of 1948, the Electoral College of 1952, Territorial Council (1957) and

Territorial Assembly (1963) provided the experience to the people in the democratic and electoral process prior to the emergence of full statehood. Yet the leaders of the Government of India entertained a notion that the people of Manipur were not mature enough for democracy and Manipur was not viable as a state. Therefore, Manipur's experience with Indian democracy from 1952-1971, produced resentment and alienation among the people. The electoral process provided the opportunity for the establishment of political parties, both national and local, including ethnic-based political parties. The aspirations and the interests of the people were to be promoted and projected by these parties.

The statehood in Manipur since 1972 saw the full working of the legislature, the cabinet form of government, the judiciary of a state of the Indian Republic. People's representatives had become the rulers of the land. People had high hopes and expectations from statehood. However, statehood was followed by frequent defections of the legislators which created instability. The eight Assembly elections held between 1972 and 2002 did not produce absolute majority for any party. Ministries were constituted by cobbling a majority of legislators. No ministry had ever completed a full term before the passage of the amended Anti - Defection Law of 2003.

Democracy hurled up new leadership from amongst the majority Meiteis, minority tribals and Muslims. The people's representatives are in the saddle of government. Luckily, Manipur had a free press and an independent judiciary which strengthened the roots of democracy. There were various civil societies which acted as pressure groups on specific issues, compelling the government to accept the people's demand. The pressure groups which sometimes created headache for the government ultimately strengthened the working of democracy.

However, one notices that democracy, democratic process, and democratic values of freedom, equality and human rights are not adequate to fulfill or accommodate the aspirations of the people for development, employment, protection of their identity and their rights. It is a test for those who believe in democracy. The electoral process was sabotaged by corrupt practices, money power, muscle power, misuse of government authority, use of gun culture both by the wielders of state power and those who are opposed to the state authority. This has weakened both the democratic system and state structure.

Moreover, the state of Manipur is a highly subsidized state. The state government is dependent on financial resources and the security provided by the Government of India. Politics have come to be more a process of capture of power through the socalled democratic election, formation of ministry with a cobbled up majority, and management of power and extraction of benefits, mostly financial, for the developmental works carried out with the assistance of the Planning Commission and other ministries. The task of government is confined to lobbying for fund in the centre and other central agencies. A successful leader in Manipur is the one who can convince the central government to give more money to the state. The huge investment of resources did not lead to development in the real sense; it created more corruption and led to the emergence of an extremely rich class of political leaders and bureaucrats who conspired to retain their position of power.

It is sad but true that the state of Manipur and its governance cannot function without the protection provided by the police and security force. Yet there is no alternative to democracy. And people now have a deep love for freedom and democracy. Democracy, can solve the problems of a pluralistic state like Manipur.

Ethnic relations

Ethnic diversity, ethnic competition, ethnic conflicts and ethnic alliance or ethnic compromise are the basic components of the ethnic relationship within a plural society. An ethnic relation was created when diverse ethnic and cultural groups, willingly or through coercion or conquest, were brought together under a state. This relationship produces both positive and negative effects. And the state imposes its power, authority and resources to keep the ethnic diversity in check in order to harmonize the relationship of the plural parts. The relationship covers both inter-ethnic and intra-ethnic relations. The greatest factor in a plural society is the capacity of the state to manage the ethnic relationship - social, economic and political - within the body politic of the state. The recent trend is that non -state structures like the church and interfaith organizations, ethnic organizations and civil societies come forward to harmonize the ethnic relationship. The state encourages the non -state groups to help manage this complex relationship.

History shows that the evolution of the state occurred in the valley of Manipur among the Meiteis, who built up chiefdom, principalities, kingdoms, nation state and even empire. In the hills, the tribes did not or could not build up states due to lack of resources, and were confined to the establishment of the village level polity. Naturally the tribes were engaged in the intra-village and inter-village relationship among themselves, mostly hostile in nature due to the practice of head-hunting. The inter-village and tribal solidarity did not emerge before the modern times. The tribes lived in independent village polity which was described by William McCulloch as "village republics". The loyalty of a tribesman and his worldview were confined to his family, his lineage, his clan, his dormitory and his village.

With the expansion of the Meitei state into the hills of Manipur, a relationship had emerged between the Meitei state

- to be more precise, the Meitei monarchy - with the hill tribes. There are traditions and historical accounts which manifest the cultural relation between the Meiteis and specific tribal groups at the clan level. Myths exist (and perhaps they were sometimes created or invented) to show the close relation between the monarch and the individual tribal villages who extended allegiance to the monarch.

The political and administrative relation was created when many hill villages were conquered and brought under the political control of the kingdom of Manipur.

The writ of the monarch was imposed on the villages situated along the lines of communication and trade routes. He imposed nominal tribute over them. As R. B. Pemberton recorded, when the Meitei forces were withdrawn again after the raid, the hill men once again returned to their free polity. It was King Garibniwaj who imposed *Lallup* (feudal service) in 1735 over the hill villages. He introduced new names for the functionaries of the hill villages like *Khullakpa,* administrator of the village, *Khunbu,* owner of the village, and *Luplakpa* among the Naga villages. And the title of '*Ningthou* (Chief) was discarded.

At the people-to-people level, the Meitei relation with the tribes was maintained through the barter trade. Commercial relationship was institutionalized into social relation system of "*Mangai'* meaning 'friendship/ relative'. A prominent tribal family always had a "*Mangai'* among the Meitei families living in the foothills or even with some families of the nobility-in the capital. The *Mangai* relationship continued for generations. The items of the barter trade were mainly the minor forest produces, bamboo products, boats hewn out of timbers, fruits and vegetables like cotton, ginger and chilly. And they were exchanged at the markets of the foothills. In return, the plainsmen exchanged salt cakes, dry fish and cotton textiles. The barter trade created commercial relationship which was mutually beneficial and socially congenial.

The Meitei traders, including women, conducted the long distance trade with the tribesmen in the hills. The Princes took shelter in the hills whenever there was political problem in the capital. There were instances of inter-marriage, which are not many, but there was no barrier.

Hinduism created a cleavage between the hill tribes and Meitei plainsmen. With the conversion of the ruling families and the people into Hinduism and the introduction of the caste system the intimate social relation between the Hindu Meitei and non Hindu tribes underwent a great change. Social barriers cropped up due to caste and difference in dietary habits; the non - Hindu tribes were looked down upon by the Kshatriya Meiteis as they were outside the Hindu Varna system. The liberal social policy of the ancient Meitei Kings was abandoned and was replaced by, orthodox caste-oriented attitude towards the hill tribes. So the population of Manipur in the 18th century was grouped into two; Hindu Meiteis and non-Hindu hill tribes.

During the colonial period, the inter-ethnic relation assumed a new dimension with the Kuki influx and the settlement of that Kuki migrants in the hills of Manipur, juxtaposed to the Naga villages and some early Kuki -Chin villages. The British Political Agents were entrusted by Maharaja Nar Singh and subsequently by Maharaja Sir Chandrakriti Singh to manage the affairs of the hill tribes. The Kukis were given land to establish villages under their chiefs. They were recruited into the Manipur army in a separate regiment known as the Kuki Irregulars. Land had become a bone of contention and cause of friction between the Nagas and the Kuki immigrants. The Nagas resented the loss of their lands and fought back against the frequent raids committed by the Kukis throughout 19th century and early 20th century. The Kuki immigration added a new complexity in the ethnic diversity and created rivalry and conflict between the two ethnic groups. The Kuki chieftainship coupled with their feudal rule were recognized by the state. The Kuki chiefs established their ownership of the land settled by the King or the Manipur State Darbar to them. After the British conquest of Manipur and introduction of British rule in Manipur, the Maharaja and his Darbar were to administer the valley of Manipur only. The Political Agent and President of the Manipur State Darbar (PMSD) were to administer the hills. Ethnicity in administration created a negative impact on interethnic relationship of Manipur. Meiteis and tribes, divided into Naga and Kuki, emerged as distinct ethnic groups.

The Kuki rebellion of 1917-19 and the Zeliangrong revolt of 1930-32 affected the inter-ethnic relations. The British were shocked at the Kuki refusal to serve as labour in France during World War I. The Nagas, some Kuki-Chin groups and the King of Manipur supported the British in the war against Germany. After the suppression of the Kuki rebellion, the British followed a lenient policy towards the former rebels. And as a consequences of the Kuki rebellion, administrative sub-divisions were created in the hills for more intensive administration. The Zeliangrong revolt was suppressed with the execution of their leader Jadonang in 1931 and imprisonment of Rani Gaidinliu.

Under the democratic rule, ethnic relations took a more friendly form. Every section of the population was given the opportunity to participate in the electoral process to promote its interests. Inter-ethnic competition, which was to get protection and benefits from the colonial authorities, was transformed under democracy in friendly alliances to obtain access to the power and resources of the state. The ethnic identity continues to be an influencing factor in the democratic process of sending representatives to the legislature. The inter-ethnic relation has been harmonized by ethnic alliances due to the mutual need to share power and resources of the state.

Bureaucracy has played an important role in influencing the political leadership. Ethnic bureaucracies in most cases define the ethnic interests and advise the leadership to achieve the ethnic goals. This role is surreptitiously played by the ethnic bureaucracy.

Further, ethnic relation has been influenced by the emergence of ethnic nationalism - Meitei nationalism, Naga nationalism and Kuki-Chin aspirations. Later, ethnic nationalism was projected and sponsored by the ethnic insurgents. There were clashes of interests between the three groups. Ethnic nationalism is opposed to Indian nationalism, but each of them is opposed to each other.

Present Scenario

A rapid survey of the inter-ethnic relations shows that the areas in which the ethnic relationship operates are in the field of people's participation in the democratic process, government employment, educational institutions, trade and commerce, interfaith interaction and the massive campaigns of the civil societies for peace, unity and development.

In the democratic state of Manipur, people participate in the electoral process. People join the political parties and contest elections to the legislature. The elected leaders become the members of the Legislative Assembly and Parliament who decide on the great issues of the state concerning the interest of the people. This electoral process involves the mobilization of masses of various ethnic groups; inter-ethnic relation is, in turn, influenced by people's participation in the electoral process. The elected representatives become ministers. The participating ethnic leaders make compromise or alliance under the law and constitution to devote to the governance of the state. The relation amongst the people was greatly influenced by the objectives given in their party manifestoes which, in most cases, harmonize their relation. Sharing of power and distribution of resources for economic development compel the elite of the ethnic groups for more involvement in the political process of the state.

The government is the greatest employer in Manipur. And government service is the most sought-after employment. Thousands of people are employed by the state. These include all sections of the population. There is a common interest among the different categories of employees and they develop solidarity and fraternity amongst themselves. The government service also covers the transfer and posting in different parts of the state - urban, rural, hill township and interior hills. These postings lead to close social and economic relation among the different sections of the people. While there is ethnic competition in the recruitment to the government services, the government employment produces positive sense of harmony and mutual benefits. The bureaucracy is the tool of the state to deal with many issues; from law and order to educational process, health care, roads and communication to rural development. So the government provides a great platform for ethnic relationship.

Educational institutions are the places where the young students of various ethnic and linguistic groups come into contact with each other. The primary and even the high schools in the hills are confined to the people of the ethnic group of the area. The schools, colleges and university in Imphal bring the students into closer contact. These institutions are the meeting place of the young minds. However, we see that the organisations of the students are segregated.

Trade and commerce continue to be a joint venture via the exchange of goods and services among the various communities of Manipur. Trade and commerce widen the ethnic relations to inter-state, national and global relations. Profit knows no boundary, caste or creed. Despite political and ethnic differences, trade is carried to the mutual benefit of all sections. Markets all over the state provide the meeting place for people of all groups as they do trade and commerce for profit and economic benefit. Imphal city, Churachandpur town and Moreh are the classic examples of the close ethnic interaction for commerce, friendship, social harmony despite the cut-throat competition among the traders and ethnic tension.

Manipur is a secular state which does not interfere in the religious pursuit of the people. Hinduism, Islam, Christianity and other religions have a limited relationship. Unfortunately religion, which is supposed to stand for spiritual uplift of man and the salvation of his soul, has not produced a friendly religious relationship. The proselytizing Christianity, the liberal Hinduism and exclusive Islam do not have a wide inter-faith interaction. The liberal among the religious leaders encourage inter-religious congregation, while some denominations are more exclusive. The inter-denominal relationship among the Christian community has emerged to some extent. The inter- religious interaction is promoted by United Religion Initiative established under the guidance of late Swami Damodar Maharaj of ISKCON. Because of the exclusivity of Christianity, the Naga- Kuki conflict occurred despite their religious commonality.

The need for harmony in ethnic relationship is greatly heightened by the need to maintain the unity of the people and integrity of Manipur. A massive campaign is continuously carried on by various civil societies to maintain peace, unity and brotherhood among the people of Manipur.

In conclusion, the shared ideals of democracy, economic interdependence, and the need for better livelihood and social coexistence will strengthen the ethnic relationship, which is bedrock of the pluralistic state of Manipur. We learn from history that Manipur has had great crises in her long history. But she had withstood them all. I would like to remind the learned audience that the classical political thinkers define the state as the people who are living in a definite territory with a government of their own, having external relation (sovereignty). I have to emphasize the role and position of the people which is the greatest factor in the making and unmaking of a state. So long as the people live unitedly in the country with full allegiance to the government, the state which is the highest form of human institutions will sustain and live on.

11

Political Status of Manipur on The Eve of Anglo-Manipur War-1891

The political status of Manipur whether she was independent or not at the outbreak of the Anglo-Manipur war of 1891 was a keenly debated issue. Even after a century of the war this highly emotive issue continues to be controversial among the historians. It has been complicated by the active participation of social activist groups in the debate. However, this paper is a fresh examination of an old problem.

The British Government took a highly partisan stand that the attack of Chief Commissioner Quinton's expeditionary forces on the palace and the fort of Manipur on 24th March, 1891 was not an act of aggression on a friendly ally, but a retaliatory action on Manipur. The execution of the British officers by the Manipur government was an act of rebellion against the British. As such the king and princes of Manipur were sentenced to death for rebellion against the Queen Empress of India. Mano Mohan Chose, the well known Barrister of Calcutta High Court argued that the king and princes of Manipur could not be punished on the charge of rebellion under the British Indian law because Manipur was an independent state not owing any allegiance to the Queen

Empress of India. Lord Landsdowne, the Viceroy of India and his council ignored the juristic and legalistic issues and made a political stand that Manipur was not an independent state and the military conflict between Manipur and the British forces was a rebellion. The then Indian vernacular press supported the view that Manipur was an independent country. The issue was debated in the British Parliament where the British Govt. endorsed the view of Lord Landsdowne. That an argument of a defence counsel was a subject matter of discussion for a policy decision of the British government both in India and Britain at the highest level clearly established the forceful logic of Ghose's argument.

Landsdowne's Contention

Lord Landsdowne in his contention that Manipur was not independent state gave the following arguments.

(i) That Manipur was liberated from the Burmese during the First Anglo-Burmese war 1824-26, and Gambhir Singh was recognised as an independent Raja by the Treaty of Yandabu, 1826.

(ii) That Maharaja Chandrakriti Singh (1850-1886) was given an assurance that his throne (gadi) would be protected by the British govrnment.

(iii) That Maharaja Chandrakriti presented a Nazarana to Viceroy Lord North Brooke in Aug 1874 during their meeting at Silchar (Zilla Darbar of Manipur's history), and that a Khillat was presented by Lord North Brooke to the Maharaja.

(iv) That on the request of Maharaja Chandrakriti Singh during his life time, the British agreed to recognise the succession of his eldest son Yubraj Surchandra Singh to the throne of Manipur after his death.

(v) That Maharaja Kullachandra Dhaja Singh in his letter of 25 March 1891 (one day after the execution of Quinton and others) to Viceroy of India admitted his subordination.

The Treaty of Yandabu Established the International personality of Manipur

Lord Landsdowne had conveniently hidden some historical facts in the history of the British relation with Manipur from the time of Maharaja Gambhir Singh to March 24, 1891. The following facts are restated for our recapitulation. The joint forces of the British and Gambhir Singh drove away the Burmese from Manipur during the first Anglo-Burmese War. The Treaty of Yandabu (1826) which concluded the war recognised Gambhir Singh as Raja of Manipur. Both the British and the king of Burma gave the recognition to the independence of Manipur. The treaty established the international personality of Manipur. That this clause was to be included in any treaty to be concluded by the British with Burma after the end of the war, was agreed upon between Gambhir Singh and David Scott, the Agent of the Governor General of British India in the Eastern frontier. The British recognised the independence of Gambhir Singh. Lord Viscount Cross, the Secretary of State for India in his reply to the Parliamentary debate in the House of Lords admitted the independence and sovereignty of Manipur by and after the Treaty of Yandabu.

Defensive Alliance

Manipur concluded two treaties with the British, one in 1762 and the other in 1833 which provided for a defensive alliance. The treaty of 1833 continued till 1891. An imperialist historian like Lee Warner described the two treaties as a defensive alliance. E.W Dun in his Gazetteer of Manipur published in 1886 as a secret document recorded that the treaty of 1833 except Art. 8 was in operation. It may be recalled that Governor General Lord William Bentinck in order to avoid further involvement in Manipur established a Political Agency to act as a channel of communication between Manipur and the British and to protect the British interests. The relation between Manipur and the British government was based on defensive alliance given in the treaty of 1833.

No Nazarana and No Khillat

Landsdowne's argument that Maharaja Chandrakriti Singh offered a Nazarana to Lord North Brooke who in turn offered a khillat to him was a historical distortion and concoction. Nazarana was the succession duty in the form of money given by a new ruler of an Indian native state and khillat was a present. We have the authority of Dr. R. Brown the British Political Agent who arranged the meeting at Silchar in August 1874 that there was usual exchange of presents between the two as friends and allies. The Cheitharol Kumbaba recorded the events including the exchange of presents and the subject matter of the talk between Lord North Brooke and Maharaja Chandrakriti was centered around the Burmese affairs. Therefore, it was neither Nazarana nor khillat but mere exchange of presents.

No Tribute, No Allegiance to the British

There was no occasion, no legal engagement, no agreement in which Maharaja Chandrakriti Singh acknowledged any allegiance to Queen Empress of India. No tribute was given to the Paramount power. In 1877 (1st Jan) there was a Darbar of Indian rulers and princes in Delhi (known as the Delhi Assemblage) during the viceroyalty of Lord Lytton. As Manipur did not owe any allegiance to the paramount power, Maharaja Chandrakriti was not invited to the said Darbar. In 1891, it was argued that Manipur was not invited because of long distance. The fact was that since Manipur was not under the British paramountcy she was not invited to the Delhi Darbar of 1877 at all. Manipur did not pay tribute to the British nor entered any agreement on that count. Therefore, the official publications of the Government of India like the Statistical Account of Assam edited by Sir W. W. Hunter, the Director General of Statistics of Govt. of India published in 1879 described Manipur as an independent state. (One should remember that W. W. Hunter was a great admirer of Lord Dalhousie's imperialism). Further, in the first edition of the Imperial Gazetteer of India in 1881, edited by Sir W. W. Hunter the same status was accorded to Manipur. (The Bengali papers highlighted this status in 1891). Even Sir Alexander Mackeniie in his celebrated, "The history of relation of the Government with tribes of North Eastern frontier of British Bengal" (1884) observed that Manipur was an "independent state". He mentioned that it was also protected. We will take up protection question later on.

Manipur: An Asiatic Power in Alliance with the Queen Empress

The judicial and legal position of the independent status of Manipur was well decreed by the judgement of the Calcutta High Court in 1865, which was cited by Mano Mohan Ghose. The Calcutta High Court decreed that "Manipur was an Asiatic power in alliance with Queen Empress". The judgement confirmed the defensive alliance of Manipur and the British mentioned above and Manipur was a friendly ally of the British Government. This status remained unchanged up to eve of the war of 1891. This fact was not contradicted nor denied by Lord Landsdowne. The history of Anglo-British relation clearly shows that Gambhir Singh helped the British in the suppression of Khasi Rebellion 1829-31, the Sadiya Uprising of 1830, and he conquered Naga Hills with British help in 1832. The Anglo-Manipur agreement of 1833 was concluded; the agreement was written in Meitei script and signed with royal seal by Maharaja Gambhir Singh in the Meitei script. The agreement was translated into English and published in the volume of Aitchison's Treaties etc. Thus, Manipur under the successive rulers like Gambhir Singh and Chandrakriti Singh rendered military help to the British in their troubles in the north eastern region and during their war against Burma. Maharaja Chandrakriti Singh helped the British in the suppression of the Naga Revolt of 1879-80. The agreement of 1833 was more beneficial to the British. The friendly ally status clearly defined by the judgement of the Calcutta High Court was maintained till 1891.

This fact was mentioned by Maharaja Kullachandra Dhaja Singh in his letter of 25, March 1891 addressed to Lord Landsdowne. He addressed the Viceroy as my friend. The Maharaja did not admit the subordinate status as alleged by Landsdowne.

No Protectorate

As to the alleged "protected state" status of Manipur ascribed by Lord Landsdowne, it is to be stated that it came out of political instability in Manipur during the reign of Chandrakriti Singh. It may be recalled that in 1850. Chandrakriti became the king of Manipur after Maharaja Debendra. But the British Political Agent Mc Culloch did not like to cooperate. Maharaja Chandrakriti Singh accordingly gave military help to the Angami Nagas in their fight against the British. Lord Dalhousie advised Chandrakriti Singh to desist from helping the Nagas and it was decided to recognise him as the Maharaja of Manipur against his uncle, Maharaja Debendra Singh who was seeking.British help. Not only this, the British made a unilateral public avowal of protection of Maharaja Chandrakriti that any pretender to the throne of Manipur against Chandrakriti Singh would be punished by the British. It was in this context that the Calcutta High Court decided "whoever conspiring against Manipur would be taken as waging war against the British as Manipur was as ally of the British." In order to strengthen the military force of Manipur the British supplied arms and ammunition. The military and political help was mutually given and taken by Manipur and the British. The protected state status was never discussed nor accepted before the war. When the issue came in the House of Lords, a member queried whether Maharaja Chandrakriti Singh ever accepted the protected status at all and no satisfactory reply was given from the British government side.

As to the guarantee for the recognition of Surchandra Singh as the successor of Maharaja Chandrakriti Singh, it was done to meet a political expediency. This did not make Manipur or her king as a protectorate or a feudatory Chief under British India. When a protected prince had to ascend the throne, an investiture ceremony was to be performed in the presence of a representative of the British Crown as was done in the case of Raja Churachand Singh in 1907. After the death of Maharaja Chandrakriti Singh his eldest son Surchandra performed the coronation ceremony at the time of his accession to the throne of Manipur. And the British Government was just informed. It was so in September, 1890, after the abdication of Surchandra Singh, Kullachandra Dhaja Singh ascended the throne and performed the coronation ceremony.

Manipur was Independent

Manipur since Gambhir Singh had maintained the status of an independent kingdom. The king performed the customary Phambalkaba (coronation ceremony) which was a compulsory state ritual to be performed by a king. Manipur had her own political and administrative system. Manipur had her own currency, Gambhir Singh, Nara Singh, Chandrakriti, Surchandra and Kullachandra Dhaja issued their own coins. Manipur had her own flags and royal insignia. There is a "coat of arms" of Maharaja Chandrakriti

Singh which is engraved with "Pakhangba" as the royal emblem.

Manipur had free hands in boundary affairs except with Burma border due to the transfer of Kabaw valley. Manipur had a minister in charge of Burmese affairs known as Aya Purel, a sort of foreign minister. Thangal General was once an Aya Purel and participated in the boundary demarcation of 1882 in which both the British and Burmese officers took part. The British endorsed the demarcation of the boundary between Manipur and Naga hills as laid down by Thangal General. The Manipur-Chin hills boundary was demarcated by Manipur in 1872. It may be recalled that Manipur participated in Lushai-Chin expedition of 1871-72. And a treaty was concluded between the king of Manipur and the Lushai-Chin Chiefs with the king of Manipur, and the treaty was drafted in English by Political Agent R. Brown.

Manipur Agents in British India

Manipur maintained two offices of her Agents in British India. One Agent was posted in Calcutta, the then capital of India and another was posted at Lakhipur in Assam. Communications between Manipur and the Government of India were maintained through the Political Agents and sometimes through the Manipur Agents at Calcutta and Lakhipur. The death of Maharaja Chandrakriti and accession of Maharaja Surchandra Singh was communicated by Major Gulap Singh, Manipur's Agent at Calcutta, to Lord Dufferin in Simla who sent condolences to Manipur through Major Gulap Singh.

No Subordinate Protected State

Without prejudice to the emotional aspects of the issue demonstrated by the British and Manipur, an independent investigation shows that Manipur by an international treaty and bilateral agreements, was an independent kingdom with all her traditional paraphernalia of independence. Of course, after the transfer of Kabaw valley, Manipur' s relation with Burma was monitored by the British. And after the British conquest of Upper Burma in 1886, Manipur was surrounded by British territories and her only foreign relation was with the Government of India.

Manipur rendered military help *to* the British who in turn provided political support and military equipments. No one can deny that Manipur's geopolitical position and limited resources made her depend on the British government in that process, the British officials tried *to* interfere in the internal affairs of Manipur. Thus, while Manipur maintained her de jure independent status, de *facto* she depended on the British. This position was well stated by Maharaja Kullachandra Dhaja Singh in his letter of March 25, 1891 that Manipur was a friendly ally of the British who got some help to Manipur.

On the ground, after the Palace Revolution of September 21, 1890, Manipur was acting as "an independent state" in the true sense of term. Quinton's encroachment on Manipur's independence was retaliated by Manipur in her defensive war against the British. However, Landsdowne's contention of the subordinate and protected status of Manipur and the right of the British government to settle disputed succession in tvlanipur was an attempt for political legitimization of the folly of Quinton with a legal fiction to punish Manipur's princes as rebels. The imperial power of the British India was so dominating that, in actuality a land locked small state like Manipur could never be equal with her in real terms, though by legal status, she was an independent state but, in reality, she had depended on the British. This was the real position of Manipur in 1891. Manipur was de jure independent of and de facto dependent on the British.

12

Tribal Administration in Manipur

1. The "Tribal Area" and "Hill Area" under the Constitution and the Laws of Manipur.

The Fifth Schedule and the Sixth Schedule of the Constitution of India provide the mechanism for the administration of the Schedule Tribes and they refer to the two areas. One is called the Schedule Areas under the Vth Scheduled and the other is called the Tribal Area of Assam, Meghalaya, Tripura and Mizoram under the VIth Schedule. The tribal areas of Manipur are included in the Scheduled Areas but not covered by the Tribal Areas of the VIth Schedule.

The Article 321 (C) of the Constitution provides a special provision for legislation and administration of the tribal people of Manipur in form of the Hill Areas Committee. According to the Manipur Legislative Assembly (Hill Areas Committee) Order 1972, the 'Hill Areas" mean the areas specified in the First Schedule of the order. The First Schedule mentions the hill districts and the subdivisions therein created by the Government of Manipur from time to time as the "Hill Areas".

The term "Hill Areas" has a historical background. During the Colonial period, the term "Hill Tribes" was used under the Rules for the Management of Manipur State and the Rules for the Management of Hill Tribes, 1935. This Rule was the application of the Chin Hills Regulation of 1896 in spirit. At the time of India's independence, the term "Hill Tribe" was substituted by the "Hill People" in the Manipur Hill People's Regulation, 1947 and the Manipur State Constitution Act, 1947. Even in the composition of 53 member Assembly, 18 seats were reserved for the hill areas. After the merger of Manipur to the Dominion of India as per the order of the President of India in 1950, the term Scheduled Tribes was used to mean Any Naga, Any Kuki and Any Lushai Tribes. The Scheduled Tribes were fragmented to 29 tribes in 1956 and 33 in 2003. In the parliament (1952), territorial Council (1957), Territorial Assembly (1963) and State Assembly (1972) seats were reserved for Scheduled Tribes on the basis of the population of the Scheduled Tribes. However, the Government of India or the State Government stick to the term "Hill Areas" in the legislation like the Manipur Hill Areas Village Authorities Act, 1956, the Manipur Land Revenue and Land Reform Act, 1960, the Manipur Hill Areas District Councils Act, 1971 or the Manipur Hill Areas Autonomous District Council Act, 2000 (since repealed in 2006). Crucial to this issue of Hill Areas or Tribal Area is the population who are the tribal people or the Scheduled Tribes. The tribal people populate the Area.., Therefore it is appropriate to adopt the term, "Tribal Area" in the administration of district or subdivision inhabited by the Scheduled Tribe population.

2. The Demographic Profile

The State of Manipur has a total area of 22,327 sq. km of which the hill areas cover 20,089 sq. km and the valley covers 2238 sq. km only. According to the census of 2001, the population of the state was 22,93,896 (excluding the population of the subdivision of Mao-Maram, PaoMata and Purul of Senapati district). The population of the hill districts was 8,82,130. The Scheduled Tribe population was 7,41,142 out of which the Scheduled Tribe population of the valley districts was 56,247 of which the urban dwellers were 28,058.

The Scheduled.Tribes population constitutes 34.2 percent of the total population of the state. Of the total Scheduled Tribe population, the Thadou is the largest tribe with 1,82,594 (24.6%) followed by the Tangkhul with 1,46,075 (19.7%), the Kabui with 82,386 (11.1 %), the Paite with 49,271 (6.6%), the Hmar with 42,013 (5.7%), Vaiphei with 38,267 (5.2%), Maring with 23,288 (3.1 %) and Anal with 21,241 (2.9%).

The Scheduled Tribe population recorded a literacy percentage of 65.9. Among the Scheduled Tribes the Hmar has recorded the highest literacy rate of 79.8%, Paite (79%), Any Mizo (74%), Anal (73%), Tangkhul (72%), Kabui (63.9%), Kom (63.9%), Vaiphei (59.8%), Thadou (57.1 %).

Of the total Scheduled Tribe literates, 6.2% are having the educational level of graduation and above. This group forms the elite of the tribal society. Among the individual tribes, the Tangkhuls have the highest number of graduates and above (8.2%) followed by the Mizo (8%).

3. Evolution of Administration in Tribal Area

(i) The Traditional Tribal Polity

The tribal people of Manipur, both the Nagas and the Kuki chins had developed their own polity. However, their polity did not grow beyond the village level. They did not develop into tribe-level polity formation. Therefore, the village is the autonomous political, social, economic and cultural unit.

There are two kinds of polity. Among the Nagas, there is a sort of democratic type of political system, which was described by the colonial writers as "small republic". Among the Kuki-Chin, the chieftainship is the main political system. The rulers of Manipur recognized this traditional polity during the pre-Colonial period. During the British rule, this polity formation was adopted as a unit of regular administration. In the post independence period, the laws of Manipur diluted the traditional polity but the people themselves still continue to profess their custom and traditions, which form the core of their polity. The traditional polity has a clear-cut boundary of the village; there was a well-regulated land ownership system, a judicial system and other social institutions based on customary laws. The land ownership includes the community land, clan land and individual land among the Nagas. There is the chiefs ownership of land among the Kuki-Chins. The traditional polity has eroded due to the Indian legislation relating to forests and revenue and with the emergence of private property in the tribal society. The tribal customary laws are very powerful guiding principles in the perpetuation of the polity in the tribal villages.

(ii) The Pre-Colonial Period

The rulers of the Meitei State always tried to gain access to and assert the command over the forest resources of the mountains surrounding Manipur valley which was the heartland and homeland of the Meitei State. There are historical references to the military expeditions and raids over the tribal villages located in the surrounding mountains. They exploited the forests, wood and timber for their house making and boat making, and the elephants for the royal stable and the armed forces. The Meitei rulers invaded the tribal villages, compelled them to accept the suzerainty of the Meitei state. However, once the Meitei forces were withdrawn the tribal villages continued to remain independent in their hills and their life was not interrupted by the Meiteis. The state imposed tributes on some selected villages which were situated on the trade routes. Thus, the policy of the Meitei state was non-interference into the hill tribes, their polity, way of life, and economic persuits. However, with the expansion of the Meitei state in terms of territory, resources and manpower, they exercised the political control over the villages which were defeated in military invasion. But they did not impose direct administration in the tribal areas. The King established personal relationship with the headmen or chiefs of large number of villages who gave loyalty and support during the time of crisis. Occasionally tributes were imposed on them. But the tributes were nominal as indicated by homage in form of Panao and Singnao (Arum roots and ginger).

With the conquest of Kabaw valley of upper Burma in 1471 A.D. the frequent invasions of Manipur by the Tripuri rulers, the Bodos and the Muslims from the West, the Meitei state had to hold on the Shan inhabited valley and to defend the western frontier upto the Barak river. They protected the trade routes between Manipur and the West (Tongjei Maril) and the Heirok route via Kwatha in the east. In the 18th century, the kingdom of Manipur possessed the military power and resources to send several military expeditions into upper Burma. King Garibaniwaz(1709–48) utilized the military services of the hill tribes in his frequent Burma expeditions. This enabled him to have control over the hill tribes though there was no direct administration.

The genesis of the administration of the tribes in the state of Manipur lay in the establishment of the Hao-Macha Loisang (the Department of hill tribes) by King Charairungba. He made his lost but recoverd son, Pamheiba (future Garibaniwaz) as the Prince-in charge of the department. This department became institutionalized and it was a part of the state administrative machinery.

When Garibaniwaz became the king of Manipur, he was intent to make the hill region of his empire a source of revenue. And he tried to curtail the independent status of the tribal village chiefs. The chronicles record that he invaded many hill villages but he befriended the chiefs of the defeated villages. The Naga chiefs were accorded the honour of riding the elephants on their journey from the foothills to the capital to have audience with the king. In 1735, Garibaniwaz, by a royal edict, introduced the Lallup system on the hill villages. The Lallup was the feudal service rendered by the subjects of the kingdom of Manipur. The Lallup service was greatly resented by the hill people. The state could impose the service on the villages that were situated on the trade routes guarded by the state forces. As per this system, the villages were compelled to supply the forest produces, timber for boat making and house making, cotton, fruits and minor forest produces.

In order to curtail the power and status of the Naga chiefs, King Garibaniwaz stopped using the title of "Ninigthou" (Chief, literal meaning King) to the heads or the chiefs of the Naga villages. He introduced the title of Khullakpa (Administrator of the village), Khunbu (Owner of the village) and Luplakpa in the polity of the tribal. Later on, the fuctionaries with Meitei titles, like Chingsanglakpa (in charge of a hill range), Mantri (minister), Meitei Lambu (interpreter) and Pakhanglak (controller of the youth) were indiscriminately introduced in the later period. In the nineteenth century, with regard to the Kuki chiefs, they continued to use the title of "Ningthou" (chief). The British interpreted the Ningthou not as a king but as a chief. But they consciously avoided using the word "King" due to the political and constitutional meaning of the term.

The Kuki influx in Manipur in the nineteenth century created tension in the hills. The Maharaja of Manipur with the assistance of the British Political Agent, W. McCulloch settled the Kukis in different parts of the hill areas. The Kuki chiefs accepted the suzerainty of the Maharaja of Manipur; they tendered loyalty and rendered service to the state of Manipur. The Kukis became the subjects of Manipur. They were even recruited into the Manipur army and they formed a regiment known as the Kuki Irregulars . Maharaj

Chandrakriti Singh (1850-85) was very friendly with the Kuki chiefs.

Throughout the pre-colonial period, the traditional tribal polity, either of the Naga or the Kuki-Chin continued to be the for m of administration. The state did not interfere, and the villages were the autonomous political entity. The hill tribes were outside the jurisdiction of the administration of the state of Manipur.

(iii) Tribes under the Colonial Rule

After the British conquest of Manipur in 1891, the hill area also came under the rule of the British Political Agent who acted on behalf of the minor Raja Churachand Singh. The British introduced the system of Indirect Rule. Under this system, the British did not rule the hill tribes directly; like the rulers of Manipur, they did not interfere into the internal affairs of the tribal villages. The British abolished the Lallup system and the slavery in 1892. They introduced the hill house tax of Rs.3/- per household per year. They made the chiefs or the headmen of the villages responsible for the administration of the village. The spirit of the Chin Hills Regulation of 1896 was the guiding principle of the hill administration.

The chief or the head of the village was made responsible for the collection of house tax, maintenance of law and order and administration of justice according to customary laws. They were made to render forced labour to the state for the construction and maintenance of the paths, roads and bridges and provide local hospitality to the touring officers, army, police and petty colonial employees. The Lallup system was reimposed on the hill tribes in a more stringent form.

The whole of the hill areas was divided into five divisions. The Political Agent in whom the authority was vested to administer the hills, appointed five Lam Subedars for the five divisions. Seven Lambus were appointed for a division under the charge of the Lam Subedar to look after the hills. The Lambu was originally an interpreter; its counterpart in Naga Hills was the Dobashi. He was employed in all aspects of the colonial administration, keeping the law and order, administration of justice, supervision of the public work. He had become the ear and eye of the government. During the pre-colonial period, the Lambu was a petty official for the administration of the rural areas. During the period of direct British management of Manipur (1891-1906) the administration of the hill tribes was looked after by the Political Agent with the help of the Lambus who oppressed the people. The British Rule ensured law and order; peace was maintained, house taxes were collected. The people could not bear the financial burden of the house tax. The monetization of the economy by the introduction of house tax was to the great hardship of the hill tribes.

When the reins of the government were handed over to Raja Churachand Singh in 1907, he was made the President of Manipur State Durbar. But the jurisdiction of the Raja and his Durbar was confined to the valley only. The Political Agent continued to administer the hill tribes. The objective of the British policy was to prevent the traditional oppression and exploitation of the hill tribes by the Raja and his government and to protect the hill tribes. They kept peace, prevented internal tribal feuds and warfare, and intra-societal conflicts, imposed tax to meet the cost of administration. They maintain the roads and bridle paths like the Cachar Road, Dimapur Road upto Mao, Moreh Road and the Tiddim Road. But in reality, the British rule through the Lambu was oppressive.

President of Manipur State Durbar (PMSD)

In 1913, there was a reorganization of the State Durbar. The Raja ceased to be the President. One British ICS officer was appointed as the President. Not the Durbar but the President in his own discretion was entrusted to administer the hill area under the overall supervision of the Political Agent. In fact, the President of the Durbar popularly known as the PMSD, with his office at the capital town of Imphal was an overburdened officer of the state. He did not have officers to assist him. He could not go on tour in the hills. He depended on the Lambus and the LamSubedars. The British imposed forced labour known as Potthang Begari and Potthang Senkhai. Very frequently, the tribal labour was subjected to physical torture. There were eighteen British PMSDs between 1913-1947. Among them were distinguished names like J.C. Higgins, Christopher Gimson, C.S.Mullan, Captain C.W.L. Harvey, G.P. Stewart and J.F. Pearson.

Creation of Sub-divisions

After the Kuki Rebellion (1917-1919), which shook the foundation of the British rule and that of the Maharaja in the hill areas, the British decided for an intensive administration and to check the oppression of the tribal people, which was not known to the higher up of the colonial administration. Two sub-divisions namely, the North West with Tamenglong as headquarter and North East with Ukhrul as the headquarter were created to administer the hill areas. The SDOs were to be recruited from amongst the Anglo-Indian officers of the Assam Provincial Civil Services. They were under the Political Agent and the PMSD. However, the officers were not easily available. And the working of the sub-divisions was not satisfactory due to the incompetence and negligence of the officers. So in 1929, the two sub-divisions were shifted to Imphal. But after the outbreak of the Zeliangrong revolt under the leadership of Haipou Jadonang and Rani Gaidinliu (1930-33) and suppression by the government it was decided to open the sub-division known as the Sadar sub-division with the headquarter at Imphal.

And the government framed the Rules for the Management of Hill Tribes in 1935.

During the Second World War, Manipur became a battlefield between the .invading Japanese forces and the Allied forces (1942-44). The administration in the hills collapsed. After the war there was a spontaneous growth of political consciousness among the people of Manipur including the hill people. There was a pressure for the establishment of a representative form of government under the monarchy. Maharaja Bodhchandra Singh promulgated two important legislations: the Manipur State Constitution Act and the Manipur Hill People's Regulation in 1947. These two laws introduced regular administration in the hill area.

(iv) The Manipur Hill Peoples' Regulation, 1947

The Manipur State Constitution Act, 1947 provided a democratic constitutional monarchy. There was a 53 member Assembly, a council of ministers headed by a Chief Minister, a chief court with a set of fundamental rights for citizens of Manipur. In the membership of the Assembly 18 seats were reserved for the hill areas. The Council of ministers had a minister-in-charge of the hills. The Hill Minister was the statutory head of the hill administration. There was a Board of Appointment, a precursor of a public service commission consisting of 3 members of which one was from the hills.

The Manipur Hill Peoples' Regulation, 1947 was a well-formulated local government system for the hill areas. The Regulation further described the powers and the function of the Hill Minister.

The Regulation provided for 3 tier judicial system. There was a village authority in a village of 20 or more tax paying houses. Thus there was a Circle Authority and then the Hill Bench. Above the Bench was the chief court.

The Regulation was a good piece of legislation for Hill Areas. The Regulation continued to operate after the Merger of Manipur into Indian Union and the abolition of the Chief Court and the Hill Bench (1956) and the Circle Authority was abolished in 1955.

4. Administrative divisions and the Instruments of Administration

After the Merger of Manipur state to the Dominion of India on 15 October, 1949, Manipur was made a "Part C" State under a Chief Commissioner. The Manipur state constitution was not abrogated; the Assembly was dissolved, the Council of ministers was dismissed, the Chief Court was abolished. The Maharaja was divested of his political and constitutional status as a Maharaja. He was retained as the head of the religious and cultural life of Manipur. He was given a privy purse.

On 26th January, 1950, Manipur was made one district state under a Chief Commissioner, a deputy Commissioner with several sub-divisional officers. There was a secretariat under a Chief Secretary.

The government retained or created the following sub-divisions the Imphal West Tahsil, Imphal East Tahsil, Thoubal Tahsil, Bishenpur Tahsil, Sardar hills Subdivision, Ukhrul, Churachandpur, Tamenglong, Mao circle, Tengnoupal circle and Jiribam Mauza. These Tahsils, circles, mauza and sub-division were constituted in November, 1969 into new districts; Manipur Central (valley and Tengnoupal), Manipur West, Manipur North, Manipur South, Manipur East. And on 29th October, 1970 more districts were created; Thoubal, Bishenpur and Tengnoupal.

And on 15th July, 1983, the names of the districts were changed as given below.

Sl. No	Old name	New name
1	Manipur North	Senapati
2	Bishnupur	Bishenpur
3	Tengnoupal	Chandel
4	Manipur East	Ukhrul
5	Manipur South	Churachandpur
6	Manipur West	Tamenglong
7	Manipur Central	Manipur Central
8	Thoubal	Thoubal

Note: Manipur Central was bifurcated into Imphal West district and Imphal East district. Total number of district is now nine

The main instruments of administration in the hill areas are the following laws:

1. The Manipur Hill Areas Village Authorities Act, 1956.

II. Manipur Hill Areas District Council Act, 1971.

[The Manipur Land Revenue and Land Reforms Act, 1960; the Indian Forest Act and the Manipur Forest Rules, 1971 relate to revenue and forest administration in the tribal areas]

I. The Village Authorities for Village Administration.

The Village Authorities Act of 1956 framed by the Parliament provided a village Authority for a village which has 20 and above house tax paying households. The Village Authority stands for the maintenance of law and order, collection of hill tax and administration of justice through the village court under the customary laws. The Act introduced democratic element in the constitution of the Authority. The Act also legitimized the feudalistic and hereditary chiefship and khullakpaship. This ex-officio chairmanship of the Authority reserved for the chief or the khullakpa is against the democratic ethos. The Act does not operate properly. The Village Authorities do not function properly, The Village Authorities were authorized by the district administration to act as a development agency and to issue certificate of land ownership to the villagers. These are extra legal role.

Talking about the statutory position of the chiefs and khullakpas under the law, we may refer to the (now redundant) Manipur Hill Areas Acquisition of the Chiefs Rights Act, 1967 passed by the Territorial Assembly. This Act provided for:

(i) the abolition of the chiefship among the Kuki-Chin villages

(ii) payment of compensation to the chiefs whose rights are to be acquired by the state

(iii) the introduction of the MLR and LR Act, 1960

This is a liberal legislation but the framers did not visualize - or understand the dangers of the MLR and LR Act and its effect on the tribal land ownership and land tenural system. The Act could not be implemented due to the opposition from the Kuki-Chin people.

II. The Manipur Hill Areas District Council Act, 1971

This Act provides a self governing district level council for the administration of the hill areas. During the movement for grant of statehood to Manipur, there was a strong demand for VIth Schedule District Council for Tribal areas of Manipur. When the statehood was granted, the Government of India passed a law for the establishment of district councils. The

District Council was a council without any autonomy. The Government of Manipur established six district councils. Each council has 18 members and 2 nominated members. The power and functioning of the council are very much limited. It has neither legislative nor judicial function.

It has executive functions on 17 subjects which are delegated by the state government to the councils. Of course, there is a Council Fund to finance the workings of the district councils.

Functions of the Council

The seventeen functions delegated by the state government consists of subjects under the head of public works, primary education, health services upto running dispensaries, public health engineering and water supply, agriculture and soil conservation, Vety and Animal husbandary including Vety dispensaries, management of markets, forest and jhum control etc.

Chairman

The Council is headed by a chairman elected by the members of the Council. He is empowered to exercise administrative authority on the delegated subjects. There may be Vice Chairman.

Chief Executive officer

The CEO is appointed on deputation from the services of the state government. He is the secretary of the Council and the officer responsible for the working of the Council.

Official language

The official language of the Council is English and/or Manipuri. The use of tribal dialect is allowed in the deliberation of the Council meetings.

Elections

There were three elections held so far to choose the members of the Council. The first election was held in 1973, second in 1978, third one in 1983. There was political instability due to constant shifting of loyalties among the members. There was frequent suspension of the council. It has been said that the history of the district council is a history of suspension. So by 1987, the six district councils were superseded by the Deputy Commissioner of the district. At that time there was a strong demand for the introduction of VI Schedule District Council.

Somehow the Central government could not be convinced and the centre refused to introduce the VI Schedule Autonomous District Council. There was opposition from the people to the holding of election. There is no election since 1989. It is sad but true that the district council had failed to deliver the goods:

5. The Constitutional Provision for legislation and Administration in Hill Areas: The Hill Areas Committee (HAC)

The Hill Areas Committee of the Manipur Legislative Assembly is empowered by the Constitution to monitor the law making and the administration for the hill areas. At the same time of movement for statehood, leaders of tribal groups wanted constitutional safeguards for the tribal people.

The Parliament provided the safeguards in Art. 371 (C) of the Constitution of India.

According to the Art. 371 (C), "The President may... provide for the constitution and functioning of a Committee of the Legislative Assembly of the State consisting of the members of the Assembly elected from the Hill Areas... for any special responsibility of the Governor in order to secure the proper functioning of the Committee".

The sub-section No (2) of this Article further states, "The Governor shall annually or whenever so required by the President, make a report to the President regarding the Hill Areas in the State of Manipur and the executive power of the Union shall extend to the giving of direction to the state as to the administration of the said area".

As per this constitutional provision,

I[st], the President of India shall constitute the Hill Area Committee of the Assembly,

2nd the Governor has been entrusted a special responsibility and power to ensure that the Hill Areas Committee functions properly,

3rd, the Governor shall report periodically to the President on the administration of the Hill Areas,

4th, the Government of India is empowered to issue direction to the state on the status of administration in the hill areas.

President V.V.Giri promulgated the Manipur Legislative Assembly (Hill Areas Committee) Order, 1972. The First Schedule of the order describes the "Hill Areas" and the Second Schedule contains the list of the Schedule Matters (13 in number).

The Hill Areas Committee has four legislative functions.

(ii) All bills except money bill containing the Schedule Matters shall be referred to HAC for consideration and report to the Assembly.

(ii) The HAC shall have the right to consider and pass resolution recommended by the government of the state, the legislative or executive action affecting the Hill Areas with respect to the Scheduled Matters.

(iii) The HAC shall have the right to discuss the Annual

Financial Statement (State Budget) in so far it relates to the Hill Areas and to facilitate discussion in the budget of the Hill Areas.

(iv) The bill recommended by the HAC may be passed by the Assembly with variation.

With regard to the general functions,

(i) The HAC shall safeguard the interest of the people of the Hill Areas particularly the accelerated development of the area.

(ii) The HAC shall promote unity between the people of the Hill Areas and other areas of the state.

(iii) The HAC has special responsibility on the development plan of the Hill Areas, "The development plan shall be placed before the HAC for its views and its views will be taken in account before the plans are finalized".

The Government shall submit quarterly report to the HAC showing the progress of the implementation of the plans.

Scheduled Matters

The Scheduled Matters which are under the jurisdiction of the HAC are:

(i) The power and functioning of the District Councils

(ii) Development and Economic Planning

(iii) Allotment, Occupation or use or selling a part of land

(iv) Management of Forest (other than Reserve Forest)

(v) Use of land and water resources for the purpose of agriculture

(vi) Regulation of the practice of Jhum or other forms of shifting cultivation

(vii) Establishment of village committee or councils and their power and other matter relating to village administration

(viii) Public health and sanitation

(ix) The appointment or succession of chief or headman

(x) Inheritance of property

(xi) Marriage and divorce

(xii) Social customs

(xiii) Any other matter which the Assembly may by resolution declare to be a matter which shall come within the provision of the Hill Areas Committee

The analysis of the power and function of the Hill Areas Committee shows that the HAC is a powerful instrument to safeguard the tribal interests and promote good governance and developmental process in the Hill Areas. However, it is necessary to examine how far the HAC has been able to protect the tribal interests.

6. The Problems of Administration

We ought to examine whether the governance of the tribal hill areas through the district administration and the general policy of the state are able to fulfill the aspirations of the people to lead a decent and dignified livelihood. How far the people's democratic aspirations are met by the laws and the working ofthe administration? There are certain issues and apprehensions felt and expressed by the tribal people.

1. The first issue is the question of autonomy in district administration. As per the directive principles of state policy of the Constitution, one aim of the Indian state to provide the self governing or autonomous institutions for administration. The Panchayati Raj Act has been introduced in the country including the

valley of Manipur. For the last forty years there has been a continuous demand for the introduction of VI Schedule Autonomous District Councils. The Government's response was the rejection of VI Schedule and introduction of the Manipur Hill Areas District Council, Act 1971. The demand for the VI Schedule was scuttled due to a strong anti VI Schedule lobby in Manipur and in the Government of India. As the 1972 District Council Act was rejected by the hill people, a new law entitled the Manipur Hill Area Autonomous District Council Act, 2000 was enacted by the Assembly. The Act has provided autonomy to the District Council by way of legislative and executive power with 29 subjects enumerated in the 73rd Amendment of the Constitution. But this important law was silently repealed by the Government of Manipur in March, 2006. The Act of 1971 which was repealed by the Act of 2000 has now been revived. But we are aware that the Act of 1971 was a useless law. It is a mockery of autonomy. Whether VI Schedule or the Act of 2000, the people have to decide.

2. The problem of Village Administration

The tribal people live in the villages. The concept of the village as the administrative, social, cultural and development unit is built into the traditional tribal polity. The existing Village Authority Act is simply inadequate and it suffers from many defects. Empowerment of the people at the village level is a basic feature of the Indian democracy. The Hill Areas of Manipur require an appropriate legislation for village administration such a law would have the following objectives:

(i) to provide local level administration in the villages

(ii) to make the village as an administrative, developmental and judicial unit

(iii) to empower the people in the development activities in the village

Such a law shall cover the judicial administration as per customary laws, the security of the people of the village, supervision and implementation of rural and tribal development programme, the supervision over the functioning of the schools, public works, public health and drinking water, rural electrification, collection of house tax and other dues payable to the state, the participation in the revenue administration, regulation of Jhum cultivation, maintenance of environment and ecological balance and management of forests.

It should be a purely democratic body. The feudalistic element in the Village Act of 1956 should be eliminated. The village authority should be renamed the Village Council.

It is suggested that the statutory Village Council Act should replace the Village Authority Act of 1956. We may also consider the establishment of village development board as it is functioning in the state of Nagaland.

3. The Manipur Land Revenue and Land Reform Act vis-a-vis the Revenue Administration

The greatest fear and apprehension in the mind of the tribal people with regard to the revenue administration in their area is the question of the introduction of the Manipur Land Reform and Land Revenue Act, 1960. The framers of the Act wanted the law to be confined to the valley district where there was an age-old revenue system. The Act does not extend to the hill areas. However, surreptiously this Act was introduced in the plain areas of the hill districts. In those areas, the lands were surveyed by the settlement department, the record of land rights was prepared, pattas were issued to the land owner, revenue were assessed and collected. There was an open attempt to extend the Act in the hill areas in the

6th Ammendment Bill of 1989. There is a strong demand among the valley based leaders to introduce the Act in the hills. The HAC stood firmly against this.

At the same time, there is equally strong opposition to the introduction of the law from amongst the tribal communities.

There is a strong lobby in the valley of Manipur and in the Revenue Department to introduce this law to the hill areas inspite of the clearcut statement that it is not applicable to hill areas. There is a feeling of mistrust. The tribal people are quite apprehensive of the outcome of the law.

The people and the legislators of the HAC in collaboration with the students organizations stand against the law. However, we have to understand that there is a need for a separate land law for the tribal in the hill areas.

4. The Development Administration

As stated in above paragraphs, the agencies of development administration in the hills are the office of the Deputy Commissioner, the District Rural Development Agency (DRDA) and other district level offices. But there is no District Planning Committee, which is provided to the Zilla Parishads under the Panchayati Raj Act. The tribal development programme under the Tribal Sub Plan has been sabotaged. The administration has become ineffective and corrupt. In the name of democracy and intervention by the legislators and leaders of the ruling party intervened in the distribution of the development programme resulting into a very high level of politicization in the administration. There is also interference from the insurgents in form of demands for large sum of money and share in the contract supply works of the engineering departments.

5. Problem of Absenteeism

Non-availability of the government employees in the

district administrative offices is a well known phenomenon. Every government employee wants posting in the urban areas, at least the headquarter and avoids the rural postings. It has led to the internal collapse of the administrative functioning. Vigilance of people on the working of the administration is needed to ensure an efficient and transparence governance.

Conclusion

This is a brief account of the evolution of the administration in tribal areas of Manipur and also problems of administration. On the one hand, the democratic aspirations of the people are rising but on the other hand, the working of the administration is weak and fails to meet the aspiration of the people.

We have seen that the tribals have their own traditional polity which was not destroyed by the rulers of the Pre-colonial and Colonial period.' But the state of Manipur after independence, had diluted the traditional system by the introduction of new laws and legislation for administration of the villages and the districts. The system of administration in the hills is the typical Indian pattern of administration. This system has eroded the traditional tribal system. They faile' to provide a viable democratic alternative. The tribal aspirations for autonomy has been scuttled and sabotaged. The tribals are facing a great danger of losing their own lands if the MLR and LR Act is indiscriminately and surreptiously enforced on the hill area. The Forest Act and Rules have destroyed the traditional ownership of land and forest. There is a need for a separate land law for the hills safeguarding the Tribal interest.

The tribals want freedom, progress and enlightenment. But with their land resources being alienated, where will they survive?

REFERENCES

Administration Report, Autonomous District Council in the Hill Areas of Manipur (1975-76).

Draft Eleventh Five Year Plan (2007-2012) Proposals. Department of Planning, Manipur, March 2007.

Gangmumei Kamei, *History of Manipur: Precolonial Period.* New Delhi 1991.

Gangmumei Kamei, *Problems of Development of Tribal Areas of Manipur in* M. Horam (Ed) *The Rising Manipur*, New Delhi.

Gangmumei Kamei, Village Administration in the Hill Areas of Manipur. *In Ethnicity and Social Change*, Imphal, 2002.

John Shakespeare, *Manipur under Direct British Management*, Shillong, 1907.

Ksh, Bimola Devi, Administrative Changes in the Hill Areas of Manipur in M. Horam (Ed) *The Rising Manipur*, New Delhi.

Lal Dena, The Constitution 73rd Ammendment Act, 1992. Vis-a-vis The Hill Areas of Manipur in M. Horam (Ed) *The Rising Manipur*, New Delhi.

Manipur Hill Areas Autonomous District Council Act,2000 (since repealed in 2006).

N, Joykumar Singh, *From Feudalism to Democracy.* Spectrum, Delhi/Guwahati, 2004.

P, Binodini Devi, *Tribal Land System of Manipur*, Centre for Manipur Studies, Manipur University and Akansha Publishing House, New Delhi, 2006.

Rajendra Kshetri, *District Council in Manipur: Formation and Functioning*, Centre for Manipur Studies, Manipur University and Akansha Publishing House, 2006, New Delhi.

Robert Reid, *History of Areas Bordering Assam*, Shillong, 1942.

Statistical Abstract, Manipur, 2005. Directoriate of Economics and Statistics. Government of Manipur, 2006.

Shyamkanhai, *Manipurgi Leingaklon Amasung Leingak Pathapki Itihas* (in Manipuri) Volume I and II.

The Census of India, 2001. The Schedule Tribes Tables for Manipur. Office of Registrar General, India

The Manipur Legislative Assembly (Hill Areas Committee) Order, 1972 published in Rules of Procedure and Conduct of Business of Manipur Legislative Assembly, 8th Edn. Imphal–2005.

PART-III

HUMAN RIGHTS AND DEVELOPMENT

13

The Rights of Indigenous Peoples

The United Nations through the International Labour Organisation (ILO) had organised two conventions on the indigenous and tribal peoples. Convention No.107 of ILO in 1957 was for the protection and integration of indigenous and other tribal population in independent countries. And ILO convention No. 163 of 1989 dealt with the indigenous and tribal peoples in independent countries and emphasized the viability and distinctiveness of the tribal and indigenous social entity. In other words, this ILO convention recognised the tribal and indigenous social entity. "tribal" is used to subsume the indigenous also. In case of the tribals, the ILO uses the term "people" (tribal people), whereas in the earlier document, in the case of indigenous, they use the term population (Indigenous Population). The "indigenous population" is used to mean the Amerindians of the two Americas, the Aborigines of Australia, Maoris of New Zealand and the other peoples of the Pacific region.

Who are the Indigenous People? The UN's view

The indigenous people means the original inhabitants of a country or a geographical region. The UN does not give any formal definition of the term "indigenous population or people". But they have a working definition. There is a background to the evolution of this working definition. In 1972, the UN Sub-Commission on Prevention of Discrimination and Protection of Minorities appointed Martinez Cobo, a Cuban, as its Special Rapporteur. The Sub-Commission was entrusted to look into the problems of the indigenous pebple. Cobo did not submit any report for 10 years. But in 1982, the UN General Assembly, decided to declare the year 1992 as the Year of Columbus to mark 500th year of the discovery of America by Christopher Columbus. It was opposed by the Amerindians and the African states on the ground that Columbus's discovery of America was the beginning of colonialism in modern times. As a soothing measure, the year 1993 was proposed as the year of World's Indigenous Population. Martinez Cobo suddenly submitted a report in 1983 which was actually written by one UN staff officer named A.D.Diaz of Guatemala. According to the report of Cobo, "the indigenous population are composed of the existing descendents of the people who inhabited the present territory of a country wholly or partially at the time when the persons of different culture of ethnic origin arrived there from other parts of the world, overcome them and by conquest, settlement or other means, reduced them to non-dominant or colonial situation". This working definition is never accepted as the official definition of the indigenous people by the UN. But selfidentification of a group as indigenous has been given overriding importance. The working group keeps the issue an open one. It has been used widely in all UN documents including the Declaration of the Rights of the Indigenous Peoples.

The Indian view

India was a signatory to the ILO Convention of 1957 and 1989. She was represented by her accredited representatives in the various. conferences organised by the UN bodies on Indigenous and Tribal peoples, including UN

Working Group on Indigenous Peoples. The Government of India in the begining does not accept the concept of the "Indigenous People" in the Indian situation. And she has made it very clear in several pronouncements. But the unofficial views are different. The Indian Council of Indigenous and Tribal Peoples (ICITP) which represents Indian indigenous people in the UN Working Group conferences, claims that the tribals of India are the indigenous people. The Council organised a national symposium on "Who are the Indigenous People?" in April, 1992 which declared in a statement by Ram Dayal Munda, a member of the Presidium of the Council, that Scheduled Tribes are indigenous people. The statement also pointed out that the Scheduled Tribe Commission (U.N. Dhebar Commission, 1960) describes the Scheduled Tribes as indigen.ous people. The World Bank unilaterally recognised the Scheduled Tribes as Indigenous People, which was condemred as a transgression on Indian sovereignty. Several Indian social scientists and thinkers express their opinion on the issue: We may note the opinion of a leading social scientist, Professor B.K. Roy Burman who observes, "without foreclosing the rights of others many tribal communities can also be considered as indigenous in the sense of their being relatively more committed to ecological ethics, more guided by the historical ethical sanction in their social relation than by the coercive power of the state, more sensitive to the muse of nature than to the guile of mammon, even more in harmony with their social self than is the case with the atomised individual of sophisticated society". He pleaded that the "Government of India could have accepted the Scheduled Tribes as a special category of indigenous people". We may remember that the criteria of "geographical isolation, distinctive culture, primitive traits, shyness of contact with other communities and economic backwardness' is a hall mark of the Scheduled Tribes.

The Government of India sponsored a massive International Meet on Tribal and Analogous People in

November, 1993 as a part of the International Year of World's Indigenous People. The determinant factor is the colonial conquest; in that many tribals in India will be indigenous.

International Year of World's Indigenous People

The observance of 1993 as the International Year of World's Indigenous Peoples was the outcome of a long process of consultation between the UN Working Group and different organisations of the indigenous peoples. In the late 1970's the World Council of Indigenous people (WCIP) had been raising the various problems of the Amerindians. The UN accorded observer status to WCIP. In 1982 the UN Economic and Social Council authorized the Human Rights Commission to establish a Working Group of Indigenous Peoples to review "the development, promotion and protection of human rights and freedom of the indigenous people and to give special attention to the evolution of standard concerning the rights of the indigenous people." In 1983, the Cobo report expanded the scope of the concept. "Indigenous" to cover isolated and marginal population in other parts of the world. In 1985, the UN General Assembly created a voluntary Fund to assist the spokesmen of the indigenous people to attend the annual meeting convened by the UN Working Group. The Working Group consisted of one representative each from Africa, Eastern Europe, Latin America and Western Europe and others like USA, Canada, Australia and New Zealand. Asia with 80% of world's indigenous peoples was represented by one member, first a Chinese and then a Japanese.

Asia Indigenous People's Pact (AIPP)

Something should be mentioned about the AIPP which is an organisation of 16 indigenous groups from Asia based in Thailand. This Pact asserted and highlighted the plight of the Asia's indigenous people. They also spoke out against the European domination over the Working Group and neglect of the Asian indigenous people. They published books, pamphlets and tracts on the Asian indigenous people. The conference of the AIPP at Chiangmai on May 18 to 23 1993 was a great landmark in the movement of the indigenous peoples. The Naga People's Movement for Human Rights played a significant role in the Pact. They among other things recommended to the UN that thei International Year of World's Indigenous people be extended to International Decade of World's Indigenous peoples 1994 to 2004, to formalize the UN Working Group on Indigenous Peoples as a permanent UN body, appoint an indigenous person to be a Special Rapporteur under Human Righis Commission, demanded an active consideration of the United Nations. The conference also made a Declaration on the rights of the Asian Indigenous and Tribal peoples.

The Issues Focussed during the Year

On December 10, 1992 Dr. Boutrous Boutrous Ghali, Secretary General of the Unia! Nations, declared 1993 as the International Year of the Indigenous People. The motto was "Indigenous Peoples: A New Partnership." The issues to be highlighted on the problem of the indigenous pertain to the following:

1. Land
2. Self Government and Self Development
3. Resources
4. Environment
5. Culture, Language and Education
6. Health
7. Human Rights
8. Social and Economic condition

These issues were discussed to make the indigenous people and the states aware of the indigenous peoples and their problems.

The Draft Declaration of the Rights of the Indigenous Peoples

The Draft Declaration on the Rights of the Indigenous Peoples was drafted in 1992 by the UN Working Group. However pursuant to the resolution of the UN Sub-Cornrnission on Human Rights, Ms. Erica Irene Diaz, Chairperson-Chief Rapporteur of the Working Group, a former Greek foreign minister, submitted a revised draft in 1993 which was ultimately adopted by the Sub-Commission in August, 1994. It was further submitted to the UN Human Rights Commission which resolved in March, 1995 to establish an inter-governmental working group on the subject. International diplomacy, the vested interests of the European and the American nations, the pressures of the African, Asian and the Pacific indigenous groups had gone into the drafting and adoption of the Declaration. Now a permanent UN Working Group on Indigenous Peoples has been established.

Issues of the Draft Declaration

The Draft Declaration contains a 19-paragraphs Preamble and forty five articles grouped into nine Parts as given below:

Part I Individual and collective rights and the right to self-determination.

Part II Right to life, sources of livelihood and identity maintenance.

Part III Cultural rights.

Part IV Educational rights of the children and some more cultural rights.

Part V Discretionary right to participate in the decision making process.

Part VI Territorial rights to land, land based resources and ecological rights.

Part VII Customary rights about self-governance structure.

Part VIII Rights to financial and technical assistance from the states, and to political, economic, social and cultural development through international cooperation.

Part IX Reaffirm the sanctity of the UN Charter, gender equality and further elaboration of rights.

The rights of the Indigenous Peoples have been applauded and criticized. But due to UN efforts the indigenous peoples have been accroded due importance. The member states of the UN had finally adopted his Declaration in 2007. The text is given in the Appendix of the book.

Protection of Human Rights of the Indigenous People in India

The indigenous and tribal peoples of India have increasingly become aware of the global attention on them due to the International Year of the Indigenous Peoples in 1993. The term Indigenous and Tribal peoples has been widely used despite the Government of India's reluctance to recognise this term. It is hoped, good sense will prevail on the Indian government. India with her 67 million indigenous and tribal population should play an active role on the problem of the indigenous people. They should be given more representation in the Working group or any other agency of the U.N.

Constitutionally, all the citizens of India including the indigenous and tribal peoples have been entitled to fundamental rights and freedoms. The national policy is to uplift the tribals of the country who are officially called the Scheduled Tribes. But due to various social, economic and political reasons, the tribes of India have been exploited by the more advanced sections and capitalist forces. This fact was admitted by various statutory commissions and committees which scrutinized, examined and criticized the working of the policy, and recommended corrective measures. Howeverl it is unfortunate to note that the observations and reconu:nendations of the various commission and committees constituted by the government, have not been taken seriously. The tribes are not satisfied with their own plight. Hence several social and political movements for autonomy and self-government have been going on. Fulfilment of the ethnic political aspirations is the springboard for securing the basic human rights and freedoms.

The right to seif-determination for the indigenous and tribal peoples has become a subject of intense debate in India which is a direct fallout of the International Year of the Indigenous Peoples. The right to selfdetermination is a universal and moral right. The existing UN Charter and Universal Declaration of Human Rights including several UN pronouncements recognize the right to self-determination. Though India accepts the right to self-determination as a principle, she is against the right to secede from the Indian union.

On the issue of violation of human rights the indigenous and tribal peoples, are against all forms of encroachment on the human rights and fundamental freedoms of any people in any part of the world. In India, there are strong human right groups including some indigenous groups which fight to protect the human rights of the people including the indigenous and tribals in insurgency prone areas. The Indian judiciary is playing a great role in protecting human rights and freedoms. But,the indigenous people do not have the resources or access to seek legal redressal of their grievances.

The government-sponsored National Human Rights Commission has started functioning. The awareness among the indigenous peoples and support from stronger human rights groups are necessary. There are strong demands for the withdrawal of draconian laws effecting human rights, introduced to keep law and order. The Armed Forces Special Powers Act which gives stringent powers to the security forces to deal with the rebels and insurgents has been misused and should be withdrawn.

There are also strong protest movements against the alienation of tribal lands and displacement of tribal and indigenous lands due to the construction of big dams which led to inundation of large tracts of tribal and indigenous lands. Two cases in point are the Narmada Bachao Andolan against. the Sardar Sarovar Project in western India and the Loktak Project Ithai Barrage in North Eastern India. The tribal and indigenous lands, their livelihood and their lifestyle should not be destroyed in the name of development and modernisation, The environment of the indigenous peoples habitat should be protected.

In order to ensure human rights and freedoms of the indigenous people, there is a need for awareness among the people themselves and intervention from the UN. We support the proposal for a permanent UN body for the Indigenous Peoples and for the continuance of the Working Group with a broad based representation of the indigenous peoples. Such action and mechanism will ensure the protection and promotion of the human rights and freedoms of the indigenous peoples.

14

Human Rights in India

The Eternal Struggle

"A large part of history is replete with struggle for human rights, an eternal struggle in which a final victory can never be won. But to tire in that struggle would mean ruin of society... These human rights are nowadays recognised, although by abundant use of formalistic legal maneuver, they are being violated to a much greater extent than a generation ago." This statement of Albert Einstein made in 1954 still holds true for the human rights scenario in India.

The National Responsibility

India as a nation has a deep commitment to fundamental human rights and also has a strong national responsibility to protect the human rights of its citizens. India has a long tradition of championing human rights throughout the world. It is rooted in her glorious national liberation struggle which endeavoured to achieve national independence based on freedom and democracy. The leaders of the national movement were influenced by the liberal principles of right to life, liberty and equality of men. The Indian National Congress after the infamous Jalianwalla Bagh massacre (1917) strongly protested against the draconian Rowllatt Act which deprived the people of their civil rights. The Congress in its Bombay Session (1918) demanded a bill of rights for the Indian people which was further reiterated in Nehru Report (1928) which was restated in its Karachi Session (1929). Gandhiji declared in the Round Table Conference (1931) that his aim was to establish a political society in India in which there would be no distinction between high class and low class people, that women should enjoy the same rights as men; and dignity and justice, social, economic and political, would be ensured to the teeming millions of Indians. He demanded that the constitutional reforms contemplated by the Simon Commission should incorporate the bill of rights. But the British government rejected such a proposal and as such it was not incorporated in-the Government of India Act, 1935. The demand for human rights was a part of the national struggle for freedom.

During the post-Second World War period, the ideals of the United Nations (1945) influenced and inspired the Indian national leaders. The first statutory step for securing human rights and freedom to the citizens of the country was taken by the Constituent Assembly when it adopted the Objective Resolution moved by the interim Prime Minister, Pandit Jawaharlal Nehru, on January, 22, 1947 which is extracted below:

"This Constituent Assembly declares its firm and solemn resolve to proclaim India as an Independent Sovereign Republic and to draw up for future governance, a Constitution wherein shall be guaranteed and secured to all people of India, Justice, social, economic and political; equality of status of opportunity and before law; freedom of thought, expression, belie£, faith, worship, vocation, association and action, subject to law and public morality."

The human rights stated in the Objective Resolution was reflected in the Preamble of the Constitution of India adopted in 1949 and in the Fundamental Rights and the Directives

Principles of State Policy in Part III and Part IV of the Constitution. India had formulated the concept of human rights and freedoms during the period 1946-49 which were quite in advance of other countries. The constitutional guarantee is a national commitment and an expression of the national responsibility to protect human rights of its citizens.

India and International Covenants on Human Rights

The foundation of the United Nations in 1945 was followed by the independence of India (1947) which opened up the process of decolonisation in Asia and Africa. India in the euphoria of her national independence became an inspired member of the UN whose ideals for protection of rights of man, both the people and the individuals, were shared by India. The UN adopted the following International Instruments of Human Rights.

1. The Universal Declaration of Human Rights with 30 articles was adopted by the UN on December 10, 1948. India with other member states was a signatory to the Declaration. (Vide Resolution No. 217 A (Ill) of December 10, 1948)
2. The United Nations adopted the International Covenant on Civil and Political Rights with 53 Articles on Dec. 16, 1966 which was enforceable in 1966 (Vide No. 2200A (XXI) of Dee. 16, 1966)
3. The UN also adopted the International Covenant on Economic, Social and Cultural Rights, December 16, 1966.
4. Optional Protocol to International Covenant on Civil and Political Rights was adopted on Dec. 16, 1966.

India had ratified the International Covenant on Civil and Political Rights on 10th April, 1979. However, she has not ratified the Optional ICCPR Protocol to which enables the Human Rights Committee set up under the Covenant to receive and consider communications from individuals claiming to be victims of human rights violations. India as per Art. 51 (C) of the Constitution is bound to 'foster respect for international law and treaty obligations in the dealings of organised peoples with one another.'

The constitutional guarantee of the fundamental rights and commitments to International Covenants have been reinforced by a sta tute known as the Protection of Human Rights Act, 1993 which takes cognizance of 'Treaties and other international instruments on human rights' which means by definition the International Covenant on Civil and Political Rights and the International Covenant on Social, Economic and Cultural Rights adopted by the UN General Assembly on 16th December, 1966.

The Human Rights

Neither the United Nations Charter nor the Universal Declaration of Human Rights gives a definition of Human Rights. The Declaration mentions "the equal and inalienable rights of all members of the human family". The Constitution of India does not define it though fundamental rights and duties are enumerated. However, according to the Protection of Human Rights Act, 1993, "human rights mean the rights relating to ,life, liberty, equality and dignity of the individual guaranteed by the Constitution or embodied in the International Covenants which are enforceable by the courts in India." D.D. Basu puts forth a definition thus: "Human rights are those minimal rights which every individual must have against the state by virtue of his being a member of the human family, irrespective of any other consideration." The human rights are deduced from natural rights created by men before the emergence of the political society; and fundamental rights are the basic human rights guaranteed by the fundamental law of the land. The human rights have two aspects:

1. The Social and Economic rights of the citizens are to be protected by the state as a duty toward its citizens:
2. The Civil and Political rights which are the sine quo non of the human rights, are rights of the individuals against the state which it has to guarantee.

The first group of social, economic and cultural rights is incorporated as the Directive Principles of State Policy of the Indian Constitution while the civil and political rights are guaranteed and secured not by an ordinary law but by the fundamental law of the land, namely the Constitution, enforceable against the state by the courts. Thus Fundamental Rights are limitation on the legislative and executive power of the state. In European and international context, both fundamental rights and fundamental freedoms are used in juxtaposition. Fundamental freedoms have been mentioned in the Universal Declaration and the International Covenants as follows:

i. Freedom of movement

ii. Freedom of thought, conscience and religion

iii. Freedom of expression

iv) Freedom of peaceable assembly

v. Freedom of association

vi. Freedom of residence

vii) Freedom from slavery or servitude

viii. Freedom from subjection to torture

ix. Freedom from hunger

Indian Constitution Art. 19 provides for right to freedoms, which are under six categories in number, namely, (i) freedom of speech and expression, (ii) peaceable assembly, (iii) association, (iv) movement, (v) residence, (vi) profession of busmess. Freedom of religion is put under a separate head.

Human rights which are approved by the UN Covenants and declarations are twenty-two in number, namely, Right to life, Right to human dignity, Right to recognition as a person before the law, Right to equality, equal protection before the law and non discrimination, Right to personal liberty, Right against torture, cruel, inhuman or degrading treatment or punishment, Freedom from slavery, forced or compulsory labour, Right to privacy, Right to fair trial, Right against ex post facto criminal law, Right against self inclination, Freedom of thought, conscience and religion, Freedom of expression, Freedom of assembly, Freedom of assembly, association, movement and residence, Right to property, Right to family, Rights of the child, Right to education, Right to work, Right to effectively remedy for the enforcement of the rights and freedoms.

The Indian Constitution groups the Fundamental Rights under six sub heads:

I. Right to equality

II. Right to freedom

III. Right against exploitation

IV. Right to freedom of religion

V. Cultural and Educational Rights

VI. Right to constitutional remedies

The enumerated individual rights or natural rights have been further recognised by the Supreme Court of India by applying the theory of emanation as Fundamental Rights. They are given below:

I. The Right to privacy

II. The Right to human dignity

III. The Right to travel abroad

IV. The Right against torture, cruel, unsual punishment or degrading treatment.

V. The Right to speedy trial

VI. The Right to free legal aid in criminal trial

VII. The Right against delayed execution

VIII. The Right against custodial violence

IX. The Right to shelter, doctor's assistance, the right to health

X. The Right to a pollution free environment

XI. The Right to education of a child until he attains the age of fourteen

XII. The freedom of press

The above rights are to be guaranteed and protected by the state in India. Do the citizens really enjoy them or are they within the reach of the common men?

Threats to Human Rights

Despite the high sounding constitutional obligations, democracy in India suffers from serious social and economic inequalities among her varied population. The Indian political and economic system has been dominated by the upper castes and classes of the feudal and capitalist groups who control the Indian state. The gap between the rich and poor has been widened; the deprived sections and minorities, both religious and ethnic, have resorted to democratic movements to improve their lot. There are violent and armed struggles in different parts of the country, the communist rebellions, ethnic insurgencies in the north east, secessionist movement in the north west, the Naxalites in middle India. These are both protest reaction against the hegemonic and chauvinistic actions of the state on the behest of the ruling classes which control it. The state, despite its high sounding human rights and freedom, has been using the colonial laws devised to suppress a colonial people in the name of keeping law and order, using police, paramilitary and armed forces to control and suppress the popular movements, social protest of a free' people in free and democratic India. Security of the state is the prime concern and not the security of the people. The wielders of the democratic political system are all from the upper castes and class. Every protest movement is in most cases viewed with suspicion and regarded as an attempt to destabilize their poor base and a conspiracy against the security of the state. The most traumatic and terrible encroachment on human ricrhts and civil liberties was the imposition of the Emergency in June, 1975 by a Presidential Proclamation and the consequent suppression of all political dissent. Jai Prakash Narain led the movement against the tyranny of the state. After the election of 1977, the Congress party was defeated and Mrs. Gandhi was ousted. Whatever she made in the form of constitutional amendments destroying the fundamental rights have been restored. The Emergency created an awareness among the free thinkers and lovers of freedom and democracy in the country to organise human rights groups for the protection of civil liberties of Indian people. There are still threats to freedom and human rights in India. Among the human rights groups, we must mention the People's Union of Civil Liberties (FUCL) founded by Jai Prakash Narain in 1976. PUCL guided by fearless members of the Bar and Bench is most extensh'e and involved national level human rights group. The Citizen for Democracy (CFD) is another organisation. In the north east, the Civil Liberties and Human Rights Organisation (CLAHRO) and Committee for Human Rights (COHR) and the Naga People's Movement for Human Rights (N~HMR) are in the forefront in the movement. The press, mostly the regional and Indian language, has been playing a very effective role in exposing the excesses of the police and state terrorism as a whole

Role of Indian Judiciary

The Supreme Court of India and many High courts in the States have through various pronouncements come out to protect the human rights of the people of India. The Social Action Litigation (SAL) or sometimes known as the Public Interest Litigation have been very successfully utilized as a strategy against encroachment on human rights. The Supreme Court had ordered that a simple letter addressed to the Chief Justice from an aggrieved person can be accepted as a writ petition; the same facility is extended to the High courts. Many cases have been settled at the intervention of the Judiciary. The Supreme Court has effectively used the power of Judicial Review to checkmate and correct the legislative and executive encroachment on human rights. The Judiciary alone cannot bear the burden. It requires an enlightened legislature and committed executive to protect the citizen's basic rights.

Human Rights Commission (HRC)

The national responsibility for protection of human rights has been the adoption of the Protection of Human Rights Act,1993 which provides for the establishment of a National Human Rights Commission and the State level Human Rights Commissions. The Act empowered the HRC to act as judicial bodies. And human rights courts will be established at the district levels. The Act enjoins upon HRC to protect human rights. However, the HRC has only recommendatory powers. The National Human Rights Commission was perhaps initially established to give a good international image for India as a reply to foreign propaganda. But the NHRC has proved to be effective in its functions. The human rights commissions have been established in many States.

National Agenda for Human Rights against State Terrorism

Unless the draconian laws operating are removed, there is no guarantee for the protection of human rights. These laws promote state terrorism in the name of fighting the insurgency and terrorists in various parts of the country or the cross border terrorism. A democracy cannot allow the violation of human rights of its own citizens by its own soldiers and policemen.

The rights of the deprived sections of the society, the backwards and weaker sections, the ethnic and religious minorities and women are to be protected.

If a national agenda for the protection of human rights against state terrorism is adopted by the government and the political parties ruling them and the Indian civil society at large, there is hope for freedom in this great country. It is in this context that, as Einstein said, the eternal struggle for human rights must continue.

15

Education in North East India: Problems of Democratization

Pre-Colonial Educational System

Education in the pre-colonial period had feudal character. The traditional education system was exclusively for the production of a priestly class which was utilized by the rulers to perpetuate their rule. The Ahom rulers, the Meitei kings, the Kachari and Tripura Rajas patronised learned people. The royal patronage to education, religion and literature was not open to everybody as education was restricted to the priestly class; the Hindu Brahmins, the Ahom Deodhais and Bailung, the Maichous of Manipur. The royal patronage succeeded in building up a rich tradition of scholarship in the field of religion, literature and history. The services of these priest-scholars were utilized by the state for religious, literary and administrative works. The ultimate objective of the royal patronage was the strengthening of the monarchy and perpetuation of the ruling dynasties. The members of the royalty and the feudal nobility were imparted education by the priest-scholars, but there Was no regular educational institution. This restricted the educational opportunity and deprived the masses of access to knowledge and learning. The Vaishnavite Satras of Assam which were established by Sankara Deva were the great centres of learning, education, religious and social activjties of the common people. The Sa tra may be regarded as the first step in taking education to the masses. The mosques provided informal educaiion to the Muslims. The Hinduized Ahoms introduced Some "Gurukulas" for the Brahmin students. In Manipur, the Maichous, the priest-scholars imparted learning to the royal princes, sons of nobility and some selected commoners in their respective residences. Among the tribal people who inhabit in hilly tracts of the eastern Himalayas, the traditional education was imparted through their dormitories, in the form of training in martial arts and welfare, handicrafts, creative arts, custom and tradition, morality and discipline. The objective of the traditional and tribal education was to produce an all rounder individual, a tribal warrior, a committed member of the village community with full knowledge of the creative arts, dance and music, well versed in the tradition and folklore of his tribe, clan and village. In other words, education was a life long continuing process in tribal society. Thus, in the traditional society, despite the absence of literacy, the social and moral fibre of the people was sustained.

Education During the Colonial Period

The introduction of western education during the early colonial period was a result of the acceptance and adoption of '"welfare" as a responsibility of the state, by the colonial government under the influence of the Utilitarian philosophy. The British conquest of the northeast India coincided with the formulation of an educational policy and decision by the government of the East India Company to introduce English education in India. The administrators sent to manage the affairs of the eastern frontier were people who were wedded to this ideology and adopted paternalism as the guiding principle of their administration. In the nineteenth century, education had become a 'social right' of the subject peoples; and the Government of India both at the centre and provinces created departments of education. Greatly influenced by the European ideas of civilizing the Asiatics, as one of the goals of imperialism, Christian evangelism was a collorary to the British colonial rule. Both the government and the Christian missionaries whose aim was to civilize the natives by converting them to Christianity took up the onerous task of spreading education among the subject peoples in North East and elsewhere. The English education was designed to inculcate the European liberal ideas, literature and science in the Indian mind, and at the same time towroduce educated persons who could be employed conveniently to run the colonial administration on the other hand, the Christian missionaries wanted to train up Christian workers from amongst the indigenous people to spread minimum literary knowledge that the people could read or understand the Bible and related literatures.

Western education was a gift and instrument of the British colonial rule whose original objectives of administration were to maintain law and order, collect revenue and adjudicate disputes among the subject people. In the North East, education was spread by three agencies: the Christian missionaries; the provincial government and the private social services bodies. The American Baptist missionaries worked in Upper Assam, in Sibsagar and among the Nagas while the Welsh mission worked among the Khasis, Garos and in Darang and Nowgong, later on the missionaries spread their activities to Manipur and Mizoram. The Government of Assam, under the inspiring leadership of dedicated administrators like David Scott, Francis Jenkins and others opened educational institutions, mostly primary schools. But it was after the famous Wood's Dispatch of 1854, that the government started grant-in-aids to the schools started with the initiative of the people. Since 1854, the new private venture schools came up and sought grants from the government. The successive chief commissioners of Assam took a special care for the promotion for education and Gauhati became the centre of western education in the region.

In the colonial period, education was theoretically made open to everybody. However, the progress of education was very slow as the sponsoring agencies did not have enough resources at their command to run the schools. But in the second half of the nineteenth century and early part of the twentieth century, the enlightened leaders of the Brahmaputra valley gradually started influencing the government in quickening the pace of educational development in Assam, starting with Gauhati Seminary to Cotton College (1901). In Manipur, western education was introduced on the initiative of the British Political Agents. It started with Nathall (1872) who started a school; Johnstone (1885) also started a school. Later on the American Baptist missionary Rev. William Pettigrew who worked in Manipur (1892-1930) started founding schools. He was the pioneer of western education in Manipur. Watkin Roberts, with his Indo-Burma Thadou Kuki Pioneer Mission worked in south Manipur Hills. Rev. Clarke was the pioneer educationist among the Nagas. Savidge and Lorrian were the pioneers in Mizoram. One should remember the royal patronage to education in the princely states of Manipur and Tripura in the Northeast and the role of the nationalist leaders of the region for spread of education among the masses.

During this period, one notices the failure or irrelevance of the traditional education system to meet the new requirement of the new regime. Yet the traditional system, especially Sanskrit education, though incorporated in the new curricula, continued to exist for the propagation of Hinduism. At the end of the colonial rule, the Northeast region made some progress in western education. A new class of English educated elite emerged; middle class emerged inAssam and Manipur. Importance of western education was well accepted as key to modernization. Education became a key determinant of wealth, status and power. And education was accepted as an instrument for economic growth, as a means to improve the quality of life, to enhance human resources, and to create new knowledge, new technology and new ways of-managing the resources.

Educational Problems of the Region

There has been a tremendous expansion of education since India's independence in 1947, at all levels, primary, secondary, higher and professional education due to the great boost given by the national government. With quantitative expansion of education came the problem of quality, standard of education, management, resource availability, contents of education. The Government of India appointed several educational commissions to examine the problem and suggest remedies. This great expansion of education was possible due to the universalization of education as a national goal. As education was for many years a state subject in Indian constitution, the responsibility of educational administration was vested in the state governments. Therefore, it was really difficult to evolve a uniform national education policy and common education system. At the same time, the cultural and linguistic character of the Indian states which were founded mostly on the basis of languages, later on ethnic and historical consideration influenced the state government to evolve education system to suit the ethos of their linguistic aspirations. During the Post independence period, along with the attempts to evolve a national education system, the Indian education assumed a regional character which was accentuated by regionalist interests and requirements. Therefore, the Indian education has become a series of educational systems with varying capabilities, policies and output.

In the North East, education assumed different patterns; and language or the medium of instruction was an important criteria in the fashioning of this pattern. In Assam, Assamese is the medium of instruction as it is the official language; the Bengali is the medium in Bengali inhabited state of Tripura and Cachar district of Assam whereas English continues to be medium in the hill states and it is Hindi in Arunachal Pradesh and Manipuri in Manipur.

The great expansion of education in the region after independence is symbolised by the establishment of Gauhati University in 1948, followed by the Universities at Dibugarh, Jorhat, Shillong, Manipur, Nagaland, Tripura,Silchar, Arunachal Pradesh and Tezpur. Gauhati, Shillong and Imphal have become three main centres of higher education. Gauhati is the greatest centre of learning. Shillong has been described as the "Mecca" of western education. Imphal with her rich cultural background and the establishment of the University, is becoming an important centre of higher education in the North East.

The central government, after the inclusion of education in the Concurrent List of the Constitution, has moved into educational field. During this period, education was imparted by the state government, central government in the Union Territories (now states of Manipur, Tripura, Mizoram and Arunachal Pradesh), the private organization, mostly the mission schools and colleges and the private venture schools. The efforts of the R.K. Mission in the education field cannot be expanded. Along with the maximum growth, many problems have come into the picture.

(1) Non-availability of enough financial resources for education is the greatest problem. At the same time, there are disparities in resources availability between different sectors. While the central government through the North East Council have given funds extravagantly to the centrally sponsored institutions, other state sponsored institutions are

not properly financed though they are discharging similar tasks.

(2) Lack of uniform and socially relevant curriculum in schools, colleges and universities has been a weakness of education in this region. The recent vigorous implementation of NCERT course and UGC guidelines on higher education in the introduction to three years degree course and rationalization of syllabi in the university provide the silver lining in this not so happy situation. The role of the State Boards of Secondary Education has to be commended in this aspect.

(3) Teaching profession has not been able to attract competent and qualified talents. Non-availability of qualified teachers in the higher levels of education has been major problems of education in all states of this region. The incentives to higher and additional degrees has given some encouragement to in service teachers. At the same time, better qualified teachers are attracted by the metropolitan universities and institutions.

(4) Extraordinary expansion of education has led to the increase of enrolment in the colleges and universities. The graduates produced by the universities cannot get employment in the region. There is no correlation between manpower recruitment and the production of graduates.

(5) Facilities for scientific and technical studies are limited. The medical, engineering and agriculture colleges and universities have not been able to meet the great rush for admission to their courses.

(6) The examination system in this region is not uniform and has been a subject matter of much criticism.

(7) Issues of medium of instruction in the schools, colleges and universities are also a problem. While in the primary level, the mother tongue is the best medium of instruction; in the secondary level, the regional languages. There is no problem for Assamese, Bengali, Manipuri, Hindi and some developed tribal languages like Khasi, Mizo and Garo: But there are manv tribal communities whose languages have not attained a high level of development. They have to adopt either a regional language or Hindi or English. For them and in the Universities, English should continue to be medium of the instruction. English cannot be easily replaced in the hill areas of this region.

(8) There are great variations in the level of literacy in different parts of this region. Mizoram is the highest and is above the national average, whereas Arunachal Pradesh and some hill districts of Nagaland, Assam and Manipur are very low.

(9) The tribal population of this region continues to suffer from economic, social and educational disabilities despite the large scale incentives given to the scheduled tribes students and tribal areas.

Problems of Democratization

India as a democratic, secular and socialist country guarantees freedom and equality to her citizens. As education is the key to the success of a democracy, there is a movement to democratize education which has been a populist slogan and used in loose terms, though not well defined, has come to mean the process of providing equal educational opportunities to all sections of the population of a democratic state, and the democratic management of a socially relevant and egalitarian education system for promoting among other things, a democratic way of life. It has two implications, the preparation of the people to inculcate and practice social democracy in all aspects of life, and the application of democratic principle in the management of the educational institutions ranging from the primary to the universities. However, it must be admitted that the translation of this ideal into reality in the Indian situation is a difficult and extremely slow process.

Despite the lack of conceptual clarity on the part of the policy planners and decision makers, one can discern, the process of democratization has been initiated in the region through several educational legislations adopted by the state legislatures and implemented through different agencies of the government. Democratization of education for the masses is to implement the universalization of education for the masses. Primary education has become free in the whole region; secondary education is highly subsidized and in the hill states, for the tribes education is free from primary to secondary except in colleges and professional colleges; where fees are reimbursed by the state government by way of scholarships. With the massive expansion of secondary education, there is always a great rush for entry into the colleges and universities which have introduced diverse courses in liberal arts and science, technical and scientific education and professional studies. Secondary education has been supervised by the State Boards of Secondary Education and the higher education is academically administered by the universities in this region. School curriculum and university syllabi have been rationalized and updated according to the guidelines provided by the NCERT and the UGC. Attempts were made to provide infrastructure in the schools and colleges, to improve the social and economic status of the teachers by giving incentives in form of revised pay scales, fellowship and advanced increments for more qualified teachers. Provisions for hostel facilities for colleges and to some extent for the schools have been made. Medium of instruction has been either the mother tongue or regional language or Hindi or English. Education has developed both quantitatively and to some extent qualitatively in the professional colleges and universities. Adult and Continuing Education Programmes have been taken up to erase illiteracy and provide non-formal education to the masses. Education for women and weaker sections including the physically handicapped and the blind has been provided. Inner democracy or semblance of it has been introduced in the management of the aided schools and colleges. The universities are given statutory autonomy.

The rosy picture of the democratization of education is one sided and mostly on paper or in the well written programmes of the governments of the region. But the social realities are quite different, there are several gaps in this process of democratization.

(1) Democratization is associated with the politicization of education. Democratization is coterminus with politicization. As state governments provide funds for the establishment and maintenance of educational institutions, both government and private aided, and appoint teachers, the political leaders, mostly the members of legislatures control the allocation of resources, implementation of educational programmes with an eye to retaining their influnce and strengthening their political base.

As the ruling party always tries to promote their own vested interests, this high level of politicization in the development administration including education has led to highly partisan politics in educational administration.

(2) Extreme poverty of the people, both in plains of Assam and the hill areas has been the major cause of slow progress of education. The poor parents

cannot send their children to the schools as they cannot maintain them as education is still costly. The children are employed by the poor parents in other productive economic activities, thus depriving their opportunities to get at least school education. On the other hand, the educational opportunities have been taken advantage of by the children of the rich parents. The rich send their children to English medium schools and private managed mission schools while the poor children have to be content with the government run schools. There is also great imbalance between the urban and rural areas including hills in the educational opportunities and facilities. This disparity would favour the rich children with better education. And they continue to control the political power, man the state bureaucracy and industrial establishments. If there is to be real democratization of education, this wide gap between these two classes has to be narrowed down. But a serious question has been raised that in the Indian social situation where there is both social hierarchy based on caste and economic status there cannot be a democratic education in the true sense of the term.

(3) The state has controlled financially and administratively the schools and colleges established by the government or by the private agencies. In the government schools and colleges which are administered by the state bureaucracy, there is no question of democracy in management. The aided institutions have to please the whims and wishes of the state educational bureaucracy and the political power wielders.

(4) In the institutions run and managed by the Christian missions and private agencies, there is no

internal democracy as the management is controlled by the Church or by the private body.

Though they give good education, commercialization of education is not conducive to the employees. Perhaps in their system efficiency i;s not sacrificed for democracy.

(5) With so much of financial dependence on the governments, the autonomy of the universities has become an academic issue only. The inner democracy of the universities depends on the policy of the state education. Luckily, in the universities of the region, there has been comparatively some respect for the university autonomy. It is due to the reluctance of the state governments rather than their lack of power to control over the universities. There is a great disparity between the funding of the universities between the central universities and state universities. This disparity has to be removed if a healthy university education is to grow in this region.

(6) The scheduled tribes have been benefited by the facilities provided by the government and a tribal elite consisting of bureaucrats, technocrats, contractors, businessmen and politicians has emerged. This elite has taken the lion share of the government facilities in education, and poorer sections of the tribals have been deprived the access to good education. While the kinship base of the tribal society is still strong, the stratification of the tribal society on economic status has created an incipient class distinction between the different sections of the tribal population. So education has gradually encroached upon the egalitarianism of the tribal society. The misguided democratization of education

has now threatened the social democracy of the tribal people.

Despite these gaps, education is so important for the survival of democracy that we cannot go back from the democratizing process of the national life. The New Education Policy, in spite of its deficiencies which will be rectified in due course, will go a long way in strengthening the educational base and promote a democratic ethos of our society.

16

Tribes of the North East India: A Historical Perspective

North East India is the most important tribal belt of the country. The great mountain ranges of the eastern Himalayas and its southern branches which form the great divide between South Asia and South East Asia, and three important river valleys, the Brahmaputra, the Imphal and the Barak, have for centuries, provided the physical ecology for the various ethnic groups who migrated to this region from the pre historic times down to the present day. The fertile river valleys are the cradles of human civilization where the migrating and conquering ethnic groups including tribes, built up their own kingdoms and principalities. In the resultant process of migration and conquering was a part of the struggle for economic and social surivial and political domination, there were contacts between various ethnic groups resulting into integration and assimilation of their respective cultural traits. Yet despite the impact of the contact with Hindu kingdoms, the conquering Ahoms, the invading and migrating Muslims and the British colonial administration, the tribes, more or less have preserved their distinctive identity.

The tribal people of the Northeast. India are referred to in the classical Indian literatures as the Kiratas. They are the Indo-Mongoloids divided ethnically and linguistically into

Austric, Tibeto Burman and Siamese Chinese who form a cultural bridge between India and South East Asia, Inner Asia and China. The Tibeto Burmans are the Bodos, the most numerous group including Dimasa, Kachari, Rabha, Mech, Tripuri and the Garos; the rest are Karbis, the Nagas, the Kuki-Chins including the Mizos and the tribes of Arunachal Pradesh like the Monpas, Daflas, Apatanis, the Adis, etc. There are several plain tribes in the Brahmaputra valley also. The representatives of the Austric are the Khasis including Jaintias who have linguistic affinity with the Nicobarese of Andaman and Nicobar, and with the Man and Mon-Khmer of South East Asia. The Siamese (Tai) speakers are the Khamti and Singphos tribes of Arunachal Pradesh who are the kith and kin of the Ahom- Tai of Upper Assam. There have been ethnic mixtures between the TIbeto-Burman and the Tais wherever they lived together either in Upper Brahmaputra valley or Manipur valley. The Indo-Aryans who migrated from the west to the Northeast India established political supremacy over the Brahmaputra valley, Hinduised the tribals wherever possible and ultimately forced the tribes to confine themselves in the interior regions of the Brahmaputra valley and the surrounding hills. The migration of the southern Mongoloids was tentatively proposed to be around 1000 B.C. But the pre-historic finds show that both paleolithic and neolithic culture existed in the Northeast. India which was one of the oldest habitats of men in the country.

Tribal States in Ancient and Medieval Period

It was in the Brahmaputra valley that the historical kingdoms grew up, the prominent being the kingdom of Pragjyotisha or Kamarupa. The first ruling dynasty belonged to the Bodo group. According to various texts, the Danava dynasty was founded by one Mairang or "Mahiranga" Danava, a non-Aryan chief. Mairang sanskritized into Maihiranga was a Bodo name. The Danavas were succeeded by another Mongoloid dynasty, Asuras who came under the influence of the Aryan religion. The founder of the Asura dynasty was a Mongoloid chief, Narakasura who was Aryanised and sanskritized later on; and all the ruling dynasties in Assam traced their descent from him. Besides Pragjyotisha, there were the kingdoms of Davaka (Nagaon), Manipur, Hidirnba and Tripura which were, except Manipur, Bodo principalities. After the downfall of the Hindu kingdom of Pragjoytisha or Kamarupa, petty tribal chiefdoms were established by the Barahis, the Chutiyas and the Kacharis who were all conquered by the new hordes of invading and migrating Ahorns from Upper Burma in the early mediaeval period. Only the Kacharis held out for a pretty long time. Another Hinduised kingdom of tribal origin was the Koch kingdom in western Assam or North Bengal which held sway over North East for sometime.

Meanwhile, the kingdoms of Manipur and Tripura emerged as powerful states by the 15!h century. The Kacharis were fighting for their survival against the Ahoms who established their political hegemony over the Brahmaputra valley by the 16th century. The Koch kingdom declined in due course and the two imperial powers, the Ahoms from the east and the Mughals from the west were locked into a protracted military conflict in the 17th century leading to the withdrawal of the Mughals from Assam. During the period, the principalities of Jaintia, Kachari, Tripura and Manipur remained intact and emerged more powerful. At the same time, the ruling families of these Mongoloid principalities were converted into Hinduism. The process of sanskritization was started giving a new dimension to the social and cultural development of the respective groups including the Ahoms who were also converted into the Sakta Hinduism. By the 18th century, next to the Ahom kingdom of Assam, Manipur was the most prominent state having conquered the upper Burma during the reign of Garibniwaz (1709-1748) who brought Hinduism to Manipur. The principality of Jaintia, of all the Khasi states, was emerging as a non-Hindu tribal state.

The kingdom of mpura had expanded while the Kacharis were under great pressure from the Ahoms.

With the decline of the Ahoms due to internal rebellions and civil war, and ultimately the Burmese invasions, the political fortunes of the tribal states were greatly affected. The Burmese conquest of the Northeast. India created a radical change in the political situation. The British conquest of the Northeast. India after the FIISt Anglo-Burmese war was a great landmark. And gradually the British were determined to occupy all the tribal areas of the region. Jaintia and Cachar were under the protection of East India Company. Tripura and Manipur were independent, Assam lost her independence.

There was, of course, strong resistance among the hill tribes to the British imperialism, starting with the Khasi rebellion under. U Tirot Singh and Sadiya uprising. But gradually the British captured the Khasi states which accepted the British paramountcy. Jaintia was annexed. Cachar Was annexed in 1832, Mattak and Moran in 1842, Upper Assam in 1838, North Cachar in 1854. Thus by the middle of the 19th century, all the tribal states were annexed into British India or brought under their paramountcy. Only Tripura maintained her independence. Though the established tribal kingdoms lost their status, a new phase in tribal history .of the Northeast. India started with the British penetration into tribal areas which were not earlier organized into principalities or states, though they had village level polity formation.

The Colonial Phase

After the British conquest, the hill tribes came under their colonial policy which aimed at the extension of the British empire, collection of revenues, maintenance of law and order, adjudication of disputes, exploitation of natural resources for capitalist enterprises, encouragement of Christian missions for proselytizing activities on the pretext of civilizing the tribal people and provision of some welfare services. The British were the heir to the previous governments. In the early phase they followed a policy of intervention, then a policy of non interference and later on a forward policy towards the hill tribes. They were either by design or circumstances, drawn into the conquest of the tribal territories. Though a personalised administration was at the ground levels, they curtailed their military feuds and raids, introduced payments of hill house taxes and exploited the natural resources especially the forest in the tribal areas.

The new British administration reduced the former tribal kingdoms into districts or smaller administrative units, destroying the political and social status of the traditional tribal rulers and the elite which supported them. At the same time, new tribes who were hitherto unadministered during the previous regime, were conquered and brought under regular administration. They started clubbing the tribes under major groups for administrative measures which produced both exogenous and endogenous impact on the tribes themselves. For the first time, the tribes were confronted with a technologically superior civilization which intended to enforce their standard law and administration, their ethical and moral values and to exploit the tribal natural wealth for their own benefit and profit. The tribal contact with the colonial administration was the beginning of their exposures to the outside world. At the same time, the colonial authorities took the burden of ensuring the moral welfare of the tribes which they called" civilizing mission". Even the nature of the ownership of land in the tribal areas was decided to suit the colonial interest or design to deal with chiefs rather than with the community or the clan.

The British relation with the hill tribes was conducted with the policy parameter mentioned above. The Khasi states with their political organization led by their Syiems were the first tribal group who resisted the British rule in North East. India. We have already referred to the Khasi Rebellion .(1829-31) under the leadership of U Tirot Singh, the Syiem of Nongkhlow which was aimed at the establishment of pan Khasi solidarity against imperialism and protect the Khasi land and independence. Though the rebellion was suppressed, the heroic struggle made the British recognize the Khasi Syiemship and made terms with them when the Khasi states accepted the British paramountcy which remained till their departure in 1947. Jaintia, a kindred tribe with monarchy was brought under the protection of the British Government. The Khasi and Jaintia states were put under the Khasi and Jaintia Hill District of Assam.

The Dimasa-Kacharis with their long history of independence in upper Assam, Maibong hills and Cachar plains with their capital at Khaspur, after the British conquest of the Northeast. India was split into plain Cachar and hill Cachar. The kingdom of Cachar was annexed by the British in 1832 and converted into the district of Cachar under one Superintendent and later on a Deputy Commissioner while the hill Cachar known as the North Cachar hills were put under the suzerainty of Tularam Senapati. In 1854, it was annexed into the British province of Assam. Thus the Kacharis lost their political status, they are now administratively confined to Maibong sub-division of the North Cachar Hill District, though some of them are scattered all over Assam.

The Garos who were the tribal group with whom, the British carne first into contact were gradually suppressed and constituted into the Garo hills district.

The most interesting tribal communities were the Nagas and the Mizos (formerly known as the Lushais) who were fiercely independent and warlike tribes with village level political organizations. They committed raids on the British territories since 1830s and the British were compelled to send in several military expeditions to the Naga Hills and later on the Lushai hills. The British policy of intervention and military control over the Naga Hills (at that time Angami and Zeme Nagas only) failed to curb the Naga raids nor maintain peace among warring Naga villages. Lord Dalhousie abandoned this policy and laid down the policy of non-interference which was followed from 1850 to 1865 but was replaced by a Forward policy. The Naga areas were constituted in 1866 into Naga Hills district with headquarters at Samaguiting (now Chumukidema) in 1877 and then shifted to Kohima, the heartland of the Angami Naga country in 1878. The British penetration under the Forward policy into Naga Hills was resisted in the form of the Naga Revolt of 1879-80 which was a serious attempt to push out the British. The revolt was suppressed with severity and since then the British gradually pushed into the interior and by the end of the 19th century, except the Tuensang area of the Konyaks, the Naga areas were brought under the regular administration. Hill house taxes and forced labour were introduced; headhunting was banned, Christian missions were sent into the hills, education was brought in. The British gave a common name to the Naga tribes. Nagaisation process was set rolling inadvertently with the British creation of the Naga identity. This process passed on to the tribes under control of the state of Manipur and Burma. Those who have affinity with the Naga tribes of Naga Hills were given a generic name "Naga" while other tribes who have affinity with Chins and Lushais were called "Kuki". From a conglomeration of tribes, speaking dialects unintelligible to each other, fighting among each other, the Nagas under the British rule, were brought under a common law and administration, and a sense of common ethnic identity was fostered. This was a remarkable outcome of the colonial rule.

Likewise, the Lushai raids led to the Lushai Hills Expedition in 1871-72 and ultimately, the Lushai Hills were conquered and constituted into the Lushai Hills District in 1896 under the province of Assam. The British adopted the Chin Hills Regulation, 1896 and recognized the Lushai chiefs and an indirect rule was introduced in the district which is now state of Mizoram. General administration and political control were exercised by the British Superintendent leaving all the village level administration including land ownership to the chief who administered the customary laws. Christian mission spread education among the Mizos, technological change came, and peace and order was maintained. The British rule produced a common identity for the Mizo people by means of the linguistic affinity and common administration. It is a unique instance of the emergence of a marginal nationality.

However the Kukis, highly dispersed tribes in the Northeast India, were originally pushed out of Mizoram by the Lushais. They made an exodus into neighbouring Tripura, Manipur and Assam where they were settled by the ruling kings on the advice of the British Political Agents. They cooperated with the host states, but they were new migrants who had occupied the lands of the indigenous Naga tribes or other communities and tension also existed. After the British conquest of Manipur, Kukis made an attempt to forge themselves into a formidable political force. They revolted in 1917-19, The Rebellion was suppressed but the British followed a lenient policy towards them. They were used by the colonial authorities as deterents on the Naga tribesmen.

Manipur hill tribes who had an autonomous status during the precolonial period under the kings of Manipur were polarised into Nagas and Kukis by the British administrators. After British conquest of Manipur, the tribes were brought under a common administrative system which was separated from the administration of the valley of Manipur inhabited by the Hindu Meiteis. The British followed a policy of protection of the hill tribes from oppression and exploitation of the plainsmen and Maharaja of Manipur, a policy which was resented by the Maharaja of Manipur. But this policy however did not easily win over the tribes who were to pay taxes to the British while they paid nothing to the Manipur Maharaja.

The tribes of Arunachal Pradesh were free people in the literal sense both during the Ahom rule and early British rule in Assam. Only the consideration of the British hegemony over Tibet and peace in the foothills made the British to make an attempt to exercise loose political control by sending out occasional expeditions being the Anglo-Adi conflict, know as Abor War in 1911.These tribes were brought under the Balipara Frontier Tract and Sadiya Frontier Tract which were later *on* combined ihto North Eastern Frontier Agency (NEFA), now Arunachal Pradesh.

The Emerging Pattern

While the hill tribes were conscious *of* the freedom struggle going on the plains of India, they did not fully participate in the movement. The Kuki Rebellion was an anti imperial movement, so also the rebellion of Jadonang and Rani Gaidinliu (1930-32). Jadonang and Rani Gaidinliu's movement was inspired by Mahatma Gandhi and the Congress nationalist movement; they confined themselves to the Zeliangrong people against the British authorities. This movement had in this sense a national dimension. But most of the tribes who were kept under the excluded or semi excluded area knew that the British were going one day and they wanted to be left out of the control of the plains meaning Assam and Manipur government. The great example is the memorandum submitted by the Naga club of Kohima in 1929 to the Indian Statutory Commission for making the Naga free when the India became independent. The failure of the National liberation struggle to penetrate into the tribal areas of North East is one of the contributing factors to the lack of understanding in the post independence period.

However, the world events like the First and Second World Wars affected the interior hills of the region. During the First World War, the tribal labourers from the Northeast were sent to Europe. This was the first opening for the tribal to the outside world. Northeast India was, as a whole affected by the Japanese invasion along with INA of Netaji Sub has Chandra Bose of the eastern frontier in Mizoram, Manipur and Nagaland. This was a rude shaking up of the isolated life of the Nagas, Mizos, Kukis and Meiteis of the region. Second World War brought foreign soldiers, machines and commodities from different parts of the World to the region. The ravages of the war, the experience of the tribal contact with the foreigners (including Phizo's and Koireng Singh's association with INA and Netaji Subhas Chandra Bose) and common suffering unleashed powerful force which influenced the future of the tribes of the Northeast India. It also hastened the freedom of India, and in this quick change which overtook them, the tribes were greatly concerned for their political future.

On the eve of India's independence, there were a number of proposals for the future political and administrative system of the Northeast India. The hill tribes were affected. The Naga National Council raised the demand for independence. The Shillong based Khasi and Garo leaders raised the demand for a hill state to be carved out of Assam hills. Tribes of Manipur and Tripura did not raise separate demands for their future and they were involved in the politics of the two princely states. Mizos were inspired to raise the demand for independence but they were fully involved in the democratic movement for the abolition of Lushai chiefship.

The Constituent Assembly of India was aware of these ethnic aspirations of the tribes of Assam hills and devised the district level autonomy in the Sixth schedule of the Indian Constitution. The Assam hill leaders accepted it while the Nagas rejected it though the basic points pertaining to land and natural resources, customary laws and judicial process incorporated in their 9-points agreement were incorporated in the Sixth Schedule of Indian Constitution. The Naga National Council revolted in 1956 for an independent Nagaland. The rebellion was serious and assumed international dimension while countries unfriendly to India gave help to the Naga insurgent. In the face of Naga rebellion, the Government of India, under the personal initiative of Pandit Jawaharlal Nehru created the state of Nagaland in 1963, a homeland for the Nagas in India. Now the Nagas have fully participated in the democratic process of the country. Mizos also revolted in 1966 for secession from India. The demand for the state for Assam hills, Tripura, Manipur and Mizoram continued. Ultimately, statehood was granted to Manipur, Tripura, Meghalaya, Arunachal Pradesh aild Mizoram. The Mizo Revolt was solved by the Mizo Accord between the Mizo National Front of Lal Denga and the Government of India.

During the post independence period, through trial and error, the Government of India have devised autonomy both the district level and state level to fulfil the aspirations of the tribes of the region who had tasted the fruits of democracy, participated in the political life of the country and in the process of nation building tasks of their respective states. Economic development, education, new technology, new found political and civic rights have made the tribes march towards modernization: They had become more conscious of their rights over their land, their traditional social institutions. It is satisfying to see that in the tribal states of the Northeast, the tribals are now well protected. But in the non-tribal majority states of Assam, Tripura and Manipur tribal struggle for autonomy either in the form of separate states or autonomy state within a state continues.

Perspective for the Future

If the past is any indication, there will be a more intense struggle for the control of the natural resources of the tribal areas between the indigenous tribes on the one hand, and the state or monopoly, both tribal and non-tribal capitalist interests. The best example is in Manipur hills and Tripura. In Manipur, the tribes are demanding the VIth Schedule district autonomy and are opposed to the introduction of the Manipur Land Revenue and Reforms Act, 1960 which they fear, will alienate the tribal lands. The demand for the autonomous state in North Cachar Hills and KarbiAnglong, the Bodoland and the continuing Naga and Meitei insurgency, the Zomi integration movement show that the tribes who are suffering from deprivation due to neglect and exploitation by the vested interests, in most cases, the capitalist forces, and the state are asserting their own right to protect their lands, culture, language and economy by raising demand for autonomy. The existing district level autonomy under the VI Schedule is not adequate to meet the tribal aspiration. The autonomous district Council in Tripura does not deter the Tripuri secessionist movement.

The reorganization of the states in tribal and hill areas of the Northeast will open the Pandora box of ethnic and community conflicts in the region. States of Uttranchal, Chhatisgarh and Jharkhand had been created. But the basic question is the tribal rights of self management of their resources and their participation in the development programme are to be fully acknowledged and implemented. India has to accommodate the aspiration of the tribes of the Northeast India to strengthen the Indian nationhood.

17

Historical Ecology and Technological Development in Manipur

Ecology is the study of the interrelationship between organisms and their environment. Ecology deals with the symbiotic relation between man and his environment which consists of physical situations like the mountains, rivers, flora and fauna including forests and the animal kingdom of birds and animals which pertain to man's struggle for survival and his utilization of the resources of nature for his needs. Historical ecology therefore, means the change and transformation in the eco-system of a geographical region or a biosphere over a length of time or centuries. Historical ecology deals with time and space. It includes the human or social environment, man's continuous encroachment on nature and the environment. Human ecology consists of the human "calling", which according to B.K. Roy Burman, "is a continuous negotiation between the man in his biosphere limitation and the man in his multi hued communion with his surroundings." Thus, historical ecology is concerned with the geological and tectonic history of an eco-system, its geographical features like mountain and river system and forests in terms of their classification and typology and man's encroachment on the eco-system for fulfilling his needs to survive and to be prosperous by exploiting the environment, thus creating disturbances in the system. Ecology also naturally covers human settlement, economic activities and social environment, migration of people and development of long distance trade providing opportunities for culture contact and transfer of technology from one region to the other.

Geographical Setting

The mountain state of Manipur has a, total area of 22,329 Sq. Km. The land mass of Manipur constitutes 0.68 percent of the geographical area and 0.19 percent of the population of India.

Geographically, Manipur is divided into two main relief features, the oval shaped central plain at an elevation of 792.4 mtr. (2600 ft.) above the sea level and the surrounding mountains which cover the 92 percent of the total geographical area of Manipur. Imphal is the capital of Manipur.

The Mountain System of Manipur

The mountain system of Manipur belongs to the eastern Himalayan system. Mount Zapvo, a peak of Barail range in Nagaland cuts a knot from where the mountain ranges branch off in different directions. These mountain ranges are young in age, highly folded and faulted. These hill ranges run from north to south with occasional spurs and ridges. The general aspects of the hill ranges is that of irregular serrated ridges, occasionally rising to conical peaks and flattened cliffs of bare rock. From Cachar to Imphal valley, there are five hill ranges, the Nunjaibund or Vangai range, Kala Naga or Oinamlong range, Chakha-Nungba range, Khoupum range and Kaubru Laimaton Range. The Old Cachar Road, the New Cachar Road and several trade routes pass through the western hills of Manipur.

In the north, there is the highest peak in Manipur, Essau (Tenipu) Peak (9824 ft.) to the west of Mao, from there a range comes down to Karong and then another range, Koubru-Laimaton range runs south to Churachandpur district to Kailam. In the east, there are the ranges from Seramati Peak running southward along the Indo Burma border across Somerah,Kasom, Mapithel and Yamadung and Chin Hills. The drainge of this areas falls into the Chindwin-Irrawaddy rivers. In the central plain, there are few hill ranges, like, Langol hills, Nongmaiching, Langathel, Waithou, Karang, Thanga islets within the Loktak lake.

The big rivers. in the western part, are the Barak, Irang, Makru and Ijei running from north to south and flow into Cachar and to Surma and the Brahmaputra. The Tuivai flows into the Barak while the Khuga flows into the Loktak system and Manipur River.

In the Imphal valley, the rivers are the Imphal Iril, Thoubal and Nambul. Iril and Imphal join at Lilong to become Manipur river and flows through a deep gorge called Chingnunghut to Chindwin and to the Irrawaddy. The Chakpi flows into Manipur River.

Geological Formation

The geological and tectonic history of Manipur can be understood as a part of the geological evolution of the Northeast India as an unit. This region includes the Himalayas of Arunachal Pradesh and its branches along the Indo-Burma border in Nagaland, Manipur, Mizoram, Tripura and the plateau of Meghalaya and the river valleys in this region. This region has the oldest crystalline rocks of the Meghalaya plateau to the youngest alluvium in the river valleys. It is presumed by the geologists that "there existed a shallow sea called the Tethys which provided a geosyclinioal environment in this part of the world during the Lower Paleaozoic and Mesozoic periods. However, the Shillong plateau of Meghalaya remained a land mass since Precambrian times. It consists mainly of granite and guess in the northern part, and is overlain by quartezite, phyllites, epideorites etc. of the Shillong groups of rocks in the southern part. On southern fringe of the plateau, volcanic rocks and cretaceous tertiary sedimentary rocks occur.

The Tethys continued to receive sediments eroded from the Archaean rocks during Paleaozoic and Mosozaic period.

"During the Cretaceaus period (60 to 110 m.y.) the Northeast India underwent erogenic movement caused by geodynamic forces. The long accumulated sediments on the floor of the Tethys were deformed as ridges and basins. This caused appearance of land on the one hand and deepening of parts of the Tethys on the other... The erogenic earth movement producing tectonic highlands, ridges and basins were followed by periods of quiesance, prolonged erosion and deposition of an enormous scale sediments were deposited in the shrinking geosynclinal shelf or newly formed lakes and lagoons". It is pointed out that the oldest rocks found in eastern Manipur belong to Cretaceous group, including shales, slates, siltstones and quartzits. This area experienced serpentine rocks. And the serpentine rocks are younger than Cretaceous. The rock types in the area are shales, mudstones and sandstones and of the Disang series.

It is said that the stratigraphy of Manipur is better understood from the Eocene period (40 to 60 m.y.) The Cretaceous formation are overlain by lower Tertiary formation belonging to Eocene period. In Chandel district, the sedimentary rocks to the west and north west of the region belong to Disang series. The Disang and Jaintia series are overlain by the Barail series which occupy the large part of Assam, Nagaland and Manipur. The Barail series consists of considerable tracts of Manipur north, Manipur east and Manipur south. In Tamenglong area, the rock types are the shale sand stones of Barail series.

The Surma and Tlpam groups of rocks belong to Meocene period (13 to 25 m.y.). The Dihing and Dupi Tilla groups belong to the Piocene (1 to 12 m. y.). The most recent forma lions belong to Pleistocene period. In Manipur, the central Imphal valley and Khoupum valley are example of high level flood plain. The formation of the central plain according to E.W. Dun was due to a stream blocked by some convulsion of nature. But the popular notion is that the plain was formed as a result of a lake being filled by river borne sediments. But the geologists explain that the plain was formed due to the uplift in the southern mountain which led to the reversal of the drainage system and impounding of water in the area where we have the lakes and swamps.

Forests

The entire forests of Manipur are included in the Himalayan system. There are different criteria of classification of forest. It is suggested that altitude is an ecological factor in classifying the various vegetational zones of region, namely, Sub-montane, Montane or Temperate zone, Sub-Alpine zone and Alpine zone. S.C. Sinha classifies the forests of Manipur in the major groups, i.e., Tropical, Montane, Sub-Tropical and Montane Temperate. Classification may be made on the basis of forest species.

Tropical Forest

1. Tropical wet evergreen forests: The tropical climate forest prevails in the valley and foothills to an altitude of 900 m. in Tamenglong, Jiri, Moreh and Kabaw valley forests are Tropical forests.
2. Moist mixed forests in western Manipur.
3. Bamboo forests are mostly found in west, south and south east Manipur and central plains.
4. Cane.

5. Grass land vegetation.
6. Swamp vegeation.
7. Sub-Tropical wet hill forests-in Langol, Koubru and Nongmaiching.
8. Sub-Tropical pine Forest in Ukhrul and Chandel.
9. Montane Wet Temperate Forests are found in the higher hills, 1800 m. in Koubru, Mao and Sirhoi.

The forests of Manipur are great natural resources of the state. R.B. Pemberton (1835) was amazed by the richness of Manipur forests. He wrote, "The surrounding mountains in most instances, covered with the noblest varieties of trees common to both tropical and colder climate. I know no spot in India which products of the forests are more varied and magnificent but their utility is entirely local, as the nature of the country precludes the possibility of transporting to foreign markets. The valley itself is practically free of forests though every village is surrounded by a grove of forest trees." Half a century later, EW. Dun in 1886 recorded almost the same plentiful forests. He described the forests thus: " The whole of the hill ranges lying between the valley of Cachar and valley of Manipur are densely clothed to their summits with tree jungles. Almost the only exception to this has been hill slopes facing Manipur valley. These slopes have been steadily cleared of their timber and present a denuded appearance. The tree forests present a great variety and in the ranges lying west of Manipur valley there are ranges of forest of trees comprising Nagesor, Jarul, India rubber, Oak etc...Bamboo is plentiful between Cachar and Manipur.

"In Yomadung range bordering Burma the jungle is more open. Very large trees are rare. Fir trees are occasionally seen. The tea plant is found in the range. Teak is common in the areas overlooking Kabaw valley. The Jiri forest and forest close to the valley were utilized. From the hills to the south of the valley timber" was obtained. Fir, Pine, U-Ningthou, Apricot were available in Somrah basin." Dun also noticed effects of the climatic change on forest, agricultural practice, village settlement and housing technology. He writes, "The climate, at once rainy and temperate, covers the hills in the western pottion with thick forests and induces the inhabitants to grow rice, causes numerous rivers, streams and marshes and encourage aquatic and water loving plants. Forest in the east is not so thick as in the west. Oaks replace bamboo, firs for nagesor, a drier climate produced a lighted and different kind of jungles .The villages in the valley are situated near banks of rivers or edge of the lakes so that every household has some water near it. Every house stands in almost an acre of land which the owner surrounds with mud wall and forth plants on interior fence of cactus, bamboo, plantain, babool and other. The houses are constructed of that, wood and bamboos. Poor houses are made of bamboo and thatch only." (Dun, Gazetteer of Manipur, 1886).

F. Kingdon Ward, the famous plant hunter in his **The Plant Hunter in Manipur,** (1958) has stated that Manipur is a part of the monsoon belt of Southeast Asia and naturally is included in the eco-system of forests of Southeast Asia. He also points out that the flora of Manipur has been identified with the flora of Assam hills and with southern hills (Manipur and Nagaland with Burma and Malaya) . He writes, "Some ten thousand years ago, the climate of Manipur, as of all eastern India was far more colder than it is today. The vegetation must have been different; no less so the flora. Another result of the constant wear and tear on the earth's crust of the heaving and squeezing, uplifting and sagging of the rocks is not only the gradual isolation of areas mountain types of example, but also the building of new line of communication between areas long divorced." According to his surmise, ten thousand years ago, the flora of whole northern hemisphere was still struggling in the grip of the ice age during which the Himalayas were heavily iced and glaciers were formed. This led to the migration of the northern flora to the south. Luckier plants went down to the plains and survived. Manipur during the ice age was ringed by ice. Manipur must have been sterile at the time of maximum glaciation. And when the Sino Himalayan ice cap vanished, the flora of Manipur was isolated on the tops of the mountains. According to Ward, "Long ago, Manipur was almost completely steriled. The problem was simple, it had no flora at all. It had been driven by the cold. As the climate improved, plant refugees began to return to their old homes from the deep valleys and plains. These established themselves, multiplied until Manipur became a part of Indo-Malaysia flora whence the bulk of its population was derived... In fact, the positions of Manipur, in the midst of a glaciated mountains and astride one of the glaciated escape routes was peculiarly favourable for receiving contribution of flora from all directions."

Human Settlement: Growth of Technology

Several archeological finds lead to the conclusion that there are some traces of Paleolithic and Neolithic culture in Manipur. Manipur was one of the routes between the South Asia and South East Asia and Central Asia. So various ethnic groups belonging to southern Mongoloid group, the Tibeto-Burman and the Indo-Aryans and a sizeable section of Tai and Shan came to Manipur from the pre-historic times down to the present day. The present ethnic groups of Manipur, namely, the Meiteis, the Naga tribes, Kuki-Chin tribes and other Indian communities are descendents of these migrating people. The Manipur valley is a very fertile area with heavy concentration of population that provided the ecological setting to build up civilization. It is clearly shown by the archeological evidences that these people lived first in the hills and gradually came down to settle in the valley of Manipur. These migrating people brought with them varying degrees of technology ranging from the old stone age rough stone tools to more refined Neolithic tools and potteries. With the coming of metal tools mostly bronze, copper and tin during the historical period from Thailand and Upper Burma cultural zone, the civilization of Manipur developed.

The chronicles of Manipur and the Meitei literary texts record the traditions of the discovery of paddy, invention of agriculture, practice of shifting agriculture, development of bronze and iron technology, mostly in making of daos, hoe axe and later on spade for agricultural purposes and later on spears, utensils and other implements including coinage made of bell metal. There was introduction of the transplantation of paddy by the Muslim migrants in the 17th century. Manipur is well known for her weaving designs during different periods of history. This transfer of technology of Manipur was possible due to the long distance trade between Manipur and neighbouring countries and Manipur was and is still one of the active trade routes between India, Southeast Asia, Tibet and China.

Long Distance.Trade and Technology

It is recorded in Greek, Latin and Chinese sources that there was trade between Northeast India and Roman world and between China and Roman empire. This trade intercourse was maintained through land routes across the mountain ranges between eastern India and Upper Burma, two of which were through Manipur hills. A French historian suggests that the route must have been by the Burma Road. Manipuri chronicles record the trade behveen Manipur and Yunan province of China in 1630 A.D. as the Chinese merchants visited the kingdom of Manipur and the art of making gunpowder was imparted to the artisans of Manipur. This caravan trade between Manipur and Yunan continued annually till 1813. Trade with Burma continued throughout nineteenth and twentieth centuries. In the ancient times, the Periplus of the Erythrean Sea record that Tezpat (Malabathrum) was sold by a tribe called Besate to the traders who brought it to south India and transported it to Rome. It is clear that Manipur was in constant trade with the Chinese, Burmese, Shan/Tai and other Indians. The trade contact, culture contact and migration into Manipur resulted in the introduction of new technology adopted by the people of Manipur.

For example, the bell metal gong and other bronze implements were imported from Upper Burma and Thailand. Iron technology was developed quite late in Manipur and was centered around Kakching. A culture hero is said to have gone to Tripura in search of tools and material for making of iron in Manipur. As stated above gunpowder and gun making were learnt from the Chinese and Burmese Shans. The tribes used the iron implements, like dao, hoe, spear etc. which were imported. For example, the hoe, the most important agricultural implement of the tribes and the spade used by the Meiteis were perhaps brought from the Upper Burma. Spade and plough were brought from India. The agriculture technology was improved when the Muslim peastant migrants introduced transplantation of seedling in cultivation of paddy.

The handloom industry appears to be an indigenous one. Spinning, weaving, dyeing were fairly developed in ancient times. Silk industry was perhaps learnt from the Chinese artisans who were settled in Kabaw valley. Silkworm rearing was indigenous industry practiced by the Meitei artisans who were descendents of Shan silk weavers of Kabaw valley who were absorbed in Meitei society. The silk industry of Phayeng and Khurkhul village shows the Shan legacy.

Housing Technology

There were three types of housing technology: one house structure constructed on flat ground of the Nagas, the stilt house of the KukiChin group and mud-house raised on foundation of the Meiteis. The chronicles record the construction of several storied royal houses. The use of brick in house construction was very rare. And it is said that the brick making was learnt from the Chinese. But the earliest brick structure in Manipur, the Vishnu Temple of Bishenpur (1474 A.D.) was perhaps made by artisans from Bengal origin or from lower Burma. The temples constructed in seventeenth to nineteenth centuries used bricks.

The houses in northern Tangkhul country are roofed with pieces of pine planks due to the availability of pine trees and absence of thatching grass. The Kukis of south west Manipur in the !rang and the Barak basin used leaves of canes and other creepers for roofing. The Meiteis of Imphal valley used a high quality thatch for roofing which lasts even thirty years.

Pottery was developed from early times. The Chakpas of Imphal valley are the best potters of Manipur. It is their traditional occupation. There was pottery developed among the Tangkhuls and the Poumai tribes also. The Neolithic site at Napachik produces interesting types of pottery like tripods, corded potsherds etc.

European Technology was imported in the nineteenth century especially, the military hardware. Manipur's failure to develop modem technology was one of the contributing factors of her loss of independence. But the British gradually introduced their tedmology in the nineteenth century. But it is to be stated that the technological development in Manipur in her long history was made possible due to trade contacts with the outside world and adoption of their technology by the local artisans under the supervision of the state. An example is the introduction of tannery and leather industry in Manipur. In the late nineteenth century, artisans were sent to Kanpur for undergoing training in tannery. These artisans met the state requirement for military use of leather, especially the cavalry. The royal workshop during the reign of Sir Chandrakriti Singh (1835-1844, 1850-1886) was a laboratory for experiments. Though European technology was used for the military hardware, Manipur could not develop her own modem industries in the pre-colonial period. After the British conquest in 1891 and fifty six years of foreign rule, Manipur started introducing or using European architecture with their house building technology. Aeroplane, gramophone, cinema, telephone were introduced. The Second World War in Manipur (1942-45) exposed Manipur to the latest modern technology, both military and non-military, and from this Manipur has not looked back in technological development. Hmvever in the second half of 20th century Manipur had entered the era of industrialization. Technology of different categories was developed.

18

The Tribal Land System: The Case of the Rongmei

The tribal land system assumes a great importance due to several reasons. The natural resources of the state, specially the vast land in the hills which constitute ten-eleventh of the total area of Manipur, the forest and the rivers and their basins are in the tribal areas of Manipur. The process of privatization of tribal land, either community and village lands or chiefs' lands is going on in full swing for development of wet rice cultivation, terrace cultivation, horticulture and forest plantations and commercial and administrative centres. There is no legislation for land tenure. There is a demand from the non-tribal political and social pressure groups to introduce the Manipur Land Reforms and Land Revenue Act, 1960 in the hill areas. There is a silent but firm resistance from the tribal communities. As an instrument of resistance, there is an attempt made by the tribal elite for the perpetuation of the rights of the chiefs, mostly Kuki-Chins, over lands, and the community and lineage rights over lands and forests to prevent the alienation of the tribal lands to the state. There is an increasing concern for the study of the tribal land tenure system. The common notion that among the Kuki-Chins, there is chiefs' ownership of village lands and among the Nagas there is community system of ownership requires empirical investigation. The Rongmei land system is a complex one, variations exist at the local level. There is a three-tier land ownership' system. The Rongmei are concentrated in Tamenglong District but they are scattered at Imphal valley, Cachar valley of Assam and Zaluke valley of Nagaland.

The Rongmeis live in the villages which were once described by McCulloch as "village republics". The Rongmei's attachment to his village and village lands is very strong. They are divided into four major clans: Kamei/Pamei, Gonmei/ Newmei, Rongmei and Gangmei.

The Rongmei village is well organised politically. But the polity is based on the land system. A Rongmei village is administered by a village council called the Pei. The Rongmei polity is a sort of gerontocracy (rule of elders). The Nampou, literally owner of the village, is theoretically the chief functionary of the village council. Other functionaries were the Namupou, a functionary in charge of agricultural rites, Rangteng Pammei, the head of the family in charge of village gate and Tingku or Taku, the priest. The members of the village council (Pei) are selected from the elders of the village from their age-grade organisations like, Banja, Gan-Chang, Khangbon etc. A traditional village has got the following functionaries:

1. Nampou : Owner or chief functionary of the village.
2. Nammu-Pou : Functionary in charge of agricultural rites.
3. Tingku : Priest.
4. Pei Kumei : Elders of the village council.
5. Changloi : Advisor-assistants.

But with the introduction of political control of Meitei kings the offices with Meitei names were introduced in the eighteenth century. They are the following:

1. Khunbu	:	Owner of the village. (Nampou)
2. Khullakpa	:	Administrator of the village.
3. Nammu	:	Functionary in charge of agricultural rites.
4. Luklakpa	:	Functionary assisting the Khullakpa.
5. Meitei Lambu	:	Functionary to deal with theMeitei/ Meitei kings.
6. Changloi	:	Advisor-assistant.

It may be noted that originally, the Nampou as the owner of the village as he was the first settler or from the first settler's family was the administrator. But when the office of the Khullakpa was introduced in most villages, the Nampou was made the Khullakpa. Since they were mostly old people with less capacity for mobility somebody was appointed Khullakpa and he was made Khunbu (owner of the village: Nampou). Thus the Nampou who could shoulder the responsibility of the Khullakpa was made Khunbu. The two officers in terms of social and ritual hierarchy are the same. They are normally addressed as the Khunbu-Khullakpa (owner and administrator of the village). But the office of the Khullakpa became more important in its relation with the government either Manipur king or the British ruler.'When the British administration was introduced in the twentieth century, they brought the concept of Headman of the village which was loosely termed Gaon Bura as in Assam hills and abbreviated to G.B. So the terms G.B., Khullakpa, Khunbu and Headman were very loosely used. In northern Rongmei country which was under the influence of the' Manipur Kings during the pre-British rule, the terms Khullakpa and Khunbu were adopted. With the introduction of Manipur Hill People's

Regulation 1947, the Khullakpa and Chief of villages were given a statutory position. The Khunbu and Gaon Bura are not accorded such a status. The village Authorities Act of 1956 made the Khullakpa the ex-officio Chairman of the village court known as the Village Authority. But the loose administration of the Government of Manipur did not care to examine the legal status of the village authorities and the government has given the same administrative responsibilities to the chairman of the village court who happens to be the Khullakpa of the village. The combination of the two roles in the single person has not been properly given a proper legal definition and delineation. So there are instances that those who are the Khullakpa who (as the ex-officio chairman of the village authority) claim the ownership of the village lands. Now in every Rongmei village, there are two administrative system: the traditional village council and statutory. The Village Authority has got the following functionaries:

1. Chairman (Khullakpa)
2. 5-12 members (According to the number of households)
3. Secretary.

The traditional village Council as mentioned earlier still exists. This has produced a great constraint on the land system of the Rongmeis.

Land Use Pattern

The lands in a Rongmei Village are classified according to the pattern of its utilization. Every village has a community forest which is to be utilized by the village community or individuals for domestic consumption. Every village has a tree grove (Rambou) around a village which acts as a fire protection belt and some time the village gates which are usually fortified. are located in the grove. These community forests are not to be utilized for cultivation.

Jhumland

Other areas of the villages either belonging to the village or clan or individual Rampou are utilized for shifting cultivation. Shifting cultivation is a long process. The village council decides the location of the area for shifting cultivation in a particular area. The cycle of Jhum cultivation in Rongmei area varies from five to ten years. These Jhum fields are made out of the forest either of trees or bamboos or both which are cut down and burnt. And paddy and other crops are planted. After harvest, the land is again left fallow to be re-cultivated in the next cycle after 5 years or lesser period.

The Village Settlement

The site of the village is normally located on the hill tops on the consideration of defence strategy and healthy climate. There is an elaborate rite for the establishment of a Rongmei village. The first important step is the location of construction of the water pond or stream or spring to supply water to the village. The ceremony is called Duikhun Khumei, (excavation of the water pond). The gates of the village are to be raised in the northern and southern sides of village. The raising of gates is called Rangteng Pammei - (embracing the post of the village gates). Every year this ceremony is to be performed. The village should have a Shong (presiding deity) who has a sacred abode. The houses are constructed in rows with enough courtyards in between. The courtyard will have stone megaliths in memory of the dead ancestors or in commemoration of some worthy occasion like victory in raid, a ceremony etc. The Rongmeis have dormitories both for the boys and girls. The institution is still working in the tradition l Rongmei society. Nowadays there are schools, churches, community hall in the village, playgrounds for the young people. The village settlements which were in the past located on the top of hills have been shifted down on the roadside where easy means of transport is available. There is no more headhunting raid; as the government is able to provide security to them. Commercial activities are also increased by these settlements on the roadside. But the dignity and beauty of a Rongmei village have vanished in these stray roadside settlements.

The Rongmeis are now great orange growers and horticultural trees are planted near the homesteads. The trees planted are mostly citrus fruits. They have also started growing papaya, jackfruit, perkia, banana, pineapple. Permanent or semi-permanent farm is necessary for horticultural development. These activities are carried on by the individual families.

Wet Paddy Cultivable Land

The need for an increase in the productivity of the soil has led the Rongmeis to take to the terrace cultivation in spite of the stiff slope of their mountain country. The *river* valleys in the Rongmei area in the Ijei basin, the Leimatak basin, the Barak and Makru valleys and the Khoupum valley have provided enough land for the introduction of plough cultivation. This has led to the private cultivation of land holdings in Rongmei village to a certain extent.

Lrnd Ownership System

The land owning system among the Rongmeis varies from village to village. The system is much dependent on the history of settlement of the village whether it was settled by an adventurous individual or clan or was started by a group of clan or individual. In most cases it was a clan effort which settled a village and it would be naturally reflected in the ownership of the land in the village. Had it been the efforts of two or more clans, the same pattern would be reflected in its land system. This variation occurred in Rongmei village. Thus there are patterns of land system (1) Clan ownership (2) Single or multiple clan system and (3) Community ownership of land. Whatever may be the nature of the formation of the village there is a three-tier system of land use among the Rongmeis.

(1) Nampou	:	Owner of the village either clan or the village community land.
(2) Rampou	:	Intermediary owner of lands within the village land (may be individual families/lineages).
(3) Laopou/ Laophunpou	:	Holders (tillers) of plot of agricultural field.

Some case studies have revealed the variation. In some villages the three-tier system exists and functions even now. The Nampou or the owner of the village is the head of the settler's clan which founded the village. The lands are actually owned by the Rampous (owner of the land). There are several Rampous in a village. They may be individual families or clans. The possession of lands by the Rarnpou family was effected due to several reasons, sharing the land with the individual family, gifting the land or transfer for some financial reason etc. The Rampous give nominal rent to the Nampou. The actual tillers of the land are the Laopous/ Laophungpou the holders of the plots which are lent out by the Rampou. The Laopous give rent of a tin of paddy to the Rampou. The Laopous are actual possessors and they have possessory right though they do not have ownership right. The possessory right is inherited by the successors of the Laopou. The Rampous do not have the right to deprive the cultivator of the right to till the land. The village community, through the village council had overall control over the whole village land. The village council decides the regulation of the Jhum land. It supervises the collection of the rents, performance of the religious rites connected with agricultural production. Moreover, there is a community forest which is the village land.

There are villages which have only the Nampou (owner of the village) who is vested with ownership of the land. Here there is no Rampou but only Laopous who pay rent to the Nampou who is actually a functionary called Khullakpa. In such a case also the village council has the supervisory power of allocation of Jhum Land, collection of rent and performance of agricultural rites.

Now who is a Nampou ? The Nampouship is a hereditary office among the settler's clan (Nampou Khong). The Nampouship does not automatically pass on to his son but to the eldest member of the settlers clan. In Khoupum, for example, the Nampou is from the Rongmei clan which is the settler clan; the present Khullakpa is the eldest male member of the clan. He is also the ex-officio chairman of the Village Authority. After him, the Nampouship of Khoupum will pass on to the eldest member of his clan.

There are villages like Awangkhul where there is neither individual nor clan Nampou. As it will be indicated in the following case study, the village council representing the village community covering all the clans and individual families is the owner of the village. The administration is also very democratic. But in such a village where community ownership of the land exists the Rampouship also emerged as the village council (pei) transferred lands particularly forest land to individuals on payment of cash or kind to meet certain crisis in the village. But the Laopous are entitled to till the land as before. Very interesting phenomenon occurred in Awangkhul; 80 % of the land of Awangkhul is now transferred to the seven Rampous; 20 % of the land remains with the village council but the individual Laopous are given the same possessory rights over their fields. The terrace cultivation, wet paddy cultivation lands which fall within the lands of the Rampous are established by individuals and the Rampous do not object to it.

The minor forest produces are also extracted by the individual at free will. Some individual Rampous sold the right of the timber extraction to outside contractors. But recently, the village council and village authority have assumed the authority of selling the rights to extract timber and bamboo to forest contractors. The money received was utilized for community purposes like the maintenance of school and other social services.

But in the neighbouring village of Noney which has multiple clan ownership of land, the Khullakpa who is the head of the Gangmei clan is taking rent from the individual cultivator and tolls for extraction of forests. The Khunbu who is the head of the Dangmei clan is asserting similar rights over the clan land. Some lands are kept reserves for community village land. As Noney is located on the New Cachar Road, (NH-53) there is strong process of privatization of clan land into the name of Khullakpa. In Thangal village, where there is no Nampou, the village community (not village authority) has assumed the power of managing all the village and clan lands. A democratic process is going on in this village.

Thangal village land system

Thangal village has Khunbu, Khullakpa and village authority. They have no authority to control over the ownership of the village land. The village Pei (village council) members decide the site for jhum cultivation. Most of the permanent residents have got their Laoru. Laorupou (Laopou) is field owner. Every household has the right to possess for cultivation; the possessors are the field owners. There is a specific day to decide the site of jhum cultivation for every year. The day is known as Nappon Neih or Charamphak pui Neih.

Recent changes in land holding system

The need for more production of food compelled the

Rongmeis to sarch for plain lands, small valleys and basin of the rivers of their mountain in which can be utilized for cultivation. The transformation of the agricultural technology from hoe using shifting cultivation to plough using wetpaddy cultivation is slow and difficult process in spite of government assistance. The wet paddy cultivation was first introduced in Khaupum valley located on the Old Cachar Road connecting Imphal valley and Cachar district of Assam which was the lifeline of Manipur. They adopted plough cultivation in the early part of the 20th century. It was adopted in Leimatak valley and the Ijei valley through which passes the New Cachar Road, which was opened in 1970s. Meanwhile, terracing is gradually introduced in all parts of the Rongmei country. Shifting to wet cultivation requires the construction of permanent fields in which a cultivator has to put in his energy and resources to make cultivation productive.

The subsistence economy of the Rongmeis was supplemented by barter trade of their horticulture and forest products. With the opening of the Rongmei hills to good transportation, the horticultural products could be marketed with greater conveniences than which was before. The establishment of horticulture farms requires permanent fields where a plant has to grow from three years to fifty years or more. The horticulture development requires individual efforts and investments the recovery of which cannot be done for several years.

The opening of new administrative units in the district and the subdivisions and transportation on the national highway and major district roads have led to the growth of administrative and marketing centres, like Tamenglong, Nungba, Tamei and Noney necessitating the location of administrative offices, hospitals, educational institutions, markets and shops. This has led to the influx of people in Tamenglong administrative headquarters.

The change in the mode of agricultural production from shifting to horticulture, terrace cultivation and wet paddy cultivation leads to the change in the land holding system. The shifting cultivators with his cultivation work has established his possessory rights over the permanent lands which resulted into the privatization of the land holding. The land holding requires to be properly sureyed and documented. Further, the coming of several development projects like Khoupum Dam and Loktak Hydro Project led to the destruction of tribal lands, forests, horticultural and homestead even and they were given compensation. The individual villager's claims were entertained by the government. The prospects of such projects have led to the scramble for the control of the village authority to have access to the village land. The 30 sq. mile Khoupum valley with its cultivable land of about 1000 hectares. was 'surveyed for land settlements. Now the rights of the village council or the Nampou of the village are just ignored to promote interest of the villagers, who have got their private cultivable land in the Khoupum valley. The same phenomenon is happening in the river valleys.

In Tamenglong, which is declared as notified area on the request of the villagers, the village has been included in town area of Tamenglong. Consequently, the allotment of land in the notified area is done by the Deputy Commissioner. The individual Rampous who are the actual land owners are demanding the price of land allotted out of their land from the allottees. They have also demanded compensation from the Revenue 'Department. This is still a disputed matter.

Such conflicts will increase when the Manipur Land Revenue and Land Reform Act. 1960, is introduced in the hill areas of Manipur both in letter and spirit. This Act is not yet introduced in the hill areas of Manipur. According to this Act all the lands which are not under physical occupation at the time of survey will be declared Khaslands which belong to the state. The forest lands are not occupied all the year round except on particular year. So, it is apprehended that the forestlands would be declared by the government as state land and in such an eventuality, the land ceiling would be implemented, 25 acres per household. So, thousands of tribesmen would be deprived of their land creating serious problems for themselves and their future generations.

Land system and institutional finance

The Rongmeis who have migrated to valley districts of Manipur, namely, Imphal, Bishenpur and Cachar districts of Assam have agricultural lands and urban lands for dwelling purposes. They have taken loans from financial institutions for house building, business, animal husbandry and industries. But the Rongmeis who live in the hills of Manipur such facilities are not available except in Tamenglong town where the individual land holdings and ownership documents are issued. The United Bank of India and Manipur Rural Bank are operating in Rongmei areas. The banks have not so far given any loans except on hypothecation basis. This was due to the absence of the statutory documentation of the ownership right of the lands. But the village council with certain modification in their legal status should be given the power of taking loan for community purposes. Individuals should be given the loans on the ownership documents issued by the village council or village authority which should be authenticated by the revenue department.

The land holding system among the Rongmeis is highly complicated. The people are eager for quicker economic development.

Land alienation

The irrigation projects like the Khoupum earth dam, the

Loktak Hydro Project with the transmission line to Assam, opening of many government offices, farms and educational institutions and roads have led to the alienation of the tribal lands. So long the land is plenty and the forests are resourceful, there is no problem. But when these development projects have taken away tribal land even on the payment of the compensation to them, the suffering of the displaced or deprived Rongmeis have tremendously increased. For instance, the Khoupum Dam submerged more than 200 acres of cultivable lands belonging to Luwanglon Khunnou. They were paid compensation and promised employment in the Dam. But now the compensation is all consumed and the people concerned are now landless. They are engaged in shifting cultivation in their limited land. Indebtedness had also tremendously increased. Their jhum lands have been taken over by the Dam authorities.

In the eventual introduction of the Manipur Land Revenue and Land Reform Act the non-tribal will be entitled to purchase and own land in hill areas of Manipur. The Tamenglong district has great prospect of plantation crops like tea, coffee and rubber and it is apprehended that big capitalist enterprises not only from Manipur valley but also big firms from other parts of the country would move into the areas and take away the Rongmei lands. Enough attention has not been paid to this imminent danger both by the government and the people of this area.

Some case studies

Tamenglong village is the biggest Rongmei village in terms of population. The land ownership is based on three-tier system of the **Nampou** (owner of the village), the **Rampou** (owner of the land) and **the Laopou.** The head of the Pamei clan is the Nampou and there are ten Rampous which include clan Rampous and family Rampous. There is, of course, community forestland in Tamenglong. The Laopous have possessory right and they pay rent in kind to the Rampous who pay nominal rents to the Nampou. Such a system exists in Dailong village, one of the northernmost Rongmei villages. Dailong's Nampou is the head of the Gonmei clan which is the settler clan. There are clans and individual Rampous and there is also community land. However, in Nungba which is one clan village (Kamei clan) the whole village is the Kamei clan land. There is the clan Nampou like others. There are no Rampous, only the Laopous are there. In Khoupum, village in south Tamenglong district, the land is owned by the ruling clan's head who is the Nampou on behalf of the clan. The Rongmei clan is the clan of the Nampou. In the 30 sq. mile valley to the eastern side of the village, the individuals had reclaimed cultivable lands, and the Nampou does not lay claim over it which is now privately owned. There grew up five hamlets within Khoupum village, Gaidimjang, Satudai, Thanagong, Taodaijang, Namgaijang and old Khoupum in the hilltop. In the jhum land, the Nampou of Khoupum is taking rents but in the valley, he does not interfere. In Khoupum, therefore, there is a Nampou and the Laopous who are individual owners of plain paddy field and shifting cultivators.

In Noney, there are two settlers clans, the Dangmei clan and the Gangmei clan. The land in Noney is divided into clan lands. There are two Rampous who possess headship and ownership of the respective clan lands. The Khunbu (Nampou: owner of the village) is from the Dangmei clan and the Khullakpa (administrator of the village) is from the Gangmei clan. There are both traditional village council (Pei) and the statutory village authority in Noney. Since the Khullakpa has been given a statutory recognition and as the ex-officio chairman of the village authority, he has gained more importance and become an authority functionary while the Khunbu of the Dangmei clan is gradually pushed into the background. A conflict has arisen between the two functionaries with regard to the collection of rent from the land tillers and tolls on the extraction of forest. At the moment, as far as the village recognizes his supremacy with regards to the Dangmei clan land which is bigger than Gangmei clan land the Khunbu is still in a dominant position. Here the Laopous (tillers of the land) pay rent in kind for agricultural fields and cash as tolls for forest products or extraction of forest to head of the clan land.

Awangkhul land holding system

Awangkhul is a Rongmei village located in central Rongmei area of Tamenglong sub-division of the same district. It is surrounded by two rivers, the Irang in the west and Ijei in the south. The National Highway 53 (Imphal to Silchar) passes through the village. According to the narrative given by the representatives of the two major clans of the village, the Kamei and the Gonmei, this village was founded by different bands of adventurous colonizers who migrated from the old village of Kajinglung which is the boundary of the Rongmei and Liangmei tribes. Awangkhul was earlier occupied by a tribe called "Koumei" (Kourang) who were perhaps the ancestors of the Kharam tribe who speaks a dialect akin to the old Kuki-Chin language. Awangkhul is a Meitei word meaning a village on a lofty height. The Rongmei name for the village is Longchum (pointed hill meaning high hill).

According to Kamei clan tradition, a group of people led by Khoupou and Nemning of the same clan migrated from Kajinglong and settled first at Danjang within the land of Awangkhul. According to Gonmei clan tradition, two brothers of Gonmei clan, namely, Charasong, Maukhun migrated from Kajinglong. They stayed for sometime at Taotep village which is one day's journey from Kajinglong. As the wife of Charasong had to have delivery of a child, the group left Taotep and settled at Gongkhum in Awangkhul. Another group of colonizers led by Maishang of Kamei clan came from Kajinglong along with his parents, brothers and their families. He made a settlement at Danjaobam popularly known as Maishang Kaiphun (the homestead of Maishang). He was a very powerful warrior and leader. He had seven wives and thirty sons. Another group of Kamei clan under the leadership of Atun who later on became popular as a culture hero came from Kajinglong to this village. Thus four settlements were established by these bands of colonizers at Awangkhul. The number of settlers also increased and they elbowed out the earlier "Koumei" inhabitants of the village either by force, harassment or persuasion. Even now there is a place called Koutenjang which is supposed to be the site of the earlier settlers of the village. There are some stone relics of the earlier settlement, some beads used by the Koumeis were excavated by the shifting cultivators.

After the completion of the emigration of the Koumei settlers, the Rongmei settlers of the different settlements decided to establish a village according to Rongmei traditional custom. As the joint efforts of all the clans and their groups had resulted in the desertion of the earlier settlers, there was not a single founder, individual or clan who could be called the Nampou, the owner of the village. Several leaders were involved and Maishang was most prominent among them all. Khoupou of Kamei clan was the person who was believed to have come first and burnt the jungle first. And Charasong of Gonmei clan was the man who opened up the village pond and he was called Duikhun Khumei (one who constructs the pond). The eldest member of his clan till now performs this rite. There was an episode in which the leaders of the earlier settlers sent two men to purchase a pig from the neighbouring village of Tamlok for the performance of the ceremony of raising the village. According to Gonmei version, Charasong (the pond opener) was one of the two persons. And it was decided that whoever would catch the pig would be declared the head of the village. But other villagers laid down a number of conditions, among which were that he had to bear all the cost of village raising ceremony; and other rites required for the maintenance of the village. He failed to fulfil the conditions, so he surrendered his claims of the headship of the village.

Other clans did not accept this episode. According to them, it was not the costumary practice of the Rongmeis to decide the headship of a village by catching pig in some neighbouring village. Usually; they decided such case by divination. According to them, Charasong was married to a woman of the Kamei clan. Everybody agreed to establish the village and village Pei (village council) was constituted and the offices were distributed among the different clans. It appears that the influence of the Meitei monarchy was felt by the inhabitants of the village as indicated by the titles of offices.

Offices	**clan**
1. Khunbu (owner of the village)	Kamei clan
2. Khullakpa (Administrator of the village)	Kamei clan
3. Nammu (Functionary in charge of	Gonmei clan agricultural rites)
4. Luplakpa (-do-)	Gonmei clan
5. Pakhanglakpa (who is in charge of youth)	(Kamei of Kaiba Kamei clan southern village)

The immigration to this village came from different villages like Rangkhong, Taobam etc. There was emigration to other villages like Imphal valley and foothills of Koubru-Leimatol hills. There was an instance of Maishang leading a team of warriors to settle at Montha village to fight against the Kuki invaders into southern Rongmei country now in Churachandpur district. During the pre-colonial period, the kings of Manipur imposed feudal dues on Awangkhul,like cutting of Nageswar trees for supply to the state. The feudal services were so oppressive that the people left the village and went down to Imphal plain or other villages where such services were lighter.

Originally; there were only two clans: the Kamei and the Gonmei. In course of time, the Kamei was broken into two groups: Kaipi Kamei (the northern Kamei) and Kaiba Kamei (the southern Kamei) and the Gonmei has two lineages: the Gonthangmei and the Gondaimei. The Gonmei clan settlement at Gongkhum and the Kamei clan settlement at Dangjaobam were later on left and villagers moved to the main village which is now called Upper Awangkhul. In course of time the households live in two sectors the Kaipi-the northern ward and Kaiba-southern ward. These two sectors have become so strong that even the clans came to be separated on sector wise basis.

Lower Awangkhul: In the late 1960s when a second life line of Manipur in the New Cachar Road was being constructed some enterprising villagers who wanted to do terrace cultivation on the banks of the Ijei river settled at Goipongbijang (the hunting place of elephants) within the land of K. Namjonang. When the road was completed, many families shifted down to the roadside at Goipongbijang which is now known as the new or lower Awangkhul.

Pattern of land ownership: Community ownership

Theoretically, any individual or householder who is a domicile of the village who shoulders the responsibilities and obligations of the village Pei (village council) has the right of access to the lands and resources of the village, either forestlands, shifting cultivation, horticulture, terrace or other form of wet cultivation. Therefore, the different clans, lineages or clusters of households in the three hamlets have the equal rights of access to the land in the village. This right comes out of the community ownership of land in Awangkhul. The village Pei (village council) representing the whole village community is the owner of the village lands. There is no Nampou (owner of the village) in Awangkhul as it exists in other Rongmei villages. This is a consequence of a historical phenomenon, as referred to in the settlement history of the village. Awangkhul village was not founded by a single individual or clan but several enterprising individuals of several clans in different parts of the land and drove away the earlier settlers. Thus the establishment of the village was the joint endeavour of all the clans and individuals; hence, the ownership of the land in the village community represented by the village council. The individuals have the possessory rights over their lands and for cultivation. They do not pay rent to the village council. Every villager has free right to hunt animal, trap bird and do fishing in the village forest. In case of hunted animal, the hunter has to make a gift of the forelegs of the animal to the village elders for their consumption. It is a sort of thanksgiving to the elders for their blessings.

Change in land ownership pattern: The emergence of the Rampous (Land owner)

The land ownership pattern had undergone change with the emergence of a few families of land owners known as the Rampous (owners of land) which was a clear indicator of the process of privatization of the community land in Awangkhul. There is no Nampou in Awangkhul. But there are seven Rampous. The emergence of the Rampous was due to the transfer or sale of land by the village council to the individuals on payment of cash or kind. The case of the seven Rampous is very interesting. At the moment, the lands of the Rampous constituted four-fifth of the total land areas of the village.

The reason for such a transfer or sale are to meet the financial emergencies in the village, shortage of money (as a result of the monetisation of the economy during the colonial rule), political incidents in which fines were imposed by the Naga insurgents and failure of the individual to pay fines imposed by the village.

Rights of the Rampous

The Rampou literally means the owner of the land. The cultivator who tills his land within the land of a particular Rampou has to pay rent (Lampon) to the Rampou. The amount of the rent was one Doukhou, equivalent to one and half tin of paddy. As an obligation, the Rampou has to meet all the expenses incurred in the performance of the rites and ceremonies connected with agricultural production in a year. He has to pay one third of the rent collected from the tenant villagers to the village council as the gifts for the services rendered for the collection of rent from the Laopous by the village elders. Nowadays, the Rampous give a nominal gift of the paddy to the village elders. The Rampous have no right to evict the Laopou (cultivator) from his plot of fields. He does or cannot object to the construction of horticulture farms and terrace field by its cultivators. He gives his land for homestead settlement by the villagers, if they so decide.

There is no clan Rampou system in Awangkhul. But the Rampouship is inherited by the successors of the Rampou. The following are the Rampous and the manner of their acquisition of their land at the field study in 1986.

Name of Rampous and Manner of acquisition

1. Namjonang Kamei purchased the land from the village council which confiscated the land from somebody who failed to pay pig fine to the village council. Namjonang paid one big pig.

2. Dibonang Gonmei inherited from his grandfather Kuripou Gonmei who was a Rampou himself.
3. Chungonglung Kamei got the land as dowry for his wife Meidinlunglu, daughter of Kuripou, a rich Rampou.
4. Jakloungam Gonmei purchased from a descendant of Kuripou who could not give fine of one pig to the village council.
5. Languichung Kamei purchased from the village council on payment of money to meet some emergency during the Naga rebellion.
6. Ningdipou Kamei-Same as above.
7. Satoulung Gonmei purchased from Khangmemjeipou to whom the village council imposed a fine of one pig:

The village council of Awangkhul still imposes its will on the Rampous in the allocation of jhum fields and extraction of the forest. A decade ago, the extraction of the forest, timber and bamboo was sold to outside contractors on payments of toll to the Rampous. But recently, the village council and the village authority resumed the authority to sell the right of extraction of the forests to forest contractors. And the tolls so collected were utilized for public purpose in the village, running the school, meeting public expenses of the village. The individuals have the rights to extract the minor forest products like vegetables, bamboo, banana leaves etc.

Introduction of horticulture, terrace cultivation and wet land cultivation

With the introduction of horticulture, terrace cultivation and wetland cultivation in Awangkhul and the basin of the Ijei river, the individuals are constructing their own fields. The government gives assistance to them. The Rampous or the village council does not object to this privatization of the lands in such agricultural product activities. The land holding system has changed from the community ownership and with the possessory rights vested in the individuals, to the control of the village lands by seven Rampous with the continuity of the individual's possessory rights, then to the emergence of private land ownership with the development of terrace cultivation, horticulture and wet land cultivation. But the village council checks the transfer to these lands to outsiders. The village council regulates the shifting agriculture production activities.

APPENDIX

UNITED NATIONS DECLARATION ON THE RIGHTS OF INDIGENOUS PEOPLES

Affirming that indigenous peoples are equal to all other peoples, while recognizing the right of all peoples to be different, to consider themselves different, and to be respected as such,

Affirming also that all peoples contribute to the diversity and richness of civilizations and cultures, which constitute the common heritage *of* humankind,

Affirmingfurther that all doctrines, policies and practices based on or advocating superiority of peoples or individuals on the basis of national origin, racial, religious, ethnic or cultural differences are racist, scientifically false, legally invalid, morally condemnable and socially unjust,

Reaffirming also that indigenous peoples, in the exercise of their rights, should be free from discrimination of any kind,

Concerned that indigenous peoples have suffered from historic injustices as a result of, inter alia, their colonization and dispossession of their lands, territories and resources, thus preventing them from exercising, in particular, their right to development in accordance with their own needs and interests,

Recognizing the urgent need to respect and promote the inherent rights of indigenous peoples which derive from their political, economic and social structures and from their cultures, spiritual traditions, histories and philosophies, especially their rights to their lands, territories and resources,

Further recognizing the urgent need to respect and promote the rights of indigenous peoples affirmed in treaties, agreements and other constructive arrangements with States,

Welcoming the fact that indigenous peoples are organizing themselves for political, economic, social and cultural enhancement and in order to bring an end.to all forms of discrimination and oppression wherever they occur,

Convinced that control by indigenous peoples over developments affecting them and their lands, territories and resources will enable them to maintain and strengthen their institutions, cultures and traditions, and to promote their development in accordance with their aspirations and needs,

Recognizing also that respect for indigenous knowledge, cultures and traditional practices contributes to sustainable and equitable development and proper management of the environment,

Emphasizing the contribution of the demilitarization of the lands and territories of indigenous peoples to peace, economic and social progress and development, understanding and friendly relations among nations and peoples of the world,

Recognizing in particular the right of indigenous families and communities to retain shared responsibility for the upbringing, training, education and well-being of their children, consistent with the rights of the child,

Recognizing also that indigenous peoples have the right freely to determine their relationships with States in a spirit of coexistence, mutual benefit and full respect,

Considering that the rights affirmed in treaties, agreements and constructive arrangements between States and indigenous peoples are, in some situations, matters of international concern, interest, responsibility and character,

Also considering that treaties, agreements and other constructive arrangements, and the relationship they represent, are the basis for a strengthened partnership between indigenous peoples and States,

Acknowledging that the Charter of the United Nations, the International Covenant on Economic, Social and Cultural Rights and the International Covenant on Civil and Political Rights affirm the fundamental importance of the right of selfdetermination of all peoples, by virtue of which they freely determine their political status and freely pursue their economic, social and cultural development,

Bearing in mind that nothing in this Declaration may be used to deny any peoples their right of self-determination, exercised in conformity with international law,

Convinced that the recognition of the rights of indigenous peoples in this Declaration will enhance harmonious and cooperative relations between the State and indigenous peoples, based on principles of justice, democracy, respect for human rights, non-discrimination and good faith,

Encouraging States to comply with and effectively implement all their obligations as they apply to indigenous peoples under international instruments, in particular those related to human rights, in consultation and cooperation with the peoples concerned,

Emphasizing that the United Nations has an important and continuing role to play in promoting and protecting the rights of indigenous peoples,

Believing that this Declaration is a further important step forward for the recognition, promotion and protection of the rights and freedoms of indigenous peoples and in the development of relevant activities of the United Nations system in this field,

Recognizing and reaffirming that indigenous individuals are entitled without discrimination to all human rights recognized in international law, and that indigenous peoples possess collective rights which are indispensable for their existence, wellbeing and integral development as peoples,

Solemnly proclaims the following United Nations Declaration on the Rights ofIndigenous Peoples as a standard of achievement to be pursued in a spirit of partnership and mutual respect,

Article 1

Indigenous peoples have the right to the full enjoyment, as a collective or as individuals, of all human rights and fundamental freedoms as recognized in the Charter of the United Nations, the Universal Declaration of Human Rights and international human rights law.

Article 2

Indigenous peoples and individuals are free and equal to all other peoples and individuals and have the right to be free from any kind of discrimination, in the exercise of their rights, in particular that based on their indigenous origin or identity.

Article 3

Indigenous peoples have the right of self-determination. By virtue of that right they freely determine their political status and freely pursue their economic, social and cultural development.

Article 4

Indigenous peoples, in exercising their right to self-determination, have the right to autonomy or self-government in matters relating to their internal and local affairs, as well as ways and means for financing their autonomous functions.

Article 5

Indigenous peoples have the right to maintain and strengthen their distinct political, legal, economic, social and cultural institutions, while retaining their rights to participate fully, if they so choose, in the political, economic, social and cultural life of the State.

Article 6

Every indigenous individual has the right to a nationality.

Article 7

1. Indigenous individuals have the rights to life, physical and mental integrity, liberty and security of person.

2. Indigenous peoples have the collective right to live in freedom, peace and security as distinct peoples and shall not be subjected to any act of genocide or any other act of violence, including forcibly removing children of the group to another group.

Article 8

1. Indigenous peoples and individuals have the right not to be subjected to forced assimilation or destruction of their culture.

2. States shall provide effective mechanisms for prevention of, and redress for:

   (a) Any action which has the aim or effect of depriving them of their integrity as distinct peoples, or of their cultural values or ethnic identities;

   (b) Any action which has the aim or effect of dispossessing them of their lands, territories or resources;

(c) Any form of forced population transfer which has the aim or effect of violating or undermining any of their rights;

(d) Any form of forced assimilation or integration by other cultures or ways of life imposed on them by legislative, administrative or other measures;

(e) Any form of propaganda designed to promote or incite racial or ethnic discrimination directed against them.

Article 9

Indigenous peoples and individuals have the right to belong to an indigenous community or nation, in accordance with the traditions and customs of the community or nation concerned. No discrimination of any kind may arise from the exercise of such a right.

Article 10

Indigenous peoples shall not be forcibly removed from their lands or territories. No relocation shall take place without the free, prior and informed consent of the indigenous peoples concerned and after agreement on just and fair compensation and, where possible, with the option of return.

Article 11

1. Indigenous peoples have the right to practice and revitalize their cultural traditions and customs. This includes the right to maintain, protect and develop the past, present and future manifestations of their cultures, such as archaeological and historical sites, artefacts, designs, ceremonies, technologies and visual and performing arts and literature.

2. States shall provide redress through effective mechanisms, which may include restitution, developed

in conjunction with indigenous peoples, with respect to their cultural, intellectual, religious and spiritual property taken without their free, prior and informed consent or in violation oftheir laws, traditions and customs.

Article 12

1. Indigenous peoples have the right to manifest, practice, develop and teach their spiritual and religious traditions, customs and ceremonies; the right to maintain, protect, and have access in privacy to their religious and cultural sites; the right to the use and control of their ceremonial objects; and the right to the repatriation of their human remains.

2. States shall seek to enable the access and/or repatriation of ceremonial objects and human remains in their possession through fair, transparent and effective mechanisms developed in conjunction with indigenous peoples concerned.

Article 13

1. Indigenous peoples have the right to revitalize, use, develop and transmit to future generations their histories, languages, oral traditions, philosophies, writing systems and literatures, and to designate and retain their own names for communities, places and persons.

2. States shall take effective measures to ensure this right is protected and also to ensure that indigenous peoples can understand and be understood in political, legal and administrative proceedings, where necessary through the provision of interpretation or by other appropriate means.

Article 14

1. Indigenous peoples have the right to establish and control their educational systems and institutions providing education in their own languages, in a manner

appropriate to their cultural methods of teaching and learning.

2. Indigenous individuals, particularly children, have the right to all levels and forms of education of the State without discrimination.

3. States shall, in conjunction with indigenous peoples, take effective measures, in order for indigenous individuals, particularly children, including those living outside their communities, to have access, when possible, to an education in their own culture and provided in their own language.

Article 15

1. Indigenous peoples have the right to the dignity and diversity of their cultures, traditions, histories and aspirations which shall be appropriately reflected in education and public information.

2. States shall take effective measures, in consultation and cooperation with the indigenous peoples concerned, to combat prejudice and eliminate discrimination and to promote tolerance, understanding and good relations among indigenous peoples and all other segments of society.

Article 16

1. Indigenous peoples have the right to establish their own media in their own languages and to have access to all forms of non-indigenous media without discrimination.

2. States shall take effective measures to ensure that State-owned media duly reflect indigenous cultural diversity. States, without prejudice to ensuring full freedom of expression, should encourage privately-owned media to adequately reflect indigenous cultural diversity.

Article 17

1. Indigenous individuals and peoples have the right to enjoy fully all rights established under applicable international and domestic labour law.
2. States shall in consultation and cooperation with indigenous peoples take specific measures to protect indigenous children from economic exploitation and from performing any work that is likely to be hazardous or to interfere with the child's education, or to be harmful to the child's health or physical, mental, spiritual, moral or social development, taking into account their special vulnerability and the importance of education for their empowerment.
3. Indigenous individuals have the right not to be subjected to any discriminatory conditions of labour and, inter alia, employment or salary.

Article 18

Indigenous peoples have the right to participate in decision-making in matters which would affect their rights, through representatives chosen by themselves in accordance with their own procedures, as well as to maintain and develop their own indigenous decision-making institutions.

Article 19

States shall consult and cooperate in good faith with the indigenous peoples concerned through their own representative institutions in order to obtain their free, prior and informed consent before adopting and implementing legislative or administrative measures that may affect them.

Article 20

1. Indigenous peoples have the right to maintain and develop their political, economic and social systems or

institutions, to be secure in the enjoyment of their own means of subsistence and development, and to engage freely in all their traditional and other economic activities.

2. Indigenous peoples deprived of their means of subsistence and development are entitled to just and fair redress.

Article 21

1. Indigenous peoples have the right, without discrimination, to the improvement of their economic and social conditions, including, inter alia, in the areas of education, employment, vocational training and retraining, housing, sanitation, health and social security.

2. States shall take effective measures and, where appropriate, special measures to ensure continuing improvement of their economic and social conditions. Particular attention shall be paid to the rights and special needs of indigenous elders, women, youth, children and persons with disabilities.

Article 22

1. Particular attention shall be paid to the rights and special needs of indigenous elders, women, youth, children and persons with disabilities in the implementation of this Declaration.

2. States shall take measures, in conjunction with indigenous peoples, to ensure that indigenous women and children enjoy the full protection and guarantees against all forms of violence and discrimination.

Article 23

Indigenous peoples have the right to determine and develop priorities and strategies for exercising their right to development. In particular, indigenous peoples have the right to be actively involved in developing and determining health, housing and other economic and social programmes affecting them and, as far as possible, to administer such programmes through their own institutions.

Article 24

1. Indigenous peoples have the right to their traditional medicines and to maintain their health practices, including the conservation of their vital medicinal plants, animals and minerals. Indigenous individuals also have the right to access, without any discrimination, to all social and health services.

2. Indigenous individuals have an equal right to the enjoyment of the highest attainable standard of physical and mental health. States shall take the necessary steps with a view to achieving progressively the full realization of this right.

Article 25

Indigenous peoples have the right to maintain and strengthen their distinctive spiritual relationship with their traditionally owned or otherwise occupied and used lands, territories, waters and coastal seas and other resources and to uphold their responsibilities to future generations in this regard.

Article 26

1. Indigenous peoples have the right to the lands, territories and resources which they have traditionally owned, occupied or otherwise used or acquired.

2. Indigenous peoples have the right to own, use, develop and control the lands, territories and resources that they possess by reason of traditional ownership or other traditional occupation or use, as well as those which they have otherwise acquired.

3. States shall give legal recognition and protection to these lands, territories and resources. Such recognition shall be conducted with due respect to the customs, traditions and land tenure systems of the indigenous peoples concerned.

Article 27

States shall establish and implement, in conjunction with indigenous peoples concerned, a fair, independent, impartial, open and transparent process, giving due recognition to indigenous peoples' laws, traditions, customs and land tenure systems, to recognize and adjudicate the rights of indigenous peoples pertaining to their lands, territories and resources, including those which were traditionally owned or otherwise occupied or used. Indigenous peoples shall have the right to participate in this process.

Article 28

1. Indigenous peoples have the right to redress, by means that can include restitution or, when this is not possible, of a just, fair and equitable compensation, for the lands, territories and resources which they have traditionally owned or otherwise occupied or used, and which have been confiscated, taken, occupied, used or damaged without their free, prior and informed consent.

2. Unless otherwise freely agreed upon by the peoples concerned, compensation shall take the form of lands, territories and resources equal in quality, size and legal status or of monetary compensation or other appropriate redress.

Article 29

1. Indigenous peoples have the right to the conservation and protection of the environment and the productive

capacity of their lands or territories and resources. States shall establish and implement assistance programmes for indigenous peoples for such conservation and protection, without discrimination.

2. States shall take effective measures to ensure that no storage or disposal of hazardous materials shall take place in the lands or territories of indigenous peoples without their free, prior and informed consent.

3. States shall also take effective measures to ensure, as needed, that programmes for monitoring, maintaining and restoring the health of indigenous peoples, as developed and implemented by the peoples affected by such materials, are duly implemented.

Article 30

1. Military activities shall not take place in the lands or territories of indigenous peoples, unless justified by a significant threat to relevant public interest or otherwise freely agreed with or requested by the indigenous peoples concerned.

2. States shall undertake effective consultations with the indigenous peoples concerned, through appropriate procedures and in particular through their representative institutions, prior to using their lands or territories for military activities.

Article 31

1. Indigenous peoples have the right to maintain, control, protect and develop their cultural heritage, traditional knowledge and traditional cultural expressions, as well as the manifestations of their sciences, technologies and cultures, including human and genetic resources, seeds, medicines, knowledge ofthe properties of fauna and flora, oral traditions, literatures, designs, sports and traditional

games and visual and performing arts. They also have the right to maintain, control, protect and develop their intellectual property over such cultural heritage, traditional knowledge, and traditional cultural expressions.

2. In conjunction with indigenous peoples, States shall take effective measures to recognize and protect the exercise of these rights.

Article 32

1. Indigenous peoples have the right to determine and develop priorities and strategies for the development or use of their lands or territories and other resources.

2. States shall consult and cooperate in good faith with the indigenous peoples concerned through their own representative institutions in order to obtain their tree and informed consent prior to the approval of any project affecting their lands or territories and other resources, particularly in connection with the development, utilization or exploitation of their mineral, water or other resources.

3. States shall provide effective mechanisms for just and fair redress for any such activities, and appropriate measures shall be taken to mitigate adverse environmental, economic, social, cultural or spiritual impact.

Article 33

1. Indigenous peoples have the right to determine their own identity or membership in accordance with their customs and traditions. This does not impair the right of indigenous individuals to obtain citizenship of the States in which they live.

2. Indigenous peoples have the right to determine the structures and to select the membership of their institutions in accordance with their own procedures.

Article 34

Indigenous peoples have the right to promote, develop and maintain their institutional structures and their distinctive customs, spirituality, traditions, procedures, practices and, in the cases where they exist, juridical systems or customs, in accordance with international human rights standards.

Article 35

Indigenous peoples have the right to determine the responsibilities of individuals to their communities.

Article 36

1. Indigenous peoples, in particular those divided by international borders, have the right to maintain and develop contacts, relations and cooperation, including activities for spiritual, cultural, political, economic and social purposes, with their own members as well as other peoples across borders.

2. States, in consultation and cooperation with indigenous peoples, shall take effective measures to facilitate the exercise and ensure the implementation of this right.

Article 37

1. Indigenous peoples have the right to the recognition, observance and enforcement of Treaties, Agreements and Other Constructive Arrangements concluded with States or their successors and to have States honour and respect such Treaties, Agreements and other Constructive Arrangements.

2. Nothing in this Declaration may be interpreted as to

diminish or eliminate the rights of Indigenous Peoples contained in Treaties, Agreements and Constructive Arrangements.

Article 38

States in consultation and cooperation with indigenous peoples, shall take the appropriate measures, including legislative measures, to achieve the ends of this Declaration.

Article 39

Indigenous peoples have the right to have access to financial and technical assistance from States and through international cooperation, for the enjoyment of the rights contained in this Declaration.

Article 40

Indigenous peoples have the right to have access to and prompt decision through just and fair procedures for the resolution of conflicts and disputes with States or other parties, as well as to effective remedies for all infringements of their individual and collective rights. Such a decision shall give due consideration to the customs, traditions, rules and legal systems of the indigenous peoples concerned and international human rights.

Article 41

The organs and specialized agencies of the United Nations system and other intergovernmental organizations shall contribute to the full realization of the provisions of this Declaration through the mobilization, inter alia, of financial cooperation and technical assistance. Ways and means of ensuring participation of indigenous peoples on issues affecting them shall be established.

Article 42

The United Nations, its bodies, including the Permanent

Forum on Indigenous Issues, and specialized agencies, including at the country level, and States, shall promote respect for and full application of the provisions of this Declaration and follow up the effectiveness of this Declaration.

Article 43

The rights recognized herein constitute the minimum standards for the survival, dignity and well-being of the indigenous peoples ofthe world.

Article 44

All the rights and freedoms recognized herein are equally guaranteed to male and female indigenous individuals.

Article 45

Nothing in this Declaration may be construed as diminishing or extinguishing the rights indigenous peoples have now or may acquire in the future.

Article 46

1. Nothing in this Declaration may be interpreted as implying for any State, people, group or person any right to engage in any activity or to perform any act contrary to the Charter of the United Nations.

2. In the exercise of the rights enunciated in the present Declaration, human rights and fundamental freedoms of all shall be respected. The exercise of the rights set forth in this Declaration shall be subject only to such limitations as are determined by law, in accordance with international human rights obligations. Any such limitations shall be non-discriminatory and strictly necessary solely for the purpose of securing due recognition and respect for the rights and freedoms of others and for meeting the just and most compelling requirements of a democratic society.

3. The provisions set forth in this Declaration shall be interpreted in accordance with the principles of justice, democracy, respect for human rights, equality, non-discrimination, good governance and good faith.

Index

■■■